DESIGN BY OPTIMIZATION IN ARCHITECTURE, BUILDING, AND CONSTRUCTION

DESIGN BY OPTIMIZATION IN ARCHITECTURE, BUILDING, AND CONSTRUCTION

Antony D. Radford
John S. Gero

DEPARTMENT OF
ARCHITECTURAL SCIENCE

THE UNIVERSITY OF SYDNEY

VNR Van Nostrand Reinhold Company
New York

Library of Congress Catalog Card Number 87-10645
ISBN 0-442-25639-6

Printed in the United States of America

Van Nostrand Reinhold Company Inc.
115 Fifth Avenue
New York, New York 10003

Van Nostrand Reinhold Company Limited
Molly Millars Lane
Wokingham, Berkshire RG11 2PY, England

Van Nostrand Reinhold
480 La Trobe Street
Melbourne, Victoria 3000, Australia

Macmillan of Canada
Division of Canada Publishing Corporation
164 Commander Boulevard
Agincourt, Ontario M1S 3C7, Canada

16 15 14 13 12 11 10 9 8 7 6 5 4 3 2 1

Library of Congress Cataloging-in-Publication Data

Radford, Antony.
Design by optimization in architecture, building, and construction.

Includes bibliographies and index.
1. Architectural design—Data processing.
2. Computer-aided design. I. Gero, John S.
II. Title.
NA2728.R344 1987 720′.28′401519 87-10645
ISBN 0-442-25639-6

The risk was usually obvious, but it always seemed worth it—better that than the tyranny of the ordinary.

Paul Theroux
Sunrise with Seamonsters

CONTENTS

PREFACE

New and different approaches to design are becoming possible through the rapidly developing technology of computers and the mathematical tools of optimization theory. Traditional design activity is based on postulating, appraising, and modifying potential solutions in order to arrive at an acceptable form. Design by optimization employs numerical models of decision-making processes in order to generate direct prescriptive information on the nature of good solutions for the satisfaction of specified objectives. It provides the potential for better design by encompassing a much wider range of possibilities, and it offers the designer an opportunity to examine the implications of subjective decisions on the specified objectives.

This book describes the current state of the art in architectural optimization and it advocates and develops some new directions. The subject matter is grouped into four parts. Part 1, Optimization in Computer-aided Architectural Design, places design as decision making within a context of design methods. Computer-based design methods are categorized as being based on one of three types of concepts: simulation concepts, generation concepts, or optimization concepts. It is shown that optimization-based methods subsume simulation and generation.

Part 2, Design by Optimization, describes some of the important techniques involved in optimization and demonstrates how they can be applied to obtain solutions to practical design problems. Three techniques are elaborated: differential calculus, linear programming, and dynamic programming. Their respective advantages and disadvantages are discussed.

Part 3, Dynamic Programming in Design, explores and extends the most useful of the optimization techniques—dynamic programming—to increase its range of applicability and value to the designer. Included in the coverage are descriptions of some case studies.

Part 4, Multicriteria Optimization in Design, addresses design situations in which several different objectives are important. It reviews a number of possible design approaches and shows that one based on Pareto optimization can be used in practical design situations involving disparate objectives. Some examples are described, and the Pareto optimization method is examined as a source of knowledge and as a means of establishing rules for design.

This book is intended for senior undergraduate and graduate students of architecture and related disciplines, as well as for researchers into design methods and for practicing architects and other designers who are concerned with rational decision making in design. Only a modicum of mathematical knowledge is necessary, since the book concentrates on concepts and applications—although readers with strong mathematical backgrounds will find novel ideas here. Worked examples are presented as vehicles for the ideas involved, and design problems covering various situations and objectives are solved by optimization. References are provided to texts that elaborate the individual techniques in more detail.

The reader of this book should get an insight into the conceptual basis and the potential of design by optimization and should gain the knowledge necessary to formulate his or her own problems for solution by this approach.

ACKNOWLEDGMENTS

This book evolved over a long period from research carried out primarily in the Department of Architectural Science at the University of Sydney. This research formed the basis of an extensive teaching program at the University of Sydney. The ideas presented here were used in courses taught by the authors at Columbia University, Harvard University, the University of California at Berkeley, the University of Strathclyde, and the University of California at Los Angeles. The students in those courses helped us refine many of these ideas.

Our research colleagues in the Department of Architectural Science produced or helped produce many of the concepts that form the backbone of this book. Particularly deserving of acknowledgment is Dr. Michael Rosenman, who always seemed to be able to take a one-line concept and develop it to its logical conclusion. Much of the work on dynamic programming that makes this technique useful in architectural problems is attributable to him. Mr. Bala M. Balachandran was responsible for many of the multicriteria optimization algorithms described in this book, while Dr. Neville D'Cruz showed how they could be applied to large-scale problems.

Support for this work came from grants from the Australian Research Grants Scheme (Australia), the National Science Foundation (United States), and the Science and Engineering Research Council (United Kingdom).

The inspiration for this work can be traced to Professor Nestor Distefano (University of California at Berkeley) and to Professor Richard Bellman (University of Southern California), both of whom demonstrated to one of the authors the intellectual depth of the optimization paradigm in general and of dynamic programming in particular.

Fay Sudweeks proved invaluable, as ever, in typing and retyping the drafts and in shaping the final manuscript in her inimitable fashion. To her, special thanks are due.

PART 1

OPTIMIZATION IN COMPUTER-AIDED ARCHITECTURAL DESIGN

Design in architecture is a goal-directed activity in which decisions are made about the physical form of buildings and their components in order to ensure their fitness for intended purposes. Computers can aid the designer in this decision-making process by providing information on the relationship between potential solutions and the desired performance characteristics. The usefulness of this computer aid depends on the scope and relevance of the information that can be provided and its accessibility to the designer. The emphasis in computer-aided architectural design must therefore be on the needs of the designer—that is, on design and design methods, rather than on the computer. In this part, we explore some pertinent aspects of design methodology and formulate a conceptual basis for computer-aided architectural design that is founded on the place of the decision-making activity in the solution process. It is important that the reader understand these concepts before proceeding to the methods and applications that are described in the following parts.

In chapter 1 we define design as being goal-directed and develop the notion of design as a decision-making activity. We suggest that design has three phases: performance generation, vocabulary and language selection, and decisions about particulars. We discuss the applicability of computer-based design aids founded on decision-making methods within this spectrum. Finally, we explore the needs and expectations of designers of such design aids. In chapter 2 we elaborate decision-making concepts and describe various ways by which we can model problems. We then go on to show that all design problems can be modeled by simulation concepts, generation concepts, or optimization concepts—depending on the location of the decision-making activity in the solution process—and we show that optimization-based methods subsume simulation and generation.

CHAPTER 1

DESIGN AS DECISION MAKING

This book is about design. *Design* is one of the highest endeavors to which we can aspire: the making of explicit proposals to reshape our environment to make it better suited to men's and women's needs. Everything we use has been designed. Specifically, this book is about the aspiration to make designs as good as possible, the desire to ensure that our design endeavors do indeed match our needs in the best possible way. Its purpose is to explore the place, the usefulness, and some of the techniques of optimization as a tool in making design as good as possible in architecture and building.

Designing is an activity that can be approached in many ways and can be the subject of many paradigms. For designers, at least, it is an intrinsically interesting topic. We shall take as our starting point the premise that its essential feature is the existence of goals (however ill-defined they may be) that make the process purposeful and necessitate decisions about the best way to fulfill them. However the process itself takes place, the outcome is a design solution (good, bad, or indifferent) that has one or more types of performance characteristics (for example, aesthetic, financial, environmental, or structural characteristics) that relate in some way to the desirability of that solution. Of course, knowledge of many different performance characteristics may be needed to judge adequately the quality of one solution, and many different solutions may have virtually the same performance characteristics.

We present, then, a picture of a designer seeking the best possible response to a design situation, where the "goodness" of the response is judged according to a mixture of articulated and unexpressed *criteria* that reflect his or her goals. It is a picture that could depict the architect Filippo Brunelleschi in the fifteenth century designing a way to keep the dome of the Florence Cathedral stable by using a chain around its base, or it could depict the architect Jørn Utzon and the engineer Ove Arup in the twentieth century finding a way to make the concrete shells of the Sydney Opera House amenable to simple construction and structural analysis by making them segments of spherical surfaces. Through most of the intervening period the tools and media used in design stayed the same: pens; pencils; paper; experimental models made of physical materials such as wood and plaster; and (latterly) slide rules, calculators, and printed tables of calculated values such as beam and column handbooks for engineers. In the last third of the twentieth century, though, computers have begun to replace many of these traditional tools. Arup's use in the 1960s of computers in the analysis of the shells of the Sydney Opera House demonstrated that this tool could help find solutions to design problems that were beyond the scope of traditional methods.

From the start, computers drew mixed reactions from designers. Some regarded them as a dangerous threat, a dehumanizing influence on both the process and the products of design. Others looked on computers as having an almost magical power to solve all problems. Still more thought that they were alright for engineers dealing with numbers but had no role for "artist" architects dealing with form and color. Part of the confusion has stemmed from the longstanding tendency of computer enthusiasts to oversell the capabilities of their favorite tool. Lest we be seen as continuing this tradition, let us state from the outset that neither computers nor optimization is capable of solving every aspect of the real and difficult task that is design. Both, though, are useful: computers, in such a wide and general sense that not to make use of them is a sign of archaic and inadequate methods; optimization, in a particular sense for particular kinds of design problems. Where it can be used, optimization produces a form of design information for designers that is quite impossible to achieve in any other way. Our desire to explain the role of optimization in design in architecture and building is the reason we wrote this book.

DESIGN SYNTHESIS

Let us put together a model of design in which the possible role of optimization can be identified. Most models of design activity agree that the activity consists of the three identifiable phases of *problem analysis, design synthesis,* and *design evaluation* and that the process is not linear but cyclical, proceeding from abstract to more concrete ideas about and descriptions of the design proposal (fig. 1-1). This is fine, but it does not help us greatly in understanding how a design takes form—how the syn-

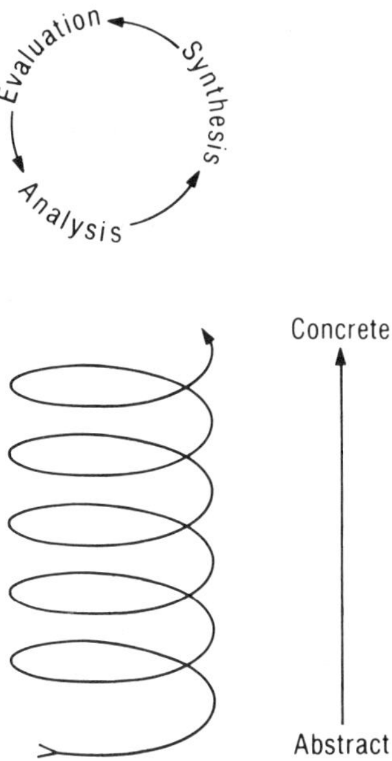

Fig. 1-1. Design as a cyclical process with phases of analysis, synthesis, and evaluation.

thesis part of this general model might operate. We need a model of design synthesis that tells us how, within what limits, and on what basis design decisions are made.

We have already argued that the essence of design is that it is purposefully directed toward the achievement of certain goals. One activity in design, then, must be the conscious or subconscious sorting out of these goals in order to express the aim of the whole exercise. In architecture some of these aims are laid out in the brief for a building, but an architect brings to design activity a multitude of design goals stemming from society's expectations and his or her own professional aspirations. Although these combined goals are never recorded in a written brief, design decisions are made according to whether they jointly further or hinder the goals' achievement. Many of the options for these decisions will tend to favor some goals while detracting from others. Consequently, whether or not to adopt such options is a tradeoff decision based on the designer's judgment of the overall picture. But the design options in any particular situation are not unlimited and cannot be treated as if they were. Constraints imposed by site conditions, regulations, and client directives limit the range of possible decisions. Moreover, architects and other designers tend to work within a *language* (or *style*) *of design* that is peculiar to an individual, a school, or an age.

This notion of a language is apparent in the documented history of architecture and building. Designers in Georgian England reacted to the "need a house" situation with a different set of architectural responses from the set used by designers in Victorian England. Writers on twentieth-century architecture compare the International, Post-Modernist, and High-Tech styles, discuss the influence of the Chicago School and note the differences between Frank Lloyd Wright's Prairie and Usonian styles of architecture. Books on construction show details and describe solutions that fit within a particular style. It is so fundamental to our view of architecture and building that we rarely attempt to define what decisions are and are not valid within a style, although writers on shape grammars and design grammars have attempted to model the work of human designers by means of a formalism that represents this work as being composed within a language analogous to written language.

We can now elaborate our description of design synthesis as the making of decisions within a language in order to further the achievement of a body of design goals. At issue are both high-level strategies (in architecture, such things as structural form and planning relationships) and low-level details (what kind of door handles to use, for example, and how wide the architrave is to be). The basis for the decision must be some kind of design information that suggests the preferability of certain options.

This design information can come from many sources: books, remembered lectures from distant college days, a colleague's advice, personal experience of successes and failures, and feedback from a tested hypothesis, to name but a few. Given equally capable designers, the best design should come from whomever tests the information available in the best form at the best time. But something else is going on that is of interest to us. Architects and many other designers do not implement their individual design decisions directly on the finished product. They work with *models* first: physical models such as drawings, numerical models such as cost plans, and verbal models such as their written report on the design to the client. Much of their design information comes from working with these and other models. Only when the models are sufficiently complete are they translated by builders into a finished reality. When we think of evaluation as being a part of the design process, and the result of that evaluation as being a form of design information, we mean not the evaluation of finished buildings (although that, too, has a role) but the evaluation of a model, whether it be a quick hand sketch or a lengthy math-

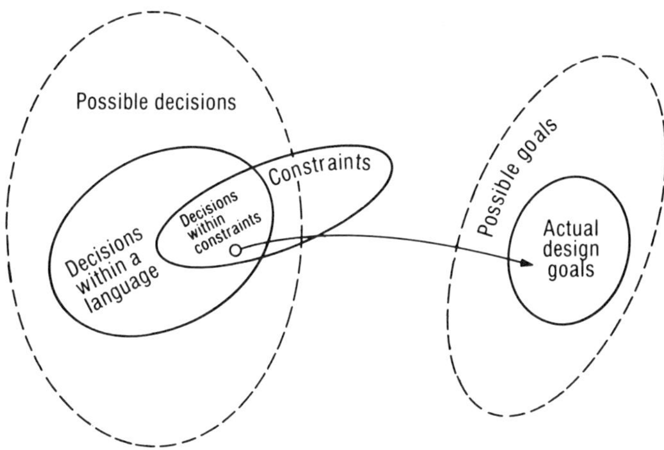

Fig. 1-2. Design synthesis as the making of decisions within a language and within constraints, using models and information that relates decisions to goals.

ematical model of thermal performance. The form of the model determines the form of the resulting design information, which involves much more than just the descriptive properties of the model.

To elaborate our description of design synthesis again, we can now express it as the making of decisions, within a design language and under project-specific constraints, using models and based on information about whether the decision will further the achievement of a body of design goals (fig. 1-2). This rather lengthy and inelegant description (and we could also apply other, equally correct descriptions) does not and is not intended to tell the whole story. Its value to us lies in the context it provides for looking at the role of *optimization*. Optimization, as a model for creating information, links the desire for good performance in the goals to the decisions that result in good performance. Consideration of its nature as a design model—and how it compares to other design models—we shall leave to the next chapter. First, we want to look at the whole notion of mapping between design decisions and design performances, at modeling characteristics in general, and at the kind of information needed for decision making.

MAPPING BETWEEN DESIGN GOALS AND DESIGN DECISIONS

To design well we need to be able to map (that is, to establish point-by-point correlations) between our design goals and the design decisions that may or may not help us achieve those goals. To build our discussion on solid foundations, we shall in this section present a theoretical view of mapping that will prove useful in later chapters.

A simple and rather artificial design problem is the vehicle for describing this mapping. (We refer generally in this book to *design problems,* although the term is not intended to suggest that design problems fit into the same scientific traditions as problems in physics, mathematics, and chemistry. The examples we use in the first two chapters of this book all relate to windows, shading, and the physical environment in building so that there is a consistency in the exposition.) Imagine an office block with continuous perimeter windows and a continuous horizontal sunshade above those windows (fig. 1-3); most cities of the world have buildings with just these characteristics. Imagine, too, that everything about the building is fixed except the height of the windows and projection of the sunshade. This gives us just two *design variables* to manipulate: we can combine different values of window height with different values of shade projection to yield tall, medium, or short windows with extensive, medium, or stubby shades. In practice, *constraints* limit the feasible values for these variables. The windows cannot extend higher than the ceiling, and the sunshades are subject to a constructional constraint that restricts projection to a maximum of, say, 2 meters or so. These constraints together define a *feasible region* within which any design must lie.

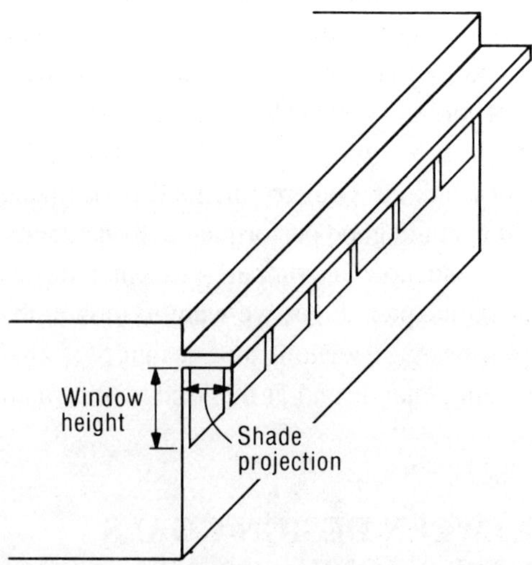

Fig. 1-3. Design variables of shade projection and window height for a window/sunshade design problem.

Windows exist for a variety of reasons, but principally to provide light, sun penetration, and a view of the world outside. These benefits are accompanied by negative effects such as the admission of noise, glare, and unwanted heat gain and loss. Let us just think about light: the designer's ideal is to create a pleasant place to work behind the windows, and one of his or her goals as a part of this ideal is to provide the best possible daylighting. But what is meant by the "best possible daylighting"? Daylighting has both quantitative and qualitative aspects. The quantity of light we can measure with a light meter; the quality of light is perhaps dependent on measurable quantities (such as those identified through analysis of the components of the light across the bands of the visible spectrum and how these components change over time), but it is not easy to establish on any commonly accepted scale. Regulations and codes on daylighting concentrate on quantity of light, setting as a criterion minimum levels of daylight factor over certain areas of the working plane. As our way of measuring the performance of our designs in meeting our design goal, we shall consider only the area of the room behind the window that has a daylight factor of more than 2 percent (a daylight factor is the lighting level at a point inside a room, expressed as a percentage of the available light outside, and is usually calculated assuming some type of standard sky conditions such as a standard overcast sky). It is important to note that this criterion is an abstraction of our original ideal and goal; good performance in satisfying the criterion is only a part of achieving the goal. This abstraction in mapping goals onto criteria is common and often useful, but the fact that it is an abstraction should be remembered.

We can represent our two design variables as axes in a *design* (or *decision*) *space,* where each point in the space will represent a particular combination of design decisions for window height and shade projection. To keep things simple, we assume there are only six feasible solutions (fig. 1-4). Each of these has an associated performance. Since we only have one criterion, our equivalent *performance space* is a vector (fig. 1-5). The result is an ordered ranking of the performances of solutions according to their position in this vector, and the whole field of feasible performances delineates a segment of the vector. Clearly, if our objective is to maximize the daylighting in the room, a solution is dominated (bettered) by any solution that offers a better performance in this criterion. We can identify a best performance, *A,* as the one that dominates all others, and we can map back from the best performance to the decisions that result in that performance.

In design, making decisions in relation to one isolated design goal while ignoring all others has very limited usefulness. Indeed, the solution may be trivial: an architect knows that the biggest window with the least shade overhang will provide the highest levels of daylight, without needing to solve the problem by extensive analysis. Such isolation of a single criterion may also be dangerous. Postwar schools in the United Kingdom contained windows designed to provide a 2 percent daylight factor over the working plane of the classrooms without sufficient concern for their other environmental consequences, leading to problems of summer solar heat gain, glare, and excessive winter heat loss.

The more interesting (and more difficult) design problems are those in which we recognize that performances with respect to two or more goals need to be explored together. In view of the United Kingdom schools' experience, we shall use summer solar heat gain as a second criterion (restricting our discussion to two criteria only to keep things simple). As with daylighting, our chosen criterion is an abstraction from the wider goal of achieving thermal comfort in the room.

The performance space with two criteria is two-dimensional. We can represent the six pairs of performances associated with our six pairs of decisions as points in this space, whose axes are "Area with 2% Daylight Factor" and "Summer Solar Heat Gain." It is useful to adopt the convention that increasing distance from the origin corresponds to increasing "goodness" of the performance, so we have drawn the "Summer Solar Heat Gain" axis with high numbers at the origin and low numbers away from the origin (fig. 1-6). The set of performances delineates an area known as the *feasible performance region*.

Now we can see that performance *A* is the best if we only consider

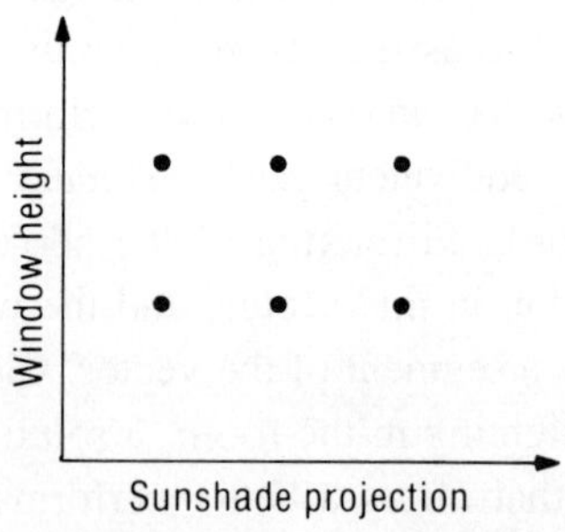

Fig. 1-4. Design or decision space for the window/sunshade problem, in which the two axes represent possible values for the decision variables. Any design solution can be represented as a point in this space.

daylighting and that performance *F* is the best if we only consider summer solar heat gain, but what about the middle ground? *E* is worse than *D* in daylighting, but it is better in solar heat gain; therefore, we cannot say that *E* is better overall than *D*, or that *D* is better overall than *E*. If we compare, *D* and *B*, however, we discover that *D* is better in both criteria. On this basis we can say that *D* dominates *B*, and we can eliminate *B* from further consideration with respect to these criteria, since we would always select *D* in preference to it. Similarly, we can eliminate *C*. The performances that remain—those that are not dominated by other performances—are known as the set of *nondominated, noninferior* or *Pareto optimal performances* (named after the nineteenth-century economist Vilfredo Pareto, who introduced the concept in welfare economics). As before, we can map back from these performances to the decisions that produce them.

In this book, we shall use the term *Pareto optimal* to mark this specific meaning of *dominance* from other uses of the word. Generalizing from two to many criteria, we reach the following definition:

> A feasible solution to a multicriteria problem is Pareto optimal if no other feasible solution exists that will yield an improvement in one criterion without causing a degradation in at least one other criterion.

For two criteria, the Pareto optimal set traces a curve along the upper right-hand edge of the performance space. For three criteria the result is a surface, each point on which satisfies the definition above. Higher dimensions are difficult to visualize, but the set of Pareto optimal solutions to a problem with *P* objectives will form a surface in *P*-dimensional space.

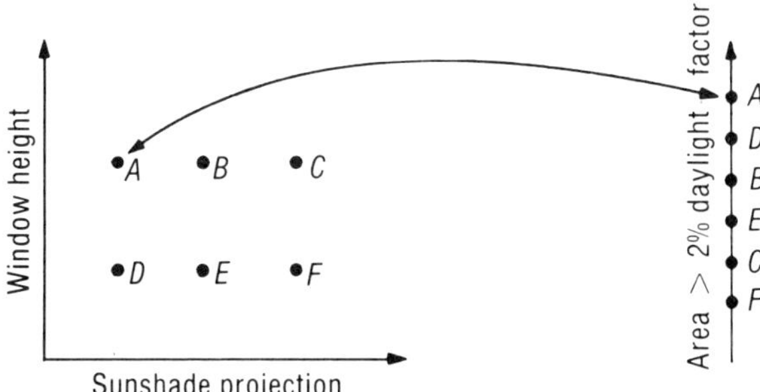

Fig. 1-5. Mapping between decisions and performances for the window/sunshade problem. With one criterion, the performance space is a vector, and there is an optimal performance and associated set of decisions.

The Pareto set is thus the nearest equivalent with two or more criteria to the concept of best or optimal solution with one criterion. Both are determined by the mechanistic application of tests of domination. But whereas one criterion yields a clear-cut best solution, multiple criteria raise a field or subset of solutions that the decision maker must investigate further. Any one of these Pareto solutions may be the best choice; which *is* best depends on the decision maker's perception of the relative importance of the performances in the different criteria.

In essence the choice comes down to one of tradeoffs. Given two goals, X and Y, how much of X is the decision maker prepared to give up in order to gain more of Y? The problem, of course, is that how much of X one is prepared to give up in order to gain more of Y depends on how much of X and Y one has. Given a tub of apples and no oranges one may be prepared to give up dozens of boring apples for the taste of an exotic orange, but if the tub contains only oranges the relative attraction is reversed. One needs to know what the options are in order to enumerate tradeoffs. A way of representing this graphically is by means of *indifference* (or *isopreference*) *curves,* which map points in the objective space that are of equal preference to the decision maker (fig. 1-7).

In figure 1-7, the indifference curves link combinations of performance in X and Y which the decision maker would rank as equal. The points on P_1 rank higher than points on P_2, however, and these in turn rank higher than those on P_3. The shape of an indifference curve indicates how the decision makers' acceptance of tradeoffs varies according to the values of X and Y. The concave (upward) graph reflects the typical case in which the tradeoff ratios are larger when X and Y are out of balance. For the general case of n criteria, the indifference curve becomes an indifference plane in n-dimensional space.

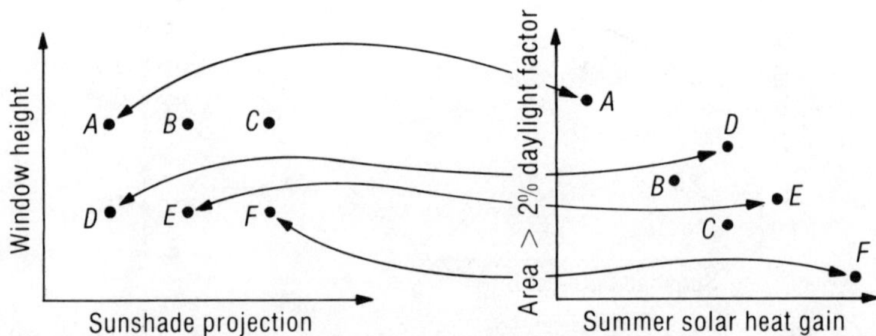

Fig. 1-6. Mapping between decisions and performances for the window/sunshade problem. With two criteria, the performance space is two-dimensional.

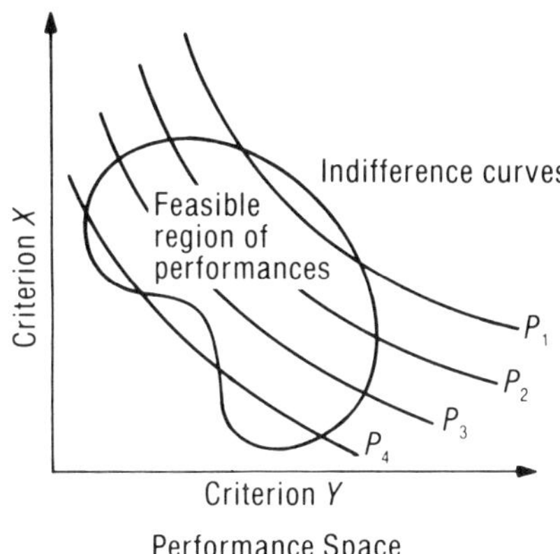

Fig. 1-7. Indifference (isopreference) curves in the performance space. Any point on the same indifference curve is equally acceptable.

Given the opportunity to continue trading off apples for oranges, we can seek a compromise position that suits our own preferences. This can be expressed graphically by superimposing indifference curves over the feasible criteria space. The *best compromise* solution is the point at which an indifference curve is tangent to the Pareto optimal set—a situation known as the *tangency condition* (fig. 1-8).

The indifference curve is only an expression of the decision maker's personal preferences; another decision maker may express these prefer-

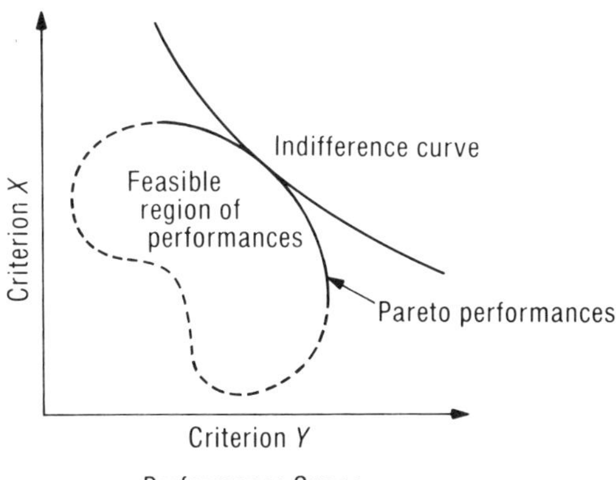

Fig. 1-8. The best compromise solution is given by the tangency condition, where the indifference curve is tangential to the Pareto set.

ences differently and hence choose a different best compromise solution. Moreover, it represents a very comprehensive statement of preferences that is extremely difficult to establish in a practical situation.

How, then, can this best compromise solution be reached? The first approach is simply to consider a graphical representation of all the Pareto optimal solutions and use the tradeoff information it portrays to arrive at a personal choice of solution. This is called a *nonpreference method* because it requires no explicit definition of relative preferences by the decision maker. The second approach is to make some prior assumption of relative importance and use this information in the generation of alternatives to identify a single choice or at most a small subset of Pareto optimal solutions. Methods based on this approach may be called *preference methods* to emphasize the difference between methods that do not require an explicit definition of preferences and methods that do.

Sometimes we can identify an obvious basis for fixing these preferences. For our window/sunshade design problem, the level of performance reached in many of the applicable criteria has direct consequences in terms of energy use and monetary cost: less daylighting implies increased use of artificial lighting; solar heat gain in summer means increased use of the cooling plant; heat loss in winter means increased use of the heating plant. One way of rationalizing preferences among different objectives is to examine their relative contribution to a common *hyperobjective*. If we interpret all objectives in terms of cost, we can identify the least-cost design, map back to the performances of this least-cost design in the contributing criteria, and then map still farther back to the design decisions that underlie a least-cost design.

In parts 2 and 3 of this book, we shall look at design problems with one criterion in mind—often a criterion that could be regarded as being derived from a hyperobjective. Then, in part 4, we shall return to looking at multicriteria problems and at ways of seeking what might be called a best compromise among conflicting goals.

SYMBOLIC MODELING

In our discussion of decision and performance spaces, we have assumed that we possess some means of establishing the performance of a design. Since in our example we do not intend to build all six possible solutions and thereafter measure the results, we need to use models.

The purpose of a model is to facilitate understanding through the description of salient features. Architects and other building designers are most familiar with physical models: two-dimensional drawings of building elevations and plans, and three-dimensional constructions of cardboard or balsa wood. Such models can either describe existing reality or predict a future or proposed reality. In making models, designers implicitly define boundaries to what is being modeled and select a level of abstraction in the way it is modeled. The typical architect's three-dimensional physical model sits on a baseboard of finite size (defining boundaries) and uses grossly simplified descriptions of the actual scene's form, color, and texture (defining a level of abstraction). Only certain selected characteristics of reality are chosen for representation in the model.

The use of the word *model* in a broader sense to encompass a range of models in addition to reduced-scale three-dimensional physical models stems from the field of operations research. Churchman, Ackoff, and Arnoff, in their book *Introduction to Operations Research,* identify three types of model: iconic, analog, and symbolic. An *iconic model* looks like what it represents; photographs, paintings, and sculptures may offer iconic models of people, objects, or scenes. We do not need a key to an iconic model, since the relationship between the parts of the model and the parts of reality is obvious. In an *analog model,* the various properties of the original are represented by properties of quite different kinds in the model. A map does not, except at a very abstract level, look like the ground it represents: roads and political boundaries are represented by lines; different heights are represented by contours, and so on. An analog model usually requires a key of some kind—something that explains the relationship between the parts of the model and the parts of reality. Architects' drawings are a mix of iconic and analog models; laymen, for example, often find it difficult to understand such drawings without having them explained.

Symbolic models use symbols to represent the parts of reality. The most common form of these are the mathematical symbols in mathematical models. Typically they consist of equations or sets of equations expressing relationships between the entities being modeled. Thus $y = mx + c$ is a symbolic model of a straight line, where the equation describes the relationship between the coordinates of points on the line. Building forms can be expressed in symbolic models that describe them (as points in space) and the links and relationships between them; the data base of a computer drafting/modeling system constitutes a symbolic model of the buildings that are drawn with the system. A symbolic model must have an accompanying key, explaining what the variable names represent and what any other symbols used mean.

Computers work with symbolic models. The models are constructed as large numbers of equations and operations, where the output from one set of operations becomes the input to another set. Such models imply unambiguity—the possibility of strict deduction and verifiability by reference back to reality—and are based on the existence of some kind of algorithm. If their purpose is to predict behavior, they need to be run (that is, to have values for input variables put through them to derive values for output variables) in order to describe reality. Their formulation involves setting the model boundaries to encompass the smallest number of components within which the behavior under study is generated, and then constructing within these boundaries the relationships responsible for the kind of behavior that is of interest. In a symbolic model constructed for design purposes, the *endogenous variables* (also called *design variables* or *decision variables*) are those over which the designer has control in determining values, while the *exogenous variables* are those fixed by factors outside the designer's control. In our illustrative window/sunshade design problem, the window height and the sunshade are the endogenous variables, while the other variables needed to describe the situation (glass type, sun path, solar radiation levels, and so on) are all exogenous variables. A *dependent variable* is one whose value is determined by the values of other variables.

Much of the rest of this book (including all of chapter 2) is devoted to the topic of constructing models. Some of these models are detailed and sophisticated; others are crude approximations for use at early stages of the design process, like the early sketches or crude cardboard models of designers' studios. However much effort goes into its construction, a model can never be a perfect or complete representation of reality, if only because we do not have perfect information about the real world. It is worthwhile to consider J. W. Forrester's description of the grounds on which the usefulness of a model can be assessed:

> The validity and usefulness of dynamic models should be judged, not against an imaginary perfection, but in comparison with the mental and descriptive models which we should otherwise use. We should judge the formal models by their clarity of structure and compare this clarity to the confusion and incompleteness so often found in a verbal description.

In our case, we are using models as a means of providing information for design. We should judge the usefulness of the models by assessing the usefulness of the information that they provide for decision making in comparison to the information that would otherwise be available.

INFORMATION FOR DECISION MAKING

What kind of information does a designer need for decision making? Clearly, prescriptive information (which prescribes the nature of good decisions) is of more value in this regard than evaluative information (which establishes whether decisions are any good only after they have been made). If designers worked with single-criterion problems, the ideal information would simply be a description of the best solution. We have argued, though, that most design problems have numerous and diverse goals, only some of which can be mapped onto measurable criteria. The best solution for one goal is still useful information—it indicates how good performance in one design aspect might be achieved, and the value of the best performance provides a yardstick against which other designs can be compared—but it is not enough.

First, the designer needs *manipulative models* that can be used to explore the relationships between design decisions and performance results. If the model does not encompass all the design goals of interest, steps must be taken to control and adapt the use of the model to take into account decisions and constraints that arise because of goals outside the model.

Second, the information derived from such models should be concerned with *fields of solutions*. This involves expressing the design options and identifying the ranges within which designers can make decisions, rather than predicting the performance of a single preselected solution or identifying a single best solution for one criterion. If simulation is used to investigate a single solution (we discuss simulation models in chapter 2), feedback information of more general use in developing the design is usually needed; just testing a preconceived idea that will not be changed is insufficient. If optimization is used to find the optimal solution, given a single criterion (we discuss optimization models further in chapter 2), the designer usually seeks to know not only the optimal solution and performance but also how sensitive the optimal performance is to changes in design parameters and how stable the optimal set of decisions is when changes are made in the assumptions on which they are selected. We are interested in close-to-optimal as well as optimal sets of decisions and performance.

Third, the information should explicate the *tradeoffs* involved in design, in order to make clear what is being lost in one group of design goals if performance is advanced in another group by making decisions to suit good performance in it.

FURTHER READING

A book that places the view of design in a broader context is:

Broadbent, G. 1973. *Design in Architecture*. New York: Wiley.

The notions of design goals are well described in:

Simon, H.A. 1975. Style in design. In *Spatial Synthesis in Computer-Aided Building Design,* ed. C. M. Eastman, pp. 287–309. London: Applied Science.

Simon has also written on the concepts that support the externalizing of decision making in:

Simon, H.A. 1969. *The Sciences of the Artificial*. Cambridge: MIT Press.

A good (though early) book on operations research is:

Churchman, C.W.; Ackoff, R.L.; and Arnoff, E.L. 1957. *Introduction to Operations Research*. New York: Wiley.

Forrester has written extensively on systems theory, and the reference in the text is drawn from:

Forrester, J.W. 1968. *Principles of Systems*. Cambridge: Wright-Allen Press.

The idea of design being modeled as language is explored in:

March, L., and Stiny, G. 1985. Spatial systems in architecture and design: some history and logic. *Environment and Planning B* 12(3): 31–53

Pareto's work has been recently republished (in translation) as:

Pareto, V. 1971. *Manual of Political Economy*. New York: A.M. Kelly.

CHAPTER 2

DESIGN MODELS

We have argued that design in architecture and building is a purposeful activity in which decisions are made about the physical form of buildings and their components in response to goals related to the building's intended purposes. Before design can begin, the designer needs some kind of model of the problem: in the mind, written down on paper, expressed as diagrams, expressed as symbols, or some combination of these. Getting the problem sorted out is among the most difficult tasks to accomplish—second only, perhaps, to recognizing that a problem exists in the first place.

Constructing a model of a problem, we have seen, does not require only that it be understood. We can understand everything about the problems of housing without having a useful model for its design. Do we begin with the roof flashing, the windows, the layout of the kitchen, or the drains? As well as understanding the problem, we need to be able to *formulate* it in a useful way so that relevant information is structured and organized and priorities are assigned. Since design is purposeful, part of the process of formulation involves relating the organization of the problem to the design goals. The system we call design includes the formulated model of the problem, the designer, and maybe other components as well. In this chapter we discuss where in this system of model and designer we can locate the objectives and the decisions, and we use this location to produce the typology of design models as simulation, generation, and optimization. We then compare these three approaches and look a little closer at the characteristics that make the optimization model of design an attractive option.

TYPOLOGY OF DESIGN MODELS

To design, we have to make some decisions, evaluate the result, and identify one or more objectives. Each of these activities can be performed inside or outside the formal model. If decisions and objectives are outside, we have a model that simply *describes* some state of the design in either static or dynamic terms. If the decisions are inside but the objectives are outside, we have a model that can *generate* designs but has no means of establishing whether those designs are any good. If the decisions, evaluation, and objectives are all inside, we have a model that can generate designs, evaluate them according to some objective, and *rank* them. We cannot put the objective inside the model and the decisions outside, since to do so would be to make a model that "knows" what the design is trying to achieve but is powerless to do anything about it.

All computer-aided design (CAD) models fall into one of three categories: simulation, generation, or optimization. In *simulation,* the computer is used to predict the performance consequences of a set of design decisions by manipulating a mathematical model that describes the design. All evaluation and decision making are external to the model. In *generation,* the computer is used to explore the consequences of recursive application of a set of decision rules. Some decision making is internal to the model but is not purposeful; all valid decisions are equally acceptable. In *optimization,* the computer is used to prescribe a set of decisions in order to achieve a specified goal as closely as possible. Some evaluation and decision making are internal to the model and are purposeful; decisions are chosen according to their ranking on an explicit measure of effectiveness (fig. 2-1).

Simulation, then, is concerned only with the description of designs. Generation is concerned with the description of designs and the application

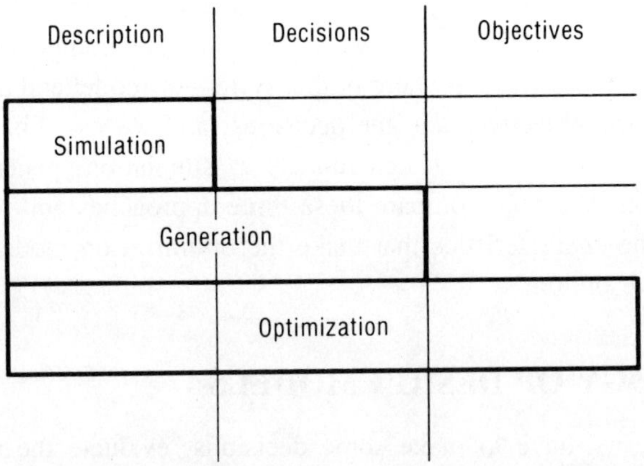

Fig. 2-1. Classification of computer-aided design models according to the location of descriptions, decisions, and objectives.

of valid decisions; the description in this case may or may not be evaluated to check whether it conforms to stated constraints. Like generation, optimization is concerned with descriptions and decisions, but in this case the results of the evaluation of different possible descriptions are ranked according to the objectives, and decisions are made according to this ranking. Thus optimization subsumes simulation and generation: we cannot have an optimization model that does not have within it the mechanisms characterizing simulation and generation. Before examining optimization, it is worth looking a bit closer at these other two kinds of models. Doing so not only helps us understand how the results from and the uses of these three kinds of models differ, but it also helps us understand the process of optimization by extracting these constituent parts and explaining what goes on within them.

SIMULATION

In the process of design, architects and designers have always created models that *simulate* things: the appearance of buildings, the cash flow during the construction process, the way a proposed building will cast shadows as the sun moves overhead. Simple manual mathematical models have long been used for describing structural performance and such environmental factors as daylighting and heat gains and losses. Computer simulation models produce the same class of information about the performance of predefined solutions as manual methods do. Consequently, they can occupy an established and well-defined position in design activity.

The great strength of simulation is that, by fixing values for all the design variables, we can examine their consequences in great detail, and on as many different aspects of the problems as there are prediction methods available. This is the usual design model in most CAD systems. The disadvantage of simulation is that it requires the user to operate by trial and error. To get any quantitative information, he or she must first have a solution; the design process therefore involves a cyclical procedure of postulation–evaluation–modification, where different possibilites are examined. Design options and sensitivity to changing assumptions can only be investigated by repeating the simulation many times with different sets of decisions.

Let us look again at the design of a window for a building. If we confine our attention to a single solution, we can predict its performance in as many performance measures as there are prediction methods available.

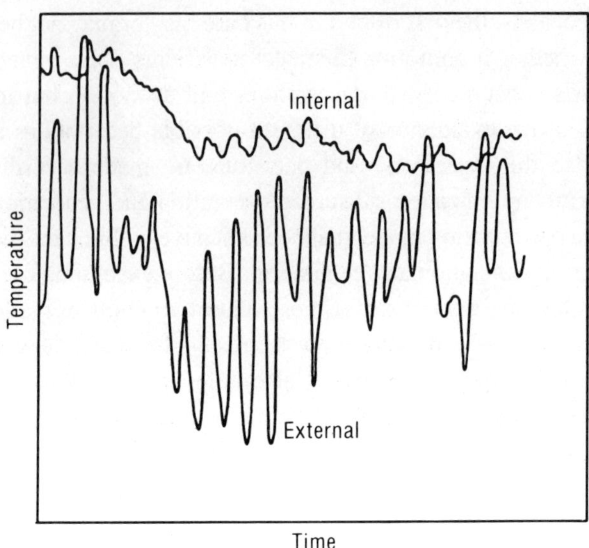

Fig. 2-2. Simulated performance represented as a graph: a profile of predicted internal air temperature in a building space, given a profile of external temperatures.

For example, for thermal performance we can predict and plot the temperature profile within a space for any hour of the day and for any day of the year, given assumed external conditions and no artificial heating and cooling (fig. 2-2); and for daylighting we can predict and plot daylight factors for every part of the room, given an assumed external sky luminance distribution (fig. 2-3). Similarly, we could predict sound intrusion at different frequencies, patterns of insolation on the walls and floors of the room at different hours and days of the year, and heat gains and losses from the space if internal temperature were to be controlled by mechanical services. We could also calculate the construction cost of a solution from a set of stored data and predict the solution's consequences in terms of energy use in operation.

If we examine the form of information produced by these simulation models, we find that results are typically presented in multivalued form—either as tables or in diagrams such as those shown in figures 2-2 and 2-3—and as neutral information, with no direct indication of the goodness or badness of the results or of how these performances compare with what may actually be achievable in the given design project. Taken alone, simulation models can only be used to check predetermined solutions against mandatory or recommended standards or to size mechanical and electrical plant in order to bridge the gap between conditions provided by the building fabric and required internal comfort conditions. To improve and develop solutions, we need to understand how to improve performance by modifying one or more of the design variables. This understanding can only be achieved by possessing a theoretical knowledge of the physical relationships involved or by comparing values for the design variables and predicted performances of many different design solutions.

In practice, any series of simulations needs to be guided by some hypothesis if it is to lead to an understanding of the relationships involved or to improvement in performance. In the process of *appraisal,* a first approximation is nominated by the designer and its performance predicted. The architect then decides whether or not modification of the solution is necessary and, if so, what form that modification should take.

The success of the process depends on the architect's ability to formulate a useful hypothesis by which to modify the solution—that is, on how much information on the relation between decision and performance variables can be established for use in the next iteration of the procedure. If the modified solution is far from the original in the solution space (for example, because it incorporates radically different values for several of the design variables), variation in performance cannot be attributed to specific design changes. If it is close to the existing solution (perhaps involving a change in only one variable in the familiar parametric process), the reasons for changes in performance are easy to understand, but the range of the solution field explored is small. Any comparison of two or more solutions also raises problems of rationalizing the multiplicity of

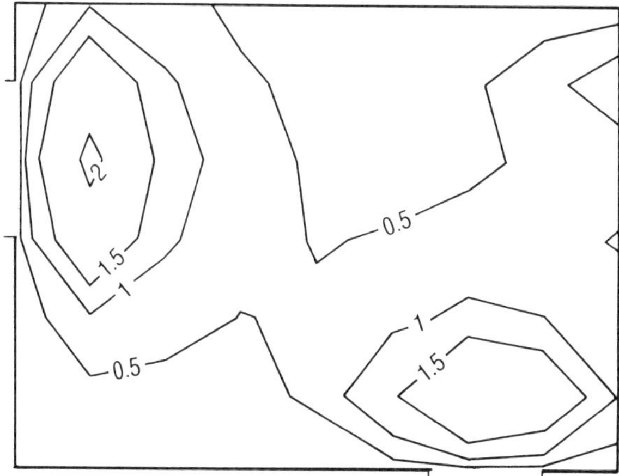

Fig. 2-3. Simulated daylight performance represented as a diagram: contours of equal daylight factor mapped onto a plan of the building space.

information given by several different performance measures each using multivalued representations of information.

With simulation, the validation of a model involves establishing that the relationships expressed in the description of the system behavior match those that exist in reality. It can be done on the basis of research on theory (checking that the components of the model are correct) or on the basis of results: if the model predicts behavior or appearances that consistently match those that occur in reality, given the same conditions, then the model is said to be validated. Hence, the validation concerns only the mechanisms employed in the description; no sense of validating the legitimacy of the intention of the model attaches to this process since no decisions or objectives are contained within it.

GENERATION

In what might be called a traditional view of design, generation comes from the human designer; he or she makes all the decisions, and these are merely described via a design medium. In a *generative model,* the model itself generates a design solution according to prescribed rules. Consider the most common methods for daylighting and artificial lighting design: in daylighting, the designer chooses a window size and checks by computer program or daylight protractor the resulting daylight factor in the room (simulation); with artificial lighting, the designer decides on a required design illuminance on the working plane and arrives at a design solution, on the basis of the lumen method, in terms of a number and layout of luminaries (generation). The type of luminaries in the latter case can be either a part of the performance specification or a part of the solution.

In a complex generative model, validating the decision rules becomes the major task. As with the descriptive part of the model, it can only be accomplished by examining the model in relation to theory and research and by comparing the results achieved by the model with those observed in reality.

By their nature, generative models provide a field of solutions that collectively demonstrate all possible design options according to the rules. The results may be evaluated, through being checked to ensure that they conform to some set of constraints, but they will not be ranked in any way. To control the generative process so that not all (and this "all" could be very large indeed) but only the best solutions are generated requires that the objectives as well as the decisions be contained within the model.

OPTIMIZATION

In *optimization* we make use of the descriptive mechanisms of simulation and the decision-according-to-rules mechanism of generation, and to these we add one or more objectives to ensure that the decision rules are chosen according to a ranking of the performance of solutions or partial solutions when measured against these objectives.

Consider again the daylight factor diagram shown in figure 2-3. To compare the daylighting performance of another solution, we need to assess whether this multivalued representation is better than, worse than, or equally good as the corresponding representation for the other solution. If the predicted daylight factors for one solution are better (or worse) than those predicted for the other solution at every point in the room, establishing which is best presents no problem. But this rarely occurs. To rank the predicted performances of two or more solutions numerically, it is usually necessary to interpret the multivalued performance representation in terms of a single-valued criterion that summarizes its contents. In chapter 1, we suggested that the information content of a daylight factor diagram could be abstracted as a single figure stating the proportion of the working plane over which the daylight factor exceeded a specified minimum level. Applying the same principle to other performance measures, the temperature profile in figure 2-2 could be summarized by an index of peak temperature; sound intrusion at different frequencies could be expressed as a single value using the *A*-weighted scale; and insolation could be summarized by a duration of insolation, measured according to fixed rules.

Optimization models effectively search the whole field of feasible solutions and identify those best suited to the designer's stated goals. Thus, optimization directly approaches an answer to the designer's fundamental question of what is the best solution. A number of examples of this approach to design now exist. Design options can be obtained by identifying near-optimal as well as optimal solutions, and formal methods are available for examining the sensitivity and stability of solutions. The disadvantage of optimization lies in the inherent difficulty of formulating meaningful quantifiable objectives in a discipline characterized by multiple and ill-defined objectives.

COMPARISON OF APPROACHES

Simulation, generation, and optimization produce very different kinds of information. Simulation can produce a great deal of information about many aspects of performance, but for only one predefined solution at a time. It tells the designer nothing about the relative merit of that solution compared with other feasible solutions, unless he or she repeats the analysis with different designs in what amounts to a process of informal optimization. Generation produces a subset of unranked feasible solutions by following a predefined sequence of rules. It tells the designer nothing about the performance or relative merit of solutions in the generated set, other than that the performance objectives ensured by the rules themselves are satisfied. Optimization encompasses the whole field of feasible solutions and produces an ordered subset of solutions that best satisfy a subset of specified performance objectives. It tells the designer nothing about performance in objectives outside this subset, unless he or she further investigates the solutions produced in a process of simulation. Which approach is appropriate depends on which kind of information is being sought. We have argued above that the designer's principal need is for information that is prescriptive—information that expresses the design options and addresses the problems of tradeoff between conflicting design goals. Optimization satisfies this need far more closely than either simulation or generation.

Although we have stressed the differences between them, simulation, generation, and optimization can be made to emulate and complement each other through the manner of their application. Thus, simulation models offer the potential for providing a field solution through repetition (including exhaustive enumeration as an extreme) and allow identification of a best solution by inspection of a set of simulated performances. Conversely, optimization emulates simulation if the feasible solution space is constrained to a single solution. Optimization subsumes generation and simulation: within an optimization model, generation is necessary to create the solution space to be searched, and simulation is necessary to describe and predict the performance to be optimized. Optimization models are therefore inherently more complex than simulation or generation models at the same degree of modeling.

OPTIMIZATION TECHNIQUES

The requirements for an optimization technique useful in this context relate to the characteristics of the information required, the types of problems encountered, and the objectives sought. Historically, optimization has been treated as a mathematical problem in which the interest lay only in the extreme value of the objective and in its offering some means of obtaining that value. What these means (the actual set of decisions required) consisted of was not particularly significant, and neither was any suboptimal solution.

In design, however, both the decisions and the suboptimal solutions are very important. The decisions represent a description of the physical form of an object or other proposal, the construction methods used, and the placement of components and other design elements; it is with the arrangement of these physical elements that the designer has traditionally been most concerned. The suboptimal solutions represent the design options and tell the designer about solution forms that are close to the optimal in terms of the stated objective but may involve more acceptable sets of decisions for their realization. Any technique adopted must therefore be able to produce fields or ranges of solutions that can be examined both in terms of their relative merit (the values of the objective function) and in terms of the sets of decisions they represent. But this is only a part of the information required. We also require good information on the stability and the sensitivity of performance of the solution choice, given possible changes in design parameters. In optimization, such information is usually obtained by methods of postoptimality analysis after optimal and suboptimal solutions have been identified.

In view of this rather demanding specification for the information required, it is unfortunate that many of the problems found in design have characteristics that are unsuited to easy application of optimization techniques. For example, architectural problems typically involve variables that are discrete and discontinuous and relationships that are nonlinear. Discrete variables can only take specific values—for example, pipe and brick sizes (to correspond with available materials) or numbers of rooms and floors (which must be integers to be meaningful). Discontinuous variables exhibit discontinuity in their range of values; for example, the required rate at which bathrooms must be provided in a building may change at threshold values imposed by building code regulations. Nonlinear relationships do not vary uniformly with the variables on which they depend—for example, area and the whole range of performance measures such as heat loss, daylighting, and cost (which are functions of area). Moreover, some relationships may be better represented as stochastic than as deterministic, requiring probability distributions for their modeling. Problems involving the movement and queuing of people frequently suggest this type of relationship, since humankind rarely behaves in a deterministic manner.

If we examine available optimization techniques, we find that—although the choice is wide—few satisfy all these requirements. *Classical calculus* provides a swift analytical solution to a range of design problems that can be formulated as continuous and differentiable equations and that are subject to few constraints. In building design, for example, it has been used to find a geometry for multistory built forms that minimizes conduction heat loss, to find the thickness of insulation required to minimize capital plus amortized running costs, and to find answers to a wide variety of structural design problems.

Linear programming is an efficient and well-developed numerical method that has been used extensively in structural design. It has been used to determine distributions of apartment types and land use in order to minimize development costs, to decide on the distribution of services within a building, and to solve other problems that can be modeled by linear relationships between variables.

For nonlinear relationships, various algorithms have been used to dimension a given floor-plan topology in order to minimize cost. In addition, a wide variety of *nonlinear programming* algorithms have been used in design situations. *Dynamic programming* has been applied to such problems as drainage design, the design of an elevator system, and the design of a floor/ceiling sandwich for multistory buildings. Dynamic programming is particularly appropriate for the kinds of problems with which design is concerned, since it can handle discrete, discontinuous, or stochastic variables and nonlinear relationships and since it is efficient with constraints. Its disadvantages are that it lacks a standard methodology and requires more thought about the structure of each separate problem than is sometimes necessary with other methods.

We look at three of these techniques—classical calculus, linear programming, and dynamic programming—in part 2 of this book, as well as offering some comments on nonlinear programming as an extension of linear programming.

FURTHER READING

Models of design are explored in:

Broadbent, G. 1973. *Design in Architecture*. New York: Wiley.

Gero, J.S., ed. 1985. *Design Optimization*. New York: Academic Press.

Gero, J.S., and Radford, A.D. 1984. The place of multicriteria optimization in design. In *Design Theory and Practice*, ed. R. Langdon and P. Purcell, pp. 81–85. London: Design Council.

March, L., ed. 1976. *The Architecture of Form*. Cambridge: Cambridge University Press.

Markus, T.A.; Whyman, P.; Morgan, J.; Whitton, D.; Maver, T.W.; Canter, D.; and Fleming, J. 1972. *Building Performance*. New York: Halsted.

Mitchell, W.J. 1977. *Computer-Aided Architectural Design*. New York: Van Nostrand Reinhold.

Radford, A.D. 1981. Optimization, simulation and multiple criteria in window design. *Computer-Aided Design* 13(6): 345–50.

Radford, A.D., and Gero, J.S. 1980. On optimization in computer-aided design. *Building and Environment* 15(2): 73–80.

The notions of appraisal within the concept of simulation are described in:

Maver, T.W. 1977. Building appraisal. In *Computer Applications in Architecture*, ed. J.S. Gero, pp. 63–94. London: Applied Science.

Generation using a grammar is described in:

Stiny, G., and Mitchell, W.J. 1978. The Palladian grammar. *Environment and Planning B* 5(1): 5–18.

PART 2

DESIGN BY OPTIMIZATION

Optimization is the search for what in some sense represents the best set of decisions about a system under study. The basis for the evaluation is an explicit objective, and the set of possible decisions is usually subject to various constraints on their practicable form. Numerous techniques can be used in conducting this search, and each one has its own advantages and disadvantages. For design by optimization, an optimization technique must be matched to the form of the problem and to the type of information being sought. In this part, we elaborate some of the most important methodologies and illustrate their suitability for different types of problems.

In chapter 3 we investigate a classical optimization method that has a long and rich history: *differential calculus*. It provides an analytical solution very quickly to a range of design problems that can be formulated as continuous and differentiable equations and that are subject to few constraints. Unfortunately, in architecture and building we are rarely able to formulate problems in this way.

Following chapter 3, we move on to numerical optimization methods that are generally grouped under the heading, *mathematical programming*. In chapter 4 we look at *linear programming*—the best developed of the mathematical programming techniques. We explain the simplex method, which provides the basis for its efficiency, and go on to show how it can be applied to design problems. Linear programming is, however, restricted to problems that can be modeled by linear relationships between the variables.

We turn to *dynamic programming,* another mathematical programming technique, in chapter 5. This technique can optimize design problems in which nonlinear relationships exist between the variables, and it is particularly well suited to design problems in which the variables can take only discrete values. It can only work, however, when the design problem is formulated in a specific way.

In each chapter, we give a verbal description of the concepts involved, a brief mathematical representation (as well as a listing of sources that develop the mathematics further), and examples to elucidate the various approaches and methods.

CHAPTER 3

DESIGN USING DIFFERENTIAL CALCULUS

The most common representation of a symbolic model is in the form of an algebraic expression that joins the problem's variables together to form a goal that can be optimized. Sometimes these algebraic expressions exhibit characteristics that make them amenable to manipulation by differential calculus. This is significant because, as we shall see, differential calculus has the potential to play an important role in locating optimal design decisions. In this chapter, we shall consider how differential calculus can aid us in this task. First, however, it will be useful to examine the graphical representations of some of these symbolic models expressed in algebraic form. This will give us an intuitive understanding of why differential calculus is important.

Suppose we have a design problem with only one variable, x, and suppose the symbolic model for this problem represented algebraically is

$$z = 10x^2 - 60x + 200 \tag{3.1}$$

where z is the goal or objective to be minimized, and the constants are derived from the particular problem. Figure 3-1 shows equation 3.1 graphically. The figure indicates that this expression can be plotted as a continuous graph—that is, it has no breaks in it. Further, the plotted expression exhibits a minimum value for the objective at the point labeled M, where $z = 110$ and $X = 3$. Clearly, this is what we are looking for. If all expressions were this simple, we could plot them and locate the optimum by inspection with a reasonable degree of accuracy. But readily plotting expressions—particularly those with more than one decision variable—is not always possible. So we need a way to find an expression's optimum irrespective of the difficulty involved in plotting and visualizing it. We shall see that differential calculus does just this for us.

Suppose a design decision problem has two decision variables, x and

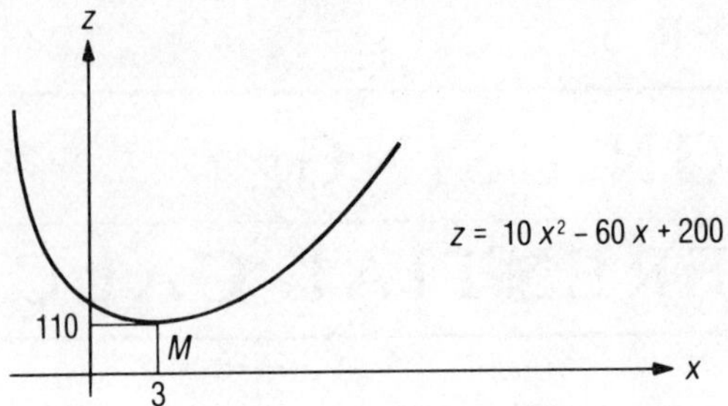

Fig. 3-1. Graphical representation of equation 3.1.

y, and a more complicated algebraic expression for the objective, z, such as

$$z = -y^2 - 2x^2 + 5x + 5 \tag{3.2}$$

Equation 3.2 can still be plotted graphically by using an orthogonal projection, as in figure 3-2. (We shall relate the abstract models represented by these equations to design problems later in this chapter.) From figure 3-2, we can observe that the objective has a maximum. From figures 3-1 and 3-2, we can reason out a requirement for a maximum or minimum to occur in the expressions that describe our problems. In both of these figures (and we could plot a great many other such expressions, as well), the optimum—that is, the maximum or minimum—occurs at the point where the graph turns around (where it starts going down instead of up, or up instead of down). We can express this more rigorously by looking at the slopes of the curves at any point and examining how they change direction. If we draw a line that touches the curve at some point, that line is called a *tangent;* its slope is the slope of the curve at that point.

Figure 3-3 is figure 3-1 with three tangents added. The tangent line, t_1,

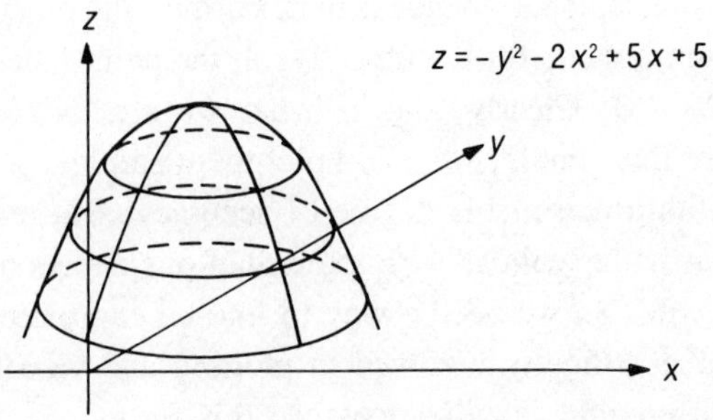

Fig. 3-2. Graphical representation of equation 3.2.

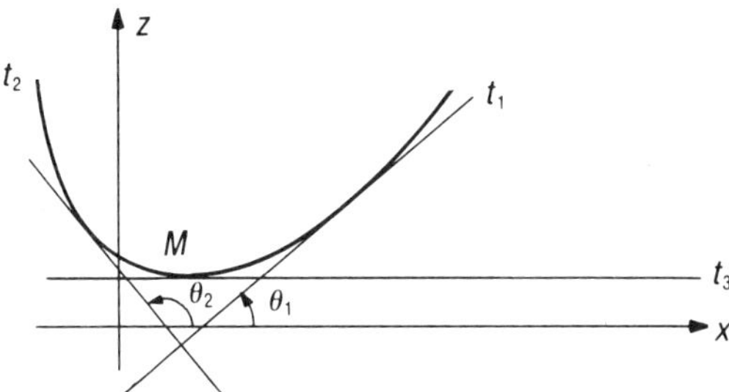

Fig. 3-3. Graph of figure 3-1 with the addition of three tangent lines.

whose slope is the trigonometric tangent (tan) of the angle θ_1, is to the right of the minimum point, M. Its slope is positive (since the tan of angles between 0° and 90° is positive). The tangent line t_2, whose slope is given by tan θ_2, is to the left of point M. Its slope is negative (since the tan of angles between 90° and 180° is negative). The third tangent line, t_3, is at the minimum point, M, and its slope is zero (since the tan of 0° is zero).

We could perform the same procedure with figure 3-2, using tangent planes instead of tangent lines, and we would discover the same result: the slopes of the curve on either side of an optimum point have opposite signs, while at the optimum point the slope is zero. Therefore, all we need to do to identify the optimum values of an expression is to locate the point at which its slope is zero. But how do we distinguish between an optimum point that is a minimum and one that is a maximum? Again we can learn by looking at graphical plots.

Figure 3-4 reproduces figure 3-1, with the slope along its length plotted directly below it. The plot shows a straight line that passes through zero at the value of x at point M and has negative values to the left of it and positive values to the right of it. We can plot below it its slope—the value of the tangents at all points along its length—but clearly, since the original slope graph is a straight line, its slope has a constant value along its length. Furthermore, this value is positive. If we had plotted the same graph for an expression that exhibited a maximum, we would have found that the slope at the optimum was negative. From this we can infer the following rules regarding the identification of optimal values of expressions:

1. An optimum occurs when the slope of the expression reaches zero.
2. An optimum is a minimum if the slope of the slope at the optimum is positive.

3. An optimum is a maximum if the slope of the slope at the optimum is negative.

Not all expressions are as simple as those in equations 3.1 and 3.2, but the rules enumerated above are still applicable. Let us now proceed to generalize and formalize an approach to the identification of optimal solutions to problems that is based on elementary calculus.

MATHEMATICAL FORAY

Calculus, invented independently by Isaac Newton and Gottfried von Leibnitz in the seventeenth century, has become a fundamental compu-

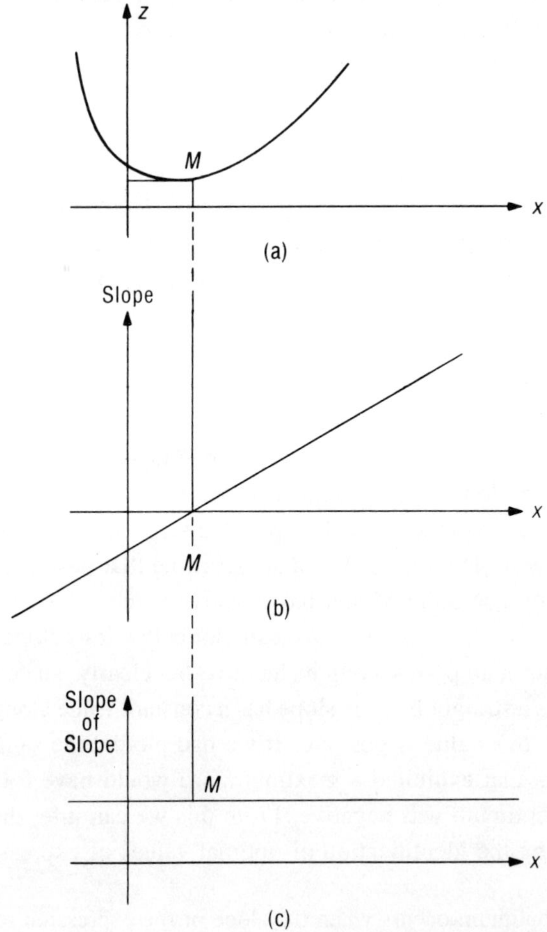

Fig. 3-4. (a) Graphical representation of the expression $z = 10x^2 - 60x + 200$. (b)Slope of the graph in (a).
(c) Slope of the slope of the graph in (a).

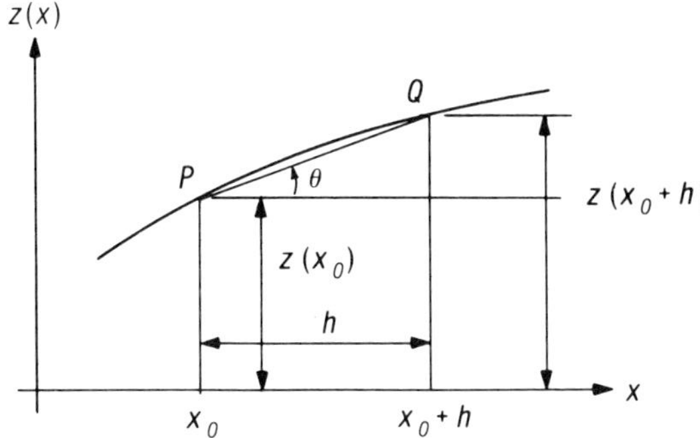

Fig. 3-5. Continuous graph where the chord *PQ* becomes the tangent to the curve as *Q* approaches *P*.

tational tool in a wide variety of applications involving algebraic expressions. Of particular interest to us is *differential calculus,* because the process of differentiation produces the slope of the tangent to a curve.

We shall begin by quickly reviewing the basis of differentiation. (Readers to whom this is well known may skip this discussion and move on to the next section.) Consider figure 3-5, where P is a point on the graph of some expression $z(x)$ (called a *function* in calculus) with an x-coordinate of x_O. Let Q be an adjacent point on the curve, whose x-coordinate is $x_O + h$. The slope of the chord PQ becomes the slope of the tangent as P and Q approach each other. This slope can be expressed as

$$\tan \theta = [z(x_O - h) - z(x_O)]/h$$

As h approaches zero in the limit, this becomes the slope of the curve, and the resulting expression is called the *derivative*. The derivative of z with respect to x is normally written as

$$\frac{dz}{dx}$$

when there is only one decision variable, and as

$$\frac{\partial z}{\partial x}$$

when there is more than one decision variable. Thus, we write

$$\frac{dz}{dx} = \frac{\lim}{h \to 0} \frac{z(x_O + h) - z(x_O)}{h} \tag{3.3}$$

as the derivative of z with respect to x in the limit as h approaches zero.

Usually, we do not need to commence differentiation at this basic level, since many rules are available to cover most situations; however, let us consider equation 3.1 and find its derivative using equation 3.3. Equation 3.1 states that

$$z = 10x^2 - 60x + 200$$

Therefore,

$$\frac{dz}{dx} = \frac{10(x + h)^2 - 60(x + h) + 200 - (10x^2 - 60x + 200)}{h}$$

$$= \frac{10x^2 + 20xh + h^2 - 60x - 60h - 200 - 10x^2 + 60x - 200}{h}$$

$$= \frac{20xh + h^2 - 60h}{h}$$

$$= 20x + h^2 - 60$$

And as h approaches zero,

$$\frac{dz}{dx} = 20x - 60$$

Equation 3.3 represents the slope at any point of the expression.

We can apply our rules to see if there is an optimum and, if there is, where it occurs by first setting the derivative to zero:

$$\frac{dz}{dx} = 20x - 60 = 0$$

Therefore, $x = 3$, so an optimum may exist.

We can check whether the suspected optimum is a maximum or a minimum (what else could it be?) by repeating the differentiation process on the derivative (called the *first derivative*) to produce the *second derivative*—the slope of the slope:

$$\frac{d}{dx}\left(\frac{dz}{dx}\right) = \frac{d^2z}{dx^2} = \frac{20(x + h) - 60 - 20x - 60}{h}$$

$$= 20$$

This is positive. Hence, an optimum exists at $x = 3$, $z = 110$, and it is a minimum in accordance with our earlier, intuitively found result.

With some restrictions, differential calculus provides a powerful means of determining optimal designs. It is not limited to producing numerical solutions, like those in the above examples, but can produce symbolic results as well. These are of special significance. Now let us turn to some design problems.

PROBLEM: PRELIMINARY SIZING OF A HOUSING ESTATE

Description

Suppose a county has a tract of land on which it intends to develop public housing. Detailed studies have been carried out to examine the benefits and costs of building estates of different sizes. The primary goal of the county is to maximize the net benefit of the project. You need to decide the size of the project in terms of cost, benefit, net benefit, and area of housing to be developed.

Formulation

Although it may look as though many decision variables are involved, they can all be expressed in terms of the area of housing to be developed, which we shall call X. Suppose the consultants have produced an equation for the benefits, B, in dollar terms, as follows:

$$B = 200 + 100X$$

Independently, you have found the cost, C, of the housing to be

$$C = 100 + 40X^2$$

B and C are expressed in millions of dollars, and X is expressed in area units (perhaps hundreds of thousands of square meters or millions of square feet). The net benefit, N, can be written as

$$\begin{aligned} N &= B - C \\ &= (200 + 100X) - (100 + 40X^2) \\ &= 100 + 100X - 40X^2 \end{aligned}$$

Thus the net benefit, N, needs to be maximized.

Solution

To begin, we need to find the first derivative of N with respect to X,

$$\frac{dN}{dX} = 100 - 80X$$

and set it to zero to determine whether an optimum may exist:

$$100 - 80X = 0$$
$$X = 1.25$$

Next, we need to check the second derivative to determine whether it is a maximum or minimum:

$$\frac{d^2N}{dX^2} = -80$$

This is negative, indicating that the decision produces a maximum. The solution is as follows:

Housing area	=	1.25 area units
Benefit	=	\$325 million
Cost	=	\$162.5 million
Net benefit	=	\$162.5 million

In this design decision problem, we found the optimal values of the variables. But, calculus has the capability of sometimes producing results that transcend the values unique to a specific problem, producing results with a wide application.

PROBLEM: DESIGNING A PREFABRICATED ROOF SYSTEM

Description

You have completed the preliminary design of a manufacturing facility. It takes the form of a square, single-story building. You have decided to select a prefabricated column-and-beam roof system to cover the building between feature end walls. You now need to decide on the number of beams, the number of columns, and the bay sizes in order to minimize the capital cost of the roof-supporting system.

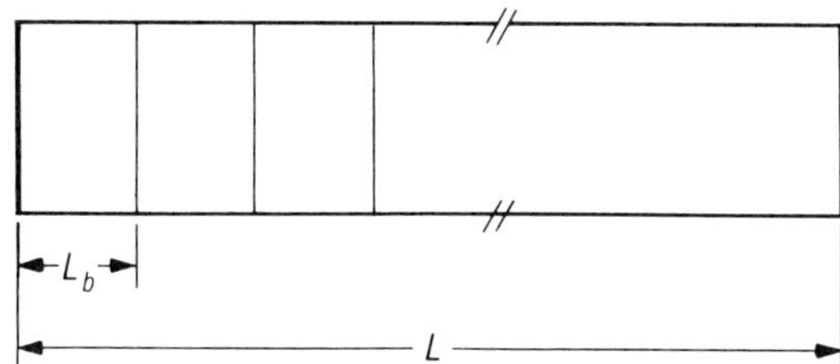

Fig. 3-6. Section of a building with a prefabricated roof system.

Formulation

For this problem it will be sufficient to consider just one row of beams and columns, since all other rows will be the same. Let us start by listing the possible decision variables (the variables for which we need values). There appear to be three: the number of beams, n_b; the number of columns, n_c; and the bay sizes, L_b.

Figure 3-6 shows the roof system. We can see that $n_c = n_b - 1$. Furthermore, we can see that $n_b L_b = L$, or $n_b = L/L_b$, where L is the wall-to-wall distance. From this we can state that—although there appear to be three decision variables—the number of columns is dependent on the number of beams, and the number of beams is dependent on the bay sizes. This leaves us with one independent decision variable: it could be any of the three, but we will arbitrarily use the bay sizes (L_b). Next we need to express the objective in terms of the decision variable.

The capital cost of the roof system, R, can be written as

$$R = n_c c_c + n_b c_b L_b$$

where c_c is the cost of one column, and c_b is the cost per unit length of a beam. This expression can be rewritten, substituting for n_c and n_b, as

$$R = [(L/L_b) - 1]c_c + (L/L_b)c_b L_b \tag{3.4}$$

Let us assume that the end walls will not change with a change in bay size. Let us further assume that the cost of a beam is directly proportional to its span

$$c_b = kL_b$$

and that the cost of a column is fixed. Now the capital cost, which is to be minimized, can be expressed as

$$R = [(L/L_b) - 1]c_c + kL_b L$$

Solution

We can now find the first derivative of the capital cost with respect to the bay size:

$$\frac{dR}{dL_b} = -Lc_c/L_b^2 + kL$$

By setting this to zero, we can determine whether an optimum may exist

$$-Lc_c/L_b^2 + kL = 0$$
$$L_b = (c_c/k)^{1/2}$$

We now need to check the second derivative to determine whether this is a maximum or a minimum:

$$\frac{d^2R}{dL_b^2} = 2Lc_c/L_b^3$$

This is always positive for any nonnegative values of L, c_c, and L_b. So we have determined that there is a minimum cost of the roof system and that it occurs when the bay size is equal to

$$(c_c/k)^{1/2}$$

We can rewrite this expression, making c_c the subject:

$$c_c = kL_b^2$$

Then, by substituting the expression that gives c_b, we get

$$c_c = c_bL_b$$

This implies that the optimum is reached when the cost of one column equals the cost of one beam. We are now in a position to calculate the number of beams and the number of columns that produce the optimum design, once we know the cost of a column and the cost per unit length of the beams. This type of result is special in that it does not depend on the values of the variables; we can infer the meaning from the symbols alone. Such results are called *field solutions,* and only calculus has the capacity to generate them.

DESIGN UNDER CONSTRAINTS

So far, we have been examining formulations in which a single relationship exists between the variables, and that relationship is the goal or objective. Far more commonly, multiple relationships are needed to describe the problem. The additional relationships normally are *constraints* because they limit the range of values the decision variables may take at the optimum solution.

The simplest form of constraints are *equality constraints*. In these, the values of the variables at the optimum solution, when substituted into the constraint expression, must equal a constant that is derived in the formulation. A designer can readily deal with an equality constraint by using it to eliminate one of the decision variables from the goal expression. We shall see how this works in the example in the next section.

Inequality constraints, which simply limit the range of individual decision variables, can also be managed fairly easily. The designer simply carries out the normal optimization and checks to make sure that the optimum does not lie on one of the boundaries defined by the constraint. Complex inequality constraints can be converted into equality constraints by the addition of new artificial variables; these are termed *slack variables* because they take up the slack between the values of the variables that satisfy the inequality relationship and the values in an equality relationship.

PROBLEM: PRELIMINARY PLAN FOR A MUSEUM BUILDING

Description

As part of a proposal for a maritime museum building, you have generated the cross section outlined in figure 3-7. It consists of three equisized quadrants of a circle, forming the main building, and a semicircle of half the radius of the other quadrants attached to the main building. You wish to keep the relative dimensions indicated, expressed in terms of a planning grid of 300-mm (1-ft) units. At this preliminary stage, you wish to get an idea of the length and width of the building that will minimize its cost, given that its volume must be 1 million cubic units. The average unit cost of the roof is \$15 per square unit. The end walls are expected to be complicated, and their average unit cost is \$30 per square unit.

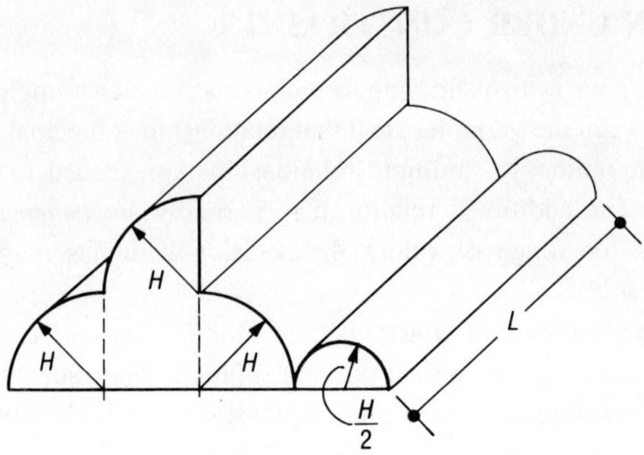

Fig. 3-7. Cross section of a preliminary design for a maritime museum, showing relative sizes.

Formulation

This preliminary design problem has two decision variables: the radius of the circles, *H;* and the length of the building, *L*. The following relationships can be established from the geometry of the cross section:

$$\text{Roof area} = (3(2\pi H/4) + H + \pi H/2)L$$

$$= 7.28HL$$

$$\text{End wall area} = 2(3(\pi H^2/4) + H^2 + \pi H^2/2)$$

$$= 9.84H^2$$

$$\text{Volume} = 4.92H^2L$$

$$\text{Cost, } C = 15 \text{ (roof area)} + 30 \text{ (end wall area)}$$

$$= 109.2HL + 295.2H^2$$

So the decision problem becomes minimizing

$$C = 109.2HL + 295.2H^2$$

subject to

$$4.92H^2L = 1{,}000{,}000$$

Solution

We can use the equality constraint to eliminate one variable. Let us choose to eliminate *L*. (It makes no difference to the result which variable is chosen.) Therefore,

$$L = (0.2 \times 10^6)/H^2$$

Substituting this into the expression for the objective, we get

$$C = [(21.8 \times 10^6)/H] + 295.2H^2$$

Now we will continue as before and differentiate C with respect to H, set the derivative to zero to locate an optimum, and then check the second derivative to ensure that it is a minimum. Differentiating C, we get

$$\frac{dC}{dH} = [(-21.8 \times 10^6)/H^2] + 590H$$

Setting dC/dH to zero and solving for H, we get

$$H = 33.3$$

We now need to check the second derivative:

$$\frac{d^2C}{dH^2} = [(53.6 \times 10^6)/H^3] + 590$$

This is always positive, so the optimum is a minimum. The solution is

Radius, H = 33.5 units

Length, L = 181 units

Cost, C = $993,800

LAGRANGIAN MULTIPLIERS

More general approaches to design under constraints using differential calculus can be adopted. The most useful one is called the *Lagrangian multiplier* method, devised by the eighteenth-century mathematician Joseph Lagrange. It commences by converting all equality constraints into equations with zero right-hand sides, and then includes them in the objective with an unknown multiplier called the Lagrangian multiplier, λ. This multiplier represents the rate of change of the objective function with respect to the constant term in the equality constraint. We shall see that it provides a measure of the sensitivity of the optimum solution with respect to the specified constraints.

Let us reexamine the museum building problem. It was formulated as minimizing

$$C = 109.2HL + 295.2H^2$$

subject to

$$4.92H^2 2L = 1{,}000{,}000$$

We commence by setting the constraint equation to zero,

$$4.92H^2L - 1{,}000{,}000 = 0$$

and including it in the objective. Since its value is always zero, it cannot affect the value of the objective function. Now our minimizing equation is

$$C = 109.2HL + 295.2H^2 - \lambda(4.92H^2L - 1{,}000{,}000)$$

The reason for the negative sign in front of λ will become clear later. Differentiating with respect to each of the three variables and setting the derivative to zero, we get

$$\frac{\partial C}{\partial H} = 109.2L + 590.4H - 9.84\lambda HL = 0$$

$$\frac{\partial C}{\partial L} = 109.2H - 4.92\lambda H^2 = 0$$

$$\frac{\partial C}{\partial \lambda} = -(4.92H^2L - 1{,}000{,}000) = 0$$

Since there are three equations in three unknown variables, we can solve for them. From $\frac{\partial C}{\partial L}$, we get

$$\lambda = 22.2/H$$

From $\frac{\partial C}{\partial H}$, after substituting for λ, we get

$$L = 5.41H$$

From $\frac{\partial C}{\partial \lambda}$, after substituting for λ, we get

$$H = 33.3 \text{ ft}$$

Therefore,

$$L = 181 \text{ ft}$$

and

$$\lambda = 0.663$$

This is the same result we arrived at by using direct substitution. The meaning of λ is that, for each unit increase in the required volume of the building, the cost will go up by \$0.663. This we can understand by examining the expression for C with a variable, X, in place of the constant, 1,000,000, in the constraint:

$$C = 109.2HL + 295.2H^2 - \lambda(4.92H^2L - X)$$

If we differentiate C with respect to X, we get the slope of C. This is also the rate of change of C with respect to X:

$$\frac{dC}{dX} = \lambda$$

Thus we can see that λ represents this rate of change.

Proving that the solution at the first derivative is a maximum or minimum, when using Lagrangian multipliers, is beyond the scope of this book. Sources for further reading are identified at the end of this chapter for readers who wish to pursue this. The use of Lagrangian multipliers allows for the inclusion of more than one constraint. It can also be generalized to handle nonnegativity and inequality constraints; the former is particularly important because, in general, negative values for decision variables have no physical meaning.

This generalization forms the basis for considering general nonlinear optimization problems. These extensions are called the *Kuhn–Tucker con-*

ditions, after the two mathematicians who developed them. Their formulation and use are beyond our scope; suffice it to say that, although they specify necessary and sufficient conditions for optimality, they produce computational difficulties in many architectural and building optimization problems.

SCOPE OF DIFFERENTIAL CALCULUS

Optimization using differential calculus promises much. The solution to design decision problems that have relatively straightforward formulations can be both simple and elegant. Often they involve very little calculation. The results can even be obtained symbolically in many cases, and sometimes these can be interpreted in the design context to produce a qualitative understanding of the solution without recourse to numerical values. We saw this in the problem involving the prefabricated roof system. If a design decision problem can be formulated in such a way as to produce an objective that is both continuous and differentiable, and if the problem has few constraints, differential calculus can fulfill its promise of providing a swift and accurate method for locating optimum designs.

Why, then, is differential calculus not used extensively for this purpose? One of the main reasons is that many architectural and building problems present themselves as discontinuous (discrete) and nondifferentiable. For example, when we have to choose the number of floors in a building, the resulting value must be an integer. Often the requirements for a design include statements such as "If the number of people per floor is less than a certain number, then so many bathroom facilities must be provided; if it is more than that number, then a specified increase in facilities is required." This statement is best modeled in a nondifferentiable way.

A more fundamental difficulty with using differential calculus has to do with the effect of constraints on the optimum. Examine the graph in figure 3-8. Calculus will find the two local optima shown in this figure, but it will fail to find the true optimum at the boundary caused by the constraint because there is no change in slope direction at that point.

While many of these difficulties can be overcome, in doing so we increase the computational complexity of obtaining a solution and lose the elegance and simplicity of the differential calculus approach. Thus, it remains of limited use in our domain.

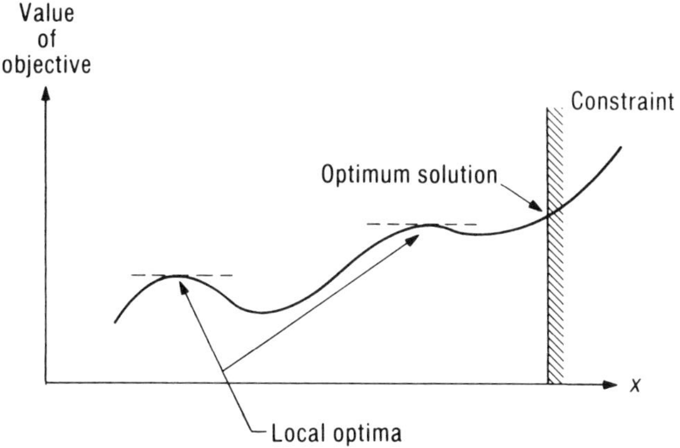

Fig. 3-8. Graph of an objective function with a single constraint.

FURTHER READING

Good discussions of design decision making by differential calculus can be found in:

Au, T., and Stelson, T.E. 1969. *Introduction to Systems Engineering: Deterministic Models*. Reading, MA: Addison-Wesley.

Stark, R.M., and Nicholls, R.L. 1972. *Mathematical Foundations for Design*. New York: McGraw-Hill.

For a better insight into the mathematics of differential calculus that are applicable to design optimization—particularly Lagrangian multipliers, constraints, and the Kuhn–Tucker conditions—the following two books are particularly good:

Beightler, C.S.; Phillips, D.T.; and Wilde, D.J. 1979. *Foundations of Optimization*. 2d ed. Englewood Cliffs, NJ: Prentice-Hall.

Hestemus, M.R. 1975. *Optimization Theory: The Finite Dimensional Case*. New York: Wiley.

Works on the use of differential calculus in design decision making include:

Bridges, A.H. 1976. The interrelationship of design and performance variables. In *CAD76*, ed. D.R. Smith and C.W. Jones, pp. 22–30. Guildford, England: IPC Science and Technology Press.

Hemp, W.S. 1973 *Optimum Structures*. Oxford: Clarendon Press.

Hennessy, R.L. 1977. Optimum wall insulation for cold climates. *American Society of Civil Engineers* 103:529–35.

Page, J.K. 1974. The optimization of building shape to conserve energy. *Journal of Architectural Research* 3(3):20–28.

CHAPTER 4

DESIGN USING LINEAR AND NONLINEAR PROGRAMMING

In chapter 3, we saw that differential calculus was a powerful analytic method under appropriate conditions. These conditions can rarely be met in design problems in architecture and building, however, because the algebraic descriptions may not be differentiable and are likely to contain large numbers of constraints, making the differential calculus method intractable. An alternate set of approaches has been developed specifically to handle problems for which differential calculus is unsuitable. These approaches, which substitute numerical calculation for symbolic analytic methods, all appear under the umbrella heading of *mathematical programming*. (Here the word *programming* bears no relation to computer programming.) In mathematical programming methods, two fundamental strategies are used for searching iteratively for solutions. The first is concerned with moving from an existing solution to an improved solution, until no better solution can be found; this is the strategy adopted by linear programming. The second enumerates (normally, only implicitly) all possible paths to solutions and selects the one that produces the best solution; this is the strategy adopted by dynamic programming (chapter 5).

CHARACTERISTICS OF LINEAR PROGRAMMING

Of all the mathematical programming techniques, linear programming is by far the best developed and the most important method to utilize the first strategy. This is because, among all those methods, it is the one most frequently used and because it guarantees to find the optimum solution in a fixed number of steps. For a problem to be amenable to solution by linear programming, it must satisfy the following three conditions:

1. The variables must be continuous and take values that are greater than or equal to zero.
2. The objective function must be a linear expression of the variables.
3. The constraints must be linear expressions of the variables.

Convex Spaces

Linear expressions, when plotted, generate a very special class of spaces called *convex spaces*. Any space bounded by continuous straight lines is convex. A nontechnical definition of the property of convexity is that a space is convex if a straight line joining any two points on the boundary always remains within the space. We can readily ascertain this by examining figure 4-1. When we go beyond two dimensions, the same concept applies; but now we need to think in terms of planes rather than lines.

The convex space, bounded by the constraints, is called the *feasible solution space,* because only solutions that lie within it satisfy the constraints, and only these solutions are feasible. When the objective function is also linear, as it moves away from the origin it is being maximized. It must not move outside the feasible solution space, however, so the problem is to move the objective function line as far from the origin as possible without moving outside the feasible solution space (fig. 4-2). Clearly, the optimum solution lies at the vertex of this convex space. In special cases,

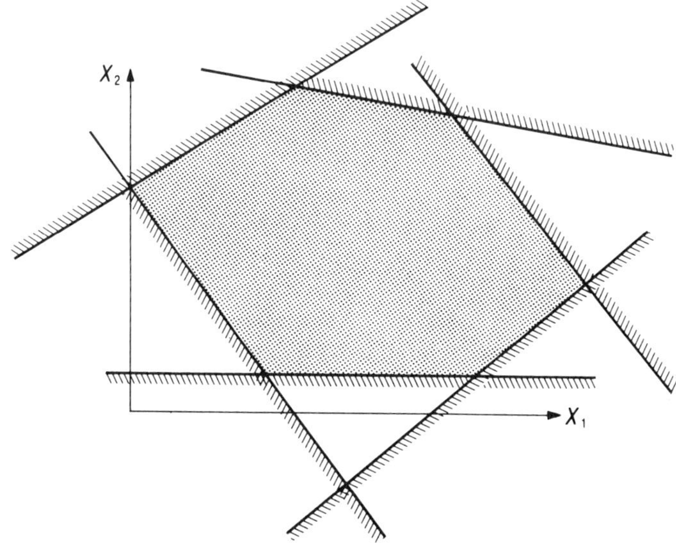

Fig. 4-1. Convex spaces produced by linear equations and inequalities.

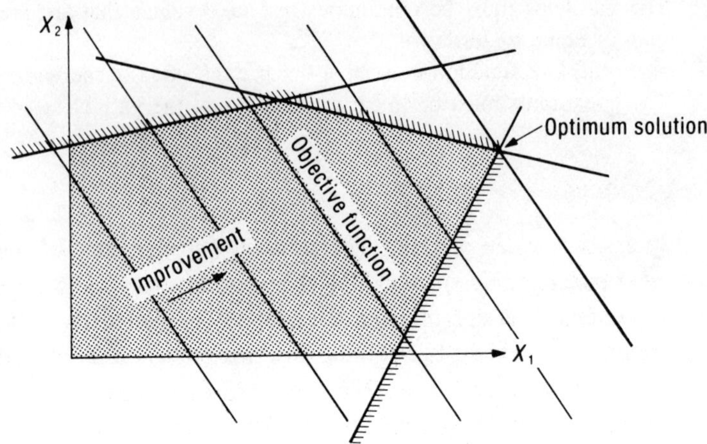

Fig. 4-2. As the objective function line moves away from the origin, its value improves.

the objective function is parallel to one of the constraints, in which case a set of equally good optimum solutions lies on the boundary between two adjacent vertices of the convex space.

Example

Suppose we have been asked to commence the preliminary design of a small complex of apartments. Our studies show that 1-bedroom and 2-bedroom apartments are the most desirable in this area. The problem is to find the number of 1-bedroom and 2-bedroom apartments that will maximize the return. We have ascertained the following costs and profits:

Apartment Type	*Capital Cost (in $1,000s)*	*Profit (in $1,000s)*
1-bedroom	90	20
2-bedroom	180	24

The available capital is $1,800,000. If maximizing profit were the only criterion, clearly it would be most advantageous if we built all 1-bedroom apartments. However, the planning authority has a planning code that discourages small apartments by placing penalties against them. For this site, the maximum number of penalty points a development can accrue is 960; the following penalties are incurred for each small unit:

Apartment Type	*Penalty Points*
1-bedroom	120
2-bedroom	60

Now it is no longer clear how many of each apartment should be included in the development to maximize profit.

The decision variables here are the number of 1-bedroom apartments and the number of 2-bedroom apartments we should design. Let us call them X_1 and X_2, respectively. We can write the objective (in thousands of dollars) in terms of these variables as maximizing

$$20X_1 + 24X_2 \tag{4.1}$$

Restrictions are imposed on the values that X_1 and X_2 can take by the constraints of available capital and of the planning policy. These constraints, too, can be expressed in terms of the decision variables. Thus, the available capital constraint (in thousands of dollars) becomes

$$90X_1 + 180X_2 \leqslant 1{,}800 \tag{4.2}$$

and the planning policy constraint becomes

$$120X_1 + 60X_2 \leqslant 960 \tag{4.3}$$

By adding the restrictions that both X_1 and X_2 take only nonnegative values, we have formulated the decision problem algebraically. Since we have only two decision variables, we can plot these expressions graphically.

Figure 4-3 shows a two-dimensional graph with the inequalities of equations 4.2 and 4.3 plotted; the feasible solution space is shown shaded. The objective function can be rewritten, as an equation, as

$$20X_1 + 24X_2 = Z \tag{4.4}$$

where Z is the value of the objective. This equation can be plotted as a series of parallel lines depending on the value of Z (fig. 4-4). The optimum solution occurs when the line representing the objective function is farthest from the origin and still within the feasible solution space. We can again see that this occurs at a vertex. We can read off the values for X_1 and X_2 from figure 4-4 as

$$X_1 = 4$$

$$X_2 = 8$$

and compute the value of the objective function as 272. Thus, the solution can be written as

Number of 1-bedroom apartments = 8
Number of 2-bedroom apartments = 4
Profit = $272,000

Thus, the solution—in terms of both decisions (values for the decision variables) and the objective—can be found by inspection. When we have more than two decision variables, however, the graphical presentation becomes difficult, and the solution can no longer be found by inspection. We need a method for locating the optimum solution that is independent of the number of decision variables. We shall develop such a method intuitively at first, and then describe it more formally.

Intuitive Method

Let us commence our intuitive method with a trivial solution: no 1-bedroom or 2-bedroom apartments. This is certainly feasible, but it produces

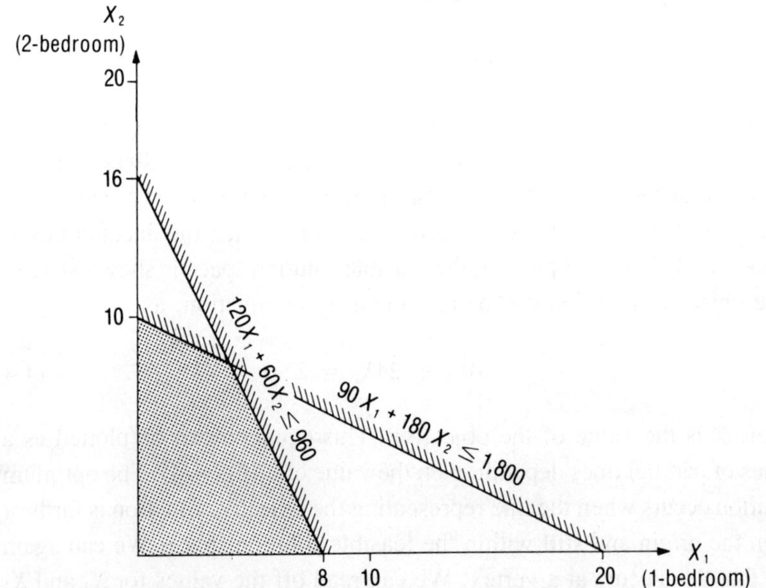

Fig. 4-3. Two-dimensional graph plotting equations 4.2 and 4.3. The shaded area is the feasible solution space.

no return and certainly does not maximize our objective. We could improve on this by having one 1-bedroom and one 2-bedroom apartment. This would produce a profit of

$$\$20{,}000(1) + \$24{,}000(1) = \$44{,}000$$

Since a unit increase in each of the apartment types generates a fixed return, why not have as many as are allowed within the constraints?

Figure 4-5 shows what happens as we do this. Our original decision to have no apartments is the corner point, Z. As we increase the number of apartments uniformly, we move to points Z_1, Z_2, and so on, until we hit the boundary of the feasible solution space. Clearly, no interior point is as good as the point on the boundary, so any strategy we adopt for our method should only include opportunities for passing along boundaries.

Let us again commence with the trivial solution; but this time, instead of moving into the interior, we will move along the axis of the decision that produces the greatest rate of return. In our example, this is the 2-bedroom axis, X_2, since each 2-bedroom apartment produces a profit of \$24,000 while each 1-bedroom apartment produces a profit of only \$20,000. We want to have as many 2-bedroom apartments as we

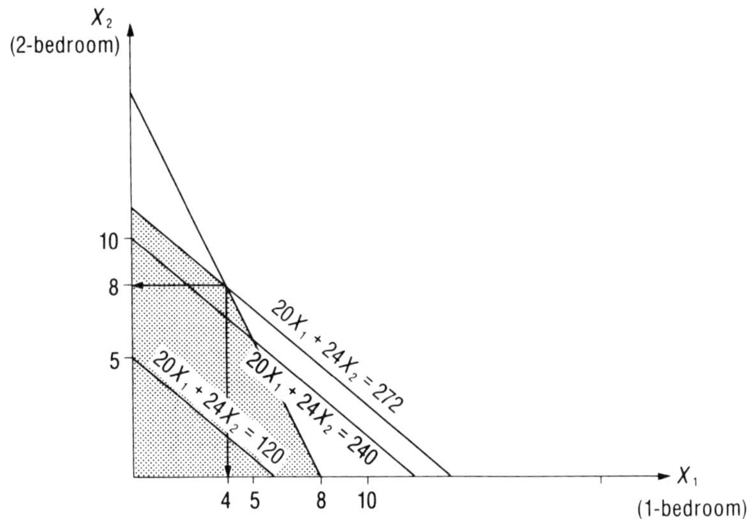

Fig. 4-4. Plot of the objective function, with different values for the return on top of the feasible solution space.

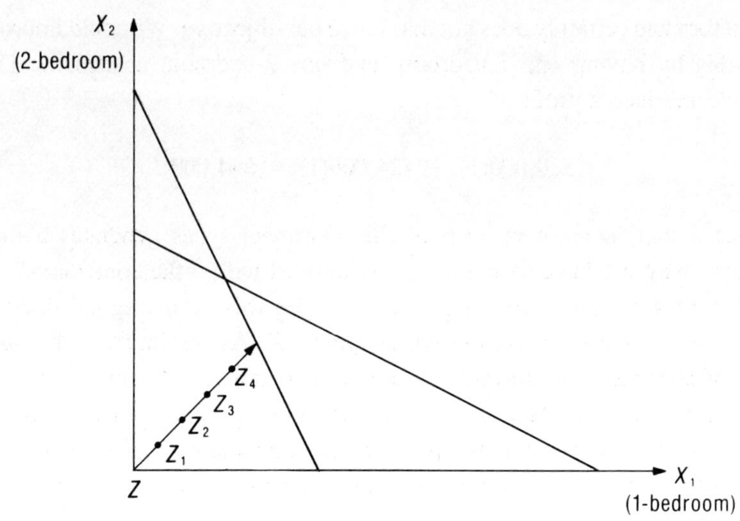

Fig. 4-5. Plot showing the effect of increasing the number of apartments in the building. Interior points are all inferior to points on the boundary.

can within the constraints. Figure 4-6 shows this move from the origin corner point, Z, to the point at which we hit the available capital constraint, A. Here, the number of 2-bedroom apartments to be designed is ten, and the number of 1-bedroom apartments is zero. The value of the objective in this case is \$240,000. While we could have stopped anywhere between

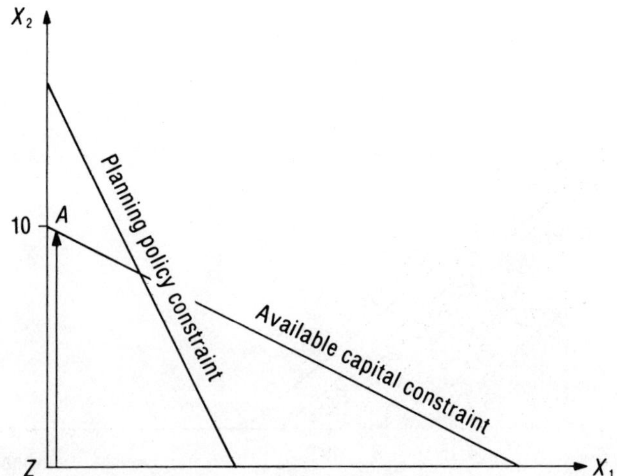

Fig. 4-6. Plot showing movement along the X_2 axis to the first vertex (from Z to A).

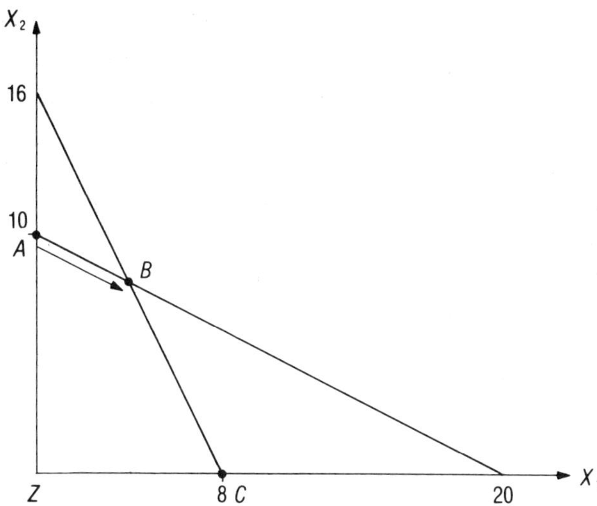

Fig. 4-7. Moving along the available capital constraint line from *A* to *B* involves trading off 2-bedroom apartments for 1-bedroom apartments, but this results in an increased profit.

Z and *A*, there is no reason to do so in view of our aim to maximize the objective.

At vertex *A*, we have used up all the available capital. But might we increase the profit by having fewer 2-bedroom apartments and in their place some 1-bedroom apartments? Can we trade 2-bedroom apartments for some 1-bedroom apartments? Moving from point *A* back toward *Z* in figure 4-7 does not add any 1-bedroom apartments; instead, though, we can move along the available capital constraint line toward vertex *B*. The slope of this line gives the tradeoff between the two decision variables. More formally this is called the *marginal rate of substitution* of 1-bedroom apartments for 2-bedroom apartments. (We can recognize this as the tangent in chapter 3.) This tradeoff is given by

$$dX_2/dX_1 = -10/20 = -\tfrac{1}{2}$$

In other words, we must give up half a 2-bedroom apartment to get one 1-bedroom apartment. This is because each 2-bedroom apartment costs as much as two 1-bedroom apartments.

What happens to the profit if we commence this tradeoff? Substituting these tradeoffs into the objective function of equation 4.1, we get

$$(1)(\$20) + (-\tfrac{1}{2})(\$24) = \$8$$

Since this value is positive, such a tradeoff is obviously beneficial. Further, since the tradeoff along this line is constant (since it is linear), we should trade off as many apartments as we can within the constraints. Thus, we will move from *A* to *B*.

But how do we locate ourselves in this geometric space so that we will be at *B*, the intersection of the two constraint lines? The way to pinpoint vertex *B* is to solve the equations for the two constraint lines simultaneously. This is because the two equations describe only one common point (the intersection point).

A usual way of solving linear equations simultaneously is to use the method of elimination and back substitution. The two equations are

$$\begin{aligned} 90X_1 + 180X_2 &= 1{,}800 \\ 120X_1 + 60X_2 &= 960 \end{aligned}$$

We will commence by eliminating X_1 from the equations. This we accomplish by dividing the first equation by 90 to produce 1 as the coefficient for X_1, and then subtracting 120 times that equation from the second one. This will eliminate X_1 from the second equation, by leaving it with a coefficient of 0. Thus, we initially get

$$\begin{aligned} 1X_1 + 2X_2 &= 20 \\ 120X_1 + 60X_2 &= 960 \end{aligned}$$

Then we get

$$\begin{aligned} 1X_1 + 2X_2 &= 20 \\ 0X_1 - 180X_2 &= -1440 \end{aligned}$$

We can find the value of X_2 from the second equation by dividing throughout by -180, and then we can find the value for X_1 by eliminating X_2 from the first equation. Thus, we get

$$\begin{aligned} 1X_1 + 2X_2 &= 20 \\ 0X_1 + 1X_2 &= 8 \end{aligned}$$

And then we get

$$\begin{aligned} 1X_1 + 0X_2 &= 4 \\ 0X_1 + 1X_2 &= 8 \end{aligned}$$

This is point B of figure 4-7, where $X_1 = 4$ and $X_2 = 8$. Now we can identify the value of the objective function as \$272,000, by substituting the values for X_1 and X_2 into equation 4.1.

Is it possible to increase the profit by moving away from vertex B and having a different mix of apartments? Moving from B back to A makes no sense; we can readily see that that will reduce the profit. But will moving to C in figure 4-7 increase the profit? The tradeoff along the planning policy constraint line is given by

$$dX_2/dX_1 = -16/8 = -2$$

This equation indicates that we need to give up two 2-bedroom apartments to get one 1-bedroom apartment. This is because the planning penalty for each 1-bedroom apartment is twice that for each 2-bedroom apartment. We can calculate the effect of this tradeoff on the profit by substituting in equation 4.1 to get

$$(1)(\$20) + (-2)(\$24) = -\$28$$

Since this value is negative, there is no reason to move toward vertex C. No other vertices exist that we could move to, so we must be at the optimum solution.

MATHEMATICAL FORAY

Clearly, we need to automate this process so that we do not have to rely on graphical representations. This process is the basis of the *simplex method* for solving linear programming problems, and we can summarize the search strategy we have used in three rules:

1. Locate a feasible solution, called the *basic feasible solution* at a vertex (usually the origin).
2. Determine the rate of change of the objective function from this vertex to each adjacent vertex. Select the vertex with the highest rate of change, and move to it.
3. Apply rule 2 until the rate of change of the objective function from this vertex to each adjacent vertex is negative or zero. The vertex then occupied defines the optimum solution.

We will now present the simplex method, since it is the basis for virtually all computer programs for linear programming.

Simplex Method Terminology

In order to move along boundary lines to vertices, we need the equations of lines—not inequalities. To convert linear inequalities into a system of linear equations, we will add one variable to each inequality. This variable is called the *slack variable* because it takes up the slack or unused amount of a constraint. If we take the capital cost constraint shown in equation 4.2, we can convert it into the following equation:

$$90X_1 + 180X_2 + S_1 = 1{,}800 \tag{4.6}$$

Here, S_1 represents the unused capital for particular values of X_1 and X_2. It is equal to the difference between the available capital and the cost of all the 1-bedroom and 2-bedroom apartments at that point. Clearly, S_1 can be zero but cannot be negative, since this would mean that the cost of the apartments was more than the available capital.

We can now rewrite the problem formulation as a set of linear equations intended to maximize

$$Z = 20X_1 + 24X_2 + OS_1 + OS_2 \tag{4.7}$$

subject to

$$90X_1 + 180X_2 + 1S_1 + 0S_2 = 1{,}800 \tag{4.8}$$

$$120X_1 + 60X_2 + 0S_1 + 1S_2 = 960 \tag{4.9}$$

and

$$X_1 \geqslant 0$$

$$X_2 \geqslant 0$$

$$S_1 \geqslant 0$$

$$S_2 \geqslant 0$$

A zero value for the coefficient of S_1 or S_2 in any of the above equations indicates that S_1 or S_2 plays no role in that equation.

We now have four variables (X_1, X_2, S_1, and S_2) but only two equations (4.8 and 4.9). For linear equations to be solvable, the number of equations must be the same as the number of variables. In general, we will have $m + n$ equations with m variables. We can solve these equations if we set n of the variables to zero. In the simplex method, we call the nonzero variables the *basic variables* or the *basis,* and we call the solution they produce the *basic solution*. There is no guarantee that a basic solution is feasible, so we can define a *basic feasible solution* as a basic solution that is located at a vertex. Each problem has a fixed number of basic feasible solutions. We already know that a *decision variable* is one whose values define solutions. Finally, we can state that the *optimum solution* is the basic feasible solution that optimizes the value of the objective function.

The Initial Simplex Tableau

The simplex method uses a structuring technique to represent the various values in the computation process. This structure is called a *tableau,* and the initial tableau takes the following form:

	X	S	
B	A	I	b
	$-c$	0	$Z = 0$

X is a list of the decision variables; S is a list of the slack variables; B is a list of the basic variables; b is a list of the right-hand sides of the constraint equations; A is the matrix of the coefficients of the decision variables in the constraint equations; and I is the matrix of the coefficients of the slack variables. In the initial simplex tableau, I will serve as the identity matrix—that is, it will have ones along its diagonals and zeros elsewhere. Z is the value of the objective function; initially it will be zero, when $X_1 = 0$ and $X_2 = 0$. Finally, c is a list of coefficients of the decision variables in the objective functions; the reason for the negative sign preceding it will become clear later.

For our example problem, the initial simplex tableau transforms into the following tableau:

	X_1	X_2	S_1	S_2	
S_1	90	180	1	0	1,800
S_2	120	60	0	1	960
	−20	−24	0	0	0

Reading the Tableau

Each row of the preceding tableau represents an equation, but we need to be aware of the values of all the variables in order to read the equation. The initial tableau is generated with the decision variables set to zero to produce the basic feasible solution. Thus, the first row of the tableau is read as

$$90(0) + 180(0) + 1S_1 + 0S_2 = 1{,}800$$

which reduces to

$$S_1 = 1{,}800$$

The basic variable whose value is obtained from this equation is on the leftmost column of that row, and the row can be directly read as left-hand column variables equals right-hand value—that is, as $S_1 = 1{,}800$. Similarly, we can read $S_2 = 960$ from the second row. The meanings of these statements are that 1,800 units (expressed in thousands of dollars) of capital remain unused, and 960 planning penalty points remain unused when the decision variables each have the value of zero.

In this tableau, S_1 and S_2 are called *solution variables*. Such variables have a one at the intersection of the column they head and the row they label, and zeros in all the other rows of the column they head.

The numbers in the columns of the tableau represent *tradeoffs* at this vertex. Let us examine the first column of the tableau:

	$\mathbf{X_1}$	X_2	S_1	S_2	
S_1	**90**	180	1	0	1,800
S_2	**120**	60	0	1	960
	−20	−24	0	0	0

In order to have a single unit of X_1, we must trade off 90 units of S_1 and 120 units of S_2; thereupon, we gain (hence the negative sign) 20 units in the objective. In this problem's terms, we can say that—in order to have one 1-bedroom apartment—we use up $90,000 of capital and 120 planning penalty points, and we make $20,000 profit.

Similarly, the second column of the tableau states that—in order to have one 2-bedroom apartment—we use up $180,000 of capital and 60 planning penalty points, and we make $24,000 profit:

	X_1	$\mathbf{X_2}$	S_1	S_2	
S_1	90	**180**	1	0	1,800
S_2	120	**60**	0	1	960
	−20	**−24**	0	0	0

The third column states that to get one unit of S_1 we have to give up one unit of S_1; consequently, the tradeoff produces no change. We get the same effect with S_2. Hence, S_1 and S_2 in this tableau are called *isolated variables*. The initial tableau corresponds to rule 1 of our search strategy.

Pivoting or Iterating

The tableau represents the situation at one vertex of the feasible solution space. In the initial tableau's case, the vertex represented is the origin. When the feasible solution space does not include the origin, additional variables are introduced—but this will not be dealt with here. Clearly, in moving from one vertex to another, one of the basic variables goes to zero in value and hence becomes nonbasic. In figure 4-7, for example, as we move from Z to A, the slack variable that measures the unused available capital goes from 1,800 to 0. At the same time, one of the nonbasic variables becomes basic; in other words, it goes from a zero value to a nonzero value. In figure 4-7, as we move from Z to A, the value of X_2 goes from 0 to 10. In terms of the tableau, one variable goes out of the basis and one variable comes in, and the values in the tableau need to be recomputed for this new situation at the new vertex. This process is called *pivoting* or *iterating*. Pivoting or iterating corresponds to rule 2 of our search strategy.

The mechanics of moving from one tableau to the next are carried out in three steps:

1. Determine which direction to move in based on the direction that produces the greatest rate of change of the objective function. This decision indicates which nonbasic variable enters the solution and becomes basic and thereby defines the pivot column.
2. Determine which previously basic variable goes to zero and leaves the solution, thereby defining the pivot row.
3. Recompute the values of the tableau.

STEP 1. If we examine the tradeoffs in the objective function (the bottom row of the tableau), we can see that 1 unit of X_1 produces a gain of 20 units in the objective, while 1 unit of X_2 produces a gain of 24 units in the objective. Therefore, we select X_2 as the variable that is to become basic and enter the solution with a nonzero value. We call the X_2 column the *pivot column*. The most negative tradeoff defines the pivot column.

STEP 2. We now know that X_2 heads the pivot column. If we examine the S_1 row, we can see that—for every X_2 we have in the solution—we must give up 180 units of S_1. There are only 1,800 units of S_1 available, so the maximum value X_2 could take to deplete all the available S_1 is $1{,}800/180 = 10$. Let us now examine the S_2 row. For every unit of X_2 we have in the solution, we must give up 60 units of S_2. There are only 960 units of S_2 available, so the maximum value X_2 could take to deplete all the available S_2 is $960/60 = 16$. Clearly, X_2 must be the smaller of these two values; otherwise, it would require more S_1 than is available. Therefore S_1 goes to zero and leaves the basic solution. We call S_1 the *pivot row*. Where the pivot column and pivot row intersect is the *pivot number*. The tableau just prior to pivoting looks like this:

		X_1	$\mathbf{X_2}$	S_1	S_2	
pivot row	$\mathbf{S_1}$	**90**	**180**	**1**	**0**	**1,800**
	S_2	120	**60**	0	1	960
		−20	**−24**	0	0	0
			pivot column			

STEP 3. We have found that X_2 comes into the solution (that is, that we are moving in the direction of X_2) and that S_1 is going out (that is, that we are going to use up all of S_1 and hit the available capital constraint). The next tableau ought to represent the tradeoffs at the next vertex, labeled *A* in figure 4-7. To obtain this representation we need to solve the equations for S_1 and X_2 simultaneously, and then recalculate the tradeoffs.

Using the method of elimination, we can solve these in a series of planned steps. First, we divide the pivot row by the pivot number to produce a 1 as the pivot number. In this example, the pivot row becomes the new first row and is relabeled with the variable that is coming into the solution (in this case, X_2). The new, partially iterated tableau now looks like this:

	X_1	X_2	S_1	S_2	
X_2	1/2	1	1/180	0	10
S_2	120	60	0	1	960
	−20	−24	0	0	0

We now eliminate X_2 from the second row by multiplying the first row by 60 (the number in the S_2 row in the pivot column), and then subtracting it from the second row. Similarly, we can eliminate X_2 from the third row by multiplying the first row by 24, and then adding it to the third row. The completed second tableau takes the following form:

	X_1	X_2	S_1	S_2	
X_2	1/2	1	1/180	0	10
S_2	90	0	− 1/3	1	360
	− 8	− 0	2/15	0	240

We have now completed one iteration, and on the graph in figure 4-7 we have moved from Z to A. At A, from the tableau, we can read that $X_1 = 0$ and $X_2 = 10$, while $S_1 = 0$ and $S_2 = 360$; consequently, we know that unused planning penalty points are available. From the bottom row, we can see that the value of the objective function is 240.

We can now repeat the same steps, commencing with the second tableau. We examine the tradeoffs in the objective function (the bottom row) and select the one with the most negative tradeoff. In this tableau, only one column has a negative tradeoff: the column headed by X_1. This becomes the pivot column, and X_1 becomes a basic variable and enters the solution. The column headed by X_2 has a zero tradeoff in the objective function, indicating that no benefit would be gained by including it again. The column headed S_1 has a positive tradeoff in the objective function, indicating that the objective function would decrease in value if that column were included.

Having decided that X_1 is to enter the solution, we need to decide which variable will leave the solution and become nonbasic. Let us examine the first row. We can see that, for every unit of X_1 we have in the solution, we must give up $\frac{1}{2}$ unit of X_2. There are only 10 units of X_2 available here, so the maximum value X_1 could take to deplete all the available X_2 is $10/\frac{1}{2} = 20$. Now let us examine the second row. We can see that, for every unit of X_1 we have in the solution, we must give up 90 units of S_2. There are only 360 units of S_2 available here, so the maximum value X_1 could take to deplete all the available S_2 is $360/90 = 4$. The smaller of these values defines the pivot row, so S_2 becomes the variable to leave the solution and 90 becomes the pivot value.

The second tableau can now be recomputed as we are moving to vertex B in figure 4.7. This we do (as before) by first dividing the pivot row by the pivot number to produce a 1 for the pivot number. Next we eliminate

X_1 from all the remaining rows to produce a 0 for all the remaining elements of the pivot column. The partial third tableau before the elimination now looks like this:

	X_1	X_2	S_1	S_2	
X_2	1/2	1	1/180	0	10
X_1	1	0	−1/270	1/90	4
	−8	0	2/15	0	240

We can eliminate X_1 from the first row by multiplying the second row by $\frac{1}{2}$, and then subtracting it from the first row. Similarly, we can eliminate X_1 from the third row by multiplying the first row by 8, and then adding it to the third row.

The completed third tableau takes the following form:

	X_1	X_2	S_1	S_2	
X_2	0	1	2/270	−1/180	8
X_1	1	0	−1/270	1/90	4
	0	0	28/270	4/45	272

As we look along the tradeoffs in the objective function, we find that no variables remain for which a change in value would produce an increase in the objective function. Therefore, we are at the optimum, and the third tableau is the final tableau.

The basic variables in the final tableau are X_1 and X_2 (shown by the row labels), and the nonbasic variables are S_1 and S_2, which are both equal to zero. Thus, from the first row we can see that $X_2 = 8$, and from the second row we can see that $X_1 = 4$. The bottom right-hand value of 272 is the value of the objective function at the optimum—or in other words, the optimum value. We can check this by substituting the values for the decision variables into the objective function (equation 4.7):

$$\$20(4) + \$24(8) + 0 + 0 = \$272$$

We can check that no unused capital or planning penalty points remain, by substituting values into the two constraint equations (4.8 and 4.9):

$$90(4) + 180(8) + 1S_1 + 0 = 1{,}800$$

$$S_1 = 0$$

and

$$120(4) + 60(8) + 0 + S_2 = 960$$

$$S_2 = 0$$

So, the *solution* to our initial problem can be expressed by the following equalities:

number of 1-bedroom apartments to build = 4
number of 2-bedroom apartments to build = 8
profit = \$272,000

We have shown how the simplex method operates on problems that are solvable by linear programming formulated in a standard or canonical form. This form consists of the following elements: a set of k decision variables, X_i $(i = 1, 2, \ldots, k)$; an objective, Z, expressed as a linear function of these variables; $Z = \max f(X)$; and a set of n linear inequality constraints of the form $g_j(X) \leqslant 0$ $(j = 1, 2, \ldots, n)$, with $X_i \geqslant 0$ $(i = 1, 2, \ldots, k)$.

Clearly, not all constraints will be in the form "less than or equal to." Constraints of other types need to be converted into this form. The way we do this depends on whether it is an inequality constraint or an equality constraint. If it is an inequality constraint of the form

$$g(X) \leqslant 0$$

then, by multiplying it by -1, we can directly produce the canonical form;

$$-g(X) \geqslant 0$$

We can then convert it into an equation by introducing a variable, S, called a *surplus variable;*

$$-g(X) + S = 0$$

If it is an equality constraint, we introduce a variable (called an *artificial variable*) that must end up with the value zero. To do this, we make sure that it becomes a nonbasic variable and remains so.

Clearly, changes in the way we make decisions in our tableau are needed. These are not conceptually significant and will not be considered further.

Nowadays, numerous computer programs are available to carry out the computations needed to find the optimum solution to problems formulated as linear programs. Almost all of these computer programs make use of the simplex method. They allow for formulations that are not in a canonical form, and they internally carry out the reformulation necessary. These computer programs can readily find solutions to problems that involve hundreds and even thousands of variables and constraints.

PROBLEM: FINDING THE MINIMUM LENGTH OF AN APARTMENT

Description

The dimensioning of floor plans is a prototypical design decision problem in architecture. Consider the dimensionless floor plan of an apartment, shown in figure 4-8. The problem is to find the minimum length of this apartment, subject to constraints on the areas of the rooms and on their lengths. If the width of the bath1, hall, and bath2 are specified, the widths of all the remaining rooms are given, and the problem becomes one of finding the length of each room. We shall again express the dimensions in 300-mm (1-ft) units. Let us state the constraints.

PLANNING:

We want the right-hand wall of bed2 to line up with the right-hand wall of bath2, for structural reasons.

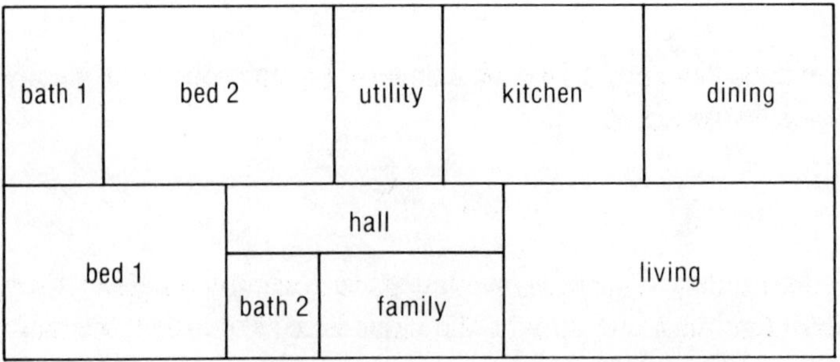

Fig. 4-8. Dimensionless floor plan of a ten-room apartment.

WIDTHS:

bath1 width = 12.00 units
hall width = 3.00 units
bath2 width = 9.00 units

AREA:

Room	*Minimum Area (square units)*	*Maximum Area (square units)*
bath1	75	80
bed2	160	180
utility	50	80
kitchen	150	200
dining	100	125
bed1	180	200
hall	—	60
living	180	200
bath2	60	80
family	100	125

Formulation

We commence by defining the *decision variables*. Here, they will be the lengths of the ten rooms. We can see, however, that the length of the hall will simply be the sum of the lengths of bath2 and family, and we can calculate it; it is not an independent decision. This leaves us with the following nine decision variables:

Room Length	*Variable*
bath1	X_1
bed2	X_2
utility	X_3
kitchen	X_4
dining	X_5
bed1	X_6
bath2	X_7
family	X_8
living	X_9

The *objective* is the sum of the lengths along one side:

$$Z = \min (X_1 + X_2 + X_3 + X_4 + X_5)$$

The *constraints* can be derived from the area restrictions, from a knowledge of the room widths, and from the wall location restriction.

AREA CONSTRAINTS:

bath1	$12X_1 \geqslant 75$
	$12X_1 \leqslant 80$
bed2	$12X_2 \geqslant 160$
	$12X_2 \leqslant 180$
utility	$12X_3 \geqslant 50$
	$12X_3 \leqslant 80$
kitchen	$12X_4 \geqslant 150$
	$12X_4 \leqslant 200$
dining	$12X_5 \geqslant 100$
	$12X_5 \leqslant 125$
bed1	$12X_6 \geqslant 180$
	$12X_6 \leqslant 200$
hall	$3X_7 + 3X_8 \leqslant 60$
living	$12X_9 \geqslant 180$
	$12X_9 \leqslant 200$
bath2	$9X_7 \geqslant 60$
	$9X_7 \leqslant 80$
family	$9X_8 \geqslant 100$
	$9X_8 \leqslant 125$

WALL LOCATION CONSTRAINTS:

left side of wall, $X_1 + X_2 = X_6 + X_7$
right side of wall, $X_8 + X_9 = X_3 + X_4 + X_5$

Thus, this problem has twenty-one constraints of all three kinds (a detailed examination reveals that the first constraint is redundant): nineteen inequality constraints, and two equality constraints.

Solution

The above formulation was solved by means of a standard computer program based on the simplex method. A total of fourteen tableaux were required in order to reach the optimum solution. The solution produced is

$$X_1 = 6.67$$
$$X_2 = 15.00$$

$$X_3 = 5.28$$
$$X_4 = 12.50$$
$$X_5 = 8.33$$
$$X_6 = 15.00$$
$$X_7 = 6.67$$
$$X_8 = 11.11$$
$$X_9 = 15.00$$

and

$$Z = 47.78$$

In the problem's terminology, the solution is:

Room Length	*Value (units)*
bath1	6.67
bed2	15.00
utility	5.28
kitchen	12.50
dining	8.33
bed1	15.00
bath2	6.67
family	11.11
living	15.00
hall	17.78 (calculated from bath2 and family)

Minimum length of apartment = 47.78 units

Thus, we have found both the optimum value of the objective function and the values that the decision variables must take in order to achieve that optimum.

PROBLEM: ARCHITECTURAL SITE FEASIBILITY ANALYSIS

Description

A client has come to you with a 120-hectare (300-acre) site to be developed as a housing estate. You must carry out a site feasibility analysis, and then report to the client in the following terms:

1. Likely maximum profit, excluding land component
2. Cost of construction, excluding land component
3. Number of dwellings to be built

Demographic studies have suggested that three types of housing, together with their site area requirements, be considered.

Housing Type	*Site Area Occupied (per dwelling unit)*
low-density—single houses	0.20 ha (0.5 acres)
medium-density—townhouses	0.08 ha (0.2 acres)
high-density—multistory apartments	0.04 ha (0.1 acres)

The market analysis indicates that the market in this area can only absorb the following number of each housing type.

Housing Type	*Marketable Number*
houses	150
townhouses	300
multistory apartments	250

Planning regulations state that 20 percent of the site must not be built upon. Furthermore, planning regulations state that the average population density of the site may not exceed 12 persons per hectare (5 persons per acre), based on 3.5 persons per house, 3.0 persons per townhouse, and 2.0 persons per apartment.

A site analysis has indicated that the site's suitability for construction can be represented under three categories: excellent, good, and adequate. These suitabilites, which will affect foundation costs, are distributed as follows:

Suitability	*Marketable Area (% of total)*
excellent	20
good	30
adequate	50

Available cost data have provided the following costs of construction per dwelling unit, including the effect of the site suitability (costs expressed in thousands of dollars):

	Site Suitability		
Housing Type	*Excellent*	*Good*	*Adequate*
houses	150	165	do not build
townhouses	98	110	do not build
apartments	85	100	115

Recent housing sales in the area suggest the following selling prices for each of the housing types:

Housing Type	*Sale Price (in $1,000s)*
houses	210
townhouses	160
apartments	133

Formulation

At first glance, there appear to be three *decision variables:* the number of houses, the number of townhouses, and the number of apartments to build. Each of these numbers is made up of two or three components, however, because of the three classes of site suitability. Thus, we must use seven decision variables:

Number of Housing Units	*Variable*
houses—excellent site	X_1
houses—good site	X_2
townhouses—excellent site	X_3
townhouses—good site	X_4
apartments—excellent site	X_5
apartments—good site	X_6
apartments—adequate site	X_7

When we report to the client, we will report as follows:

number of houses $= X_1 + X_2$
number of townhouses $= X_3 + X_4$
number of apartments $= X_5 + X_6 + X_7$

The *objective* is to maximize the profit, which is determined for each type of dwelling unit by subtracting the construction cost from the sale price. The following profit figures have been calculated:

Type of Dwelling Unit	*Profit (in $1,000s)*
house—excellent site	60
house—good site	45
townhouse—excellent site	62

(continued)

Type of Dwelling Unit	*Profit (in $1,000s)* (*continued*)
townhouse—good site	50
apartment—excellent site	48
apartment—good site	32
apartment—adequate site	18

Thus, the objective (in thousands of dollars) can be written as

$$Z = \text{maximize } (60X_1 + 45X_2 + 62X_3 + 50X_4 + 48X_5 + 32X_6 + 18X_7)$$

The *constraints* can be derived from the restrictions on area, maximum number of units to be built, and population density.

AREA CONSTRAINTS:

$$0.2(X_1 + X_2) + 0.08(X_3 + X_4) + 0.04\,(X_5 + X_6 + X_7) \leq 96$$

NUMBER OF DWELLING UNITS:

$$X_1 + X_2 \leq 150$$

$$X_3 + X_4 \leq 300$$

$$X_5 + X_6 + X_7 = \leq 250$$

POPULATION:

$$3.5(X_1 + X_2) + 3.0(X_3 + X_4) + 2.0(X_5 + X_6 + X_7) \leq 1500$$

Thus, this problem has seven variables and five constraints.

Solution

The above formulation was solved using a standard computer program based on the simplex method—although it is simple enough to solve by hand. The following solution is produced:

$$X_1 = 28.5$$
$$X_2 = 0.0$$
$$X_3 = 300.0$$
$$X_4 = 0.0$$
$$X_5 = 250.0$$
$$X_6 = 0.0$$
$$X_7 = 0.0$$

and

$$Z = 32{,}314.0$$

In the problem's terminology, the solution (after rounding X_1 to 28, since half houses cannot be built) is given the following expression:

1. Maximum profit = \$32,280,000
2. Cost of construction = \$54,850,000
3. Number of dwellings to be built = 578

Normally, site feasibility studies have many more constraints and variables than are present in this example.

POSTOPTIMALITY ANALYSIS

As designers, we cannot expect simply to be told, after we have formulated our problem as an optimization problem, what the decisions are that produce the optimum solution. We are also concerned with two behavioral aspects of the optimum solution: the *sensitivity* of the solution to variations in the problem environment; and the *stability* of the solution with respect to the decisions defining it.

Sensitivity Analysis

A simple statement of the solution omits a wide variety of information of use to a designer in supporting his or her decisions. Often it is important to know whether a particular constraint is preventing a better performance from emerging and to know which constraint should be relaxed first to improve the solution. For example, we gain nothing in arguing with the planning authority, say, to allow us to increase the site coverage, if it turns out that the constraint at issue is not one that affects the decisions. Examination of these issues once the optimum has been determined is called *sensitivity analysis*. Most of these issues can be resolved by means of a detailed study based on the final tableau of the simplex method.

Let us study the final tableau of the preliminary design of a small complex of apartments, solved by the simplex method earlier in this chapter. This tableau has the following form:

	X_1	X_2	S_1	S_2	
X_2	0	1	2/270	−1/180	8
X_1	1	0	−1/270	1/90	4
	0	0	28/270	4/45	272

The right-hand column contains the solution:

X_2	8
X_1	4
Z	272

The columns for the nonbasic variables contain tradeoff information at the solution, showing the sensitivity of the solution with respect to changes in that variable. Let us first consider the S_1 column:

	S_1		
X_2	2/270		0.0074
X_1	−1/270	or	−0.0037
Z	28/270		0.1037

This column shows that, for each additional $1,000 of available capital, we should design 0.0074 additional 2-bedroom apartments (X_2) and concurrently design 0.0037 fewer 1-bedroom apartments (X_1). Such a tradeoff would result in an increase in profit of $0.1037 \times 1{,}000$. Thus, if the client had an additional $1,000 available, this column indicates the most efficient use of that resource and its effect on the objective and on the decisions.

Similarly, let us consider the S_2 column:

	S_2		
X_2	−1/180		−0.0055
X_1	1/90	*or*	0.0111
Z	4/45		0.0888

This column shows that, if an additional planning penalty point were available, we should design 0.0111 additional 1-bedroom apartments (X_1) and 0.0055 fewer 2-bedroom apartments (X_2). This tradeoff would result in an increase in profit of $0.0888 \times 1{,}000$. Thus, if we could persuade the planning authority to increase the number of planning points available for this site, the S_2 column indicates the most efficient use of that resource and the effect on the objective and on the decisions.

The change in the values of the decision variables at the solution can be readily computed for each of the two constraints. The results are

$$\begin{array}{c} \\ X_2 \\ X_1 \\ Z \end{array} \begin{array}{c} \textit{Original Solution} \\ \left|\begin{array}{c} 8 \\ 4 \\ 272 \end{array}\right| \end{array} + 1 \times \begin{array}{c} \textit{Tradeoff } S_1 \\ \left|\begin{array}{c} 0.0074 \\ -0.0037 \\ 0.1037 \end{array}\right| \end{array} = \begin{array}{c} \textit{New Solution} \\ \left|\begin{array}{c} 8.0074 \\ 3.9963 \\ 272.1037 \end{array}\right| \end{array}$$

and

$$\begin{array}{c} \\ X_2 \\ X_1 \\ Z \end{array} \begin{array}{c} \textit{Original Solution} \\ \left|\begin{array}{c} 8 \\ 4 \\ 272 \end{array}\right| \end{array} + 1 \times \begin{array}{c} \textit{Tradeoff } S_1 \\ \left|\begin{array}{c} -0.0055 \\ 0.0111 \\ 0.0888 \end{array}\right| \end{array} = \begin{array}{c} \textit{New Solution} \\ \left|\begin{array}{c} 7.9945 \\ 4.0111 \\ 272.0888 \end{array}\right| \end{array}$$

Since all the constraints are linear, we get the same tradeoff for each unit increase in availability of a resource. We cannot presume, however, that we can simply continue to improve the value of the objective with increasing availability of each resource. Let us examine this situation with regard to S_1. Figure 4-9 shows the effect of increasing the available capital. As the available capital is increased, the optimum solution (which was at B, the intersection of the two constraint equations) changes to B'—still at the intersection of these two constraints. The solution continues to move up the planning policy constraint, given increasingly available capital, until it reaches the point marked D—the intersection of the planning policy constraint with the vertical axis. Any increase in available capital beyond this point has no effect; in this example D occurs at $X_1 = 0$.

We can see by looking at the tradeoffs for S_1 that, for every unit increase in S_1, there is a corresponding reduction in X_1. We can calculate how many units of S_1, U_1, are required to make X_1 go to zero, by looking at the S_1 column of the final tableau to get

$$\begin{array}{lr} & \boldsymbol{S_I} \\ \mathbf{X}_1 & 4 + U_1(-1/270) = 0 \\ & U_1 = 1{,}080 \end{array}$$

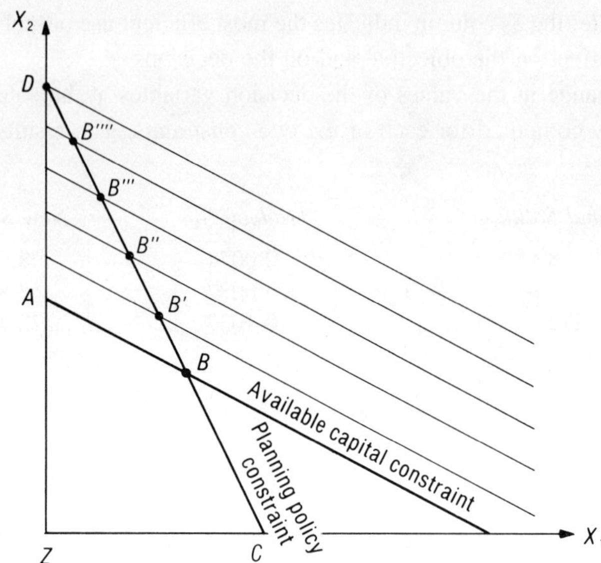

Fig. 4-9. Graphical representation of increasing the available capital.

This provides the upper bound for the right-hand side of the available capital constraint, as the original amount of 1,800 + 1,080 = 2,980. More capital than that will not increase the profit.

We can find the lower bound by taking units of resource away. A one-unit decrease in the available capital produces this new solution:

	Original Solution		*Tradeoff* S_1		*New Solution*
X_2	8		0.0074		7.9926
X_1	4	$-1\times$	-0.0037	=	4.0037
Z	272		0.1037		271.8923

We can find the value of the lower bound, L_1, analogously to how we found the upper bound.

$$\begin{array}{ll} & S_1 \\ \mathbf{X}_2 & 8 + L_1(2/270) = 0 \\ & L_1 = 1{,}080 \end{array}$$

We can observe this in figure 4-10. So the lower bound becomes 1,800 − 1,080 = 720. Thus, a value for the available capital in the range of $720,000–$2,980,000 has an effect on the solution. Outside that range, there is no effect.

At the optimum solution, the final tableau thus gives us the sensitivity of the objective to changes in the available resources.

Stability Analysis

We know that, as one of the decision variables goes to zero, it leaves the solution and another variable enters; thus, the bounds also tell us when this will happen. This is a measure of the *stability* of the solution with respect to the decisions that define it. If the range is very small, the solution is less stable than if the range is large, since different decisions will appear in the solution.

So far we have been examining variations in the right-hand sides of the constraints—that is, in the amount of available resources. Let us now examine the effects of varying the values of the coefficients of the decision variables in the objective function. We can readily understand these effects graphically. Figure 4-11 shows our example with the objective function at the optimum solution, B.

It is clear from this figure that, as long as the slope of the objective function lies between the slopes of the available capital constraint and the planning policy constraint, the decisions at the optimum solution remain unchanged. A change of slope within this range will only produce a different value for the objective function at the optimum.

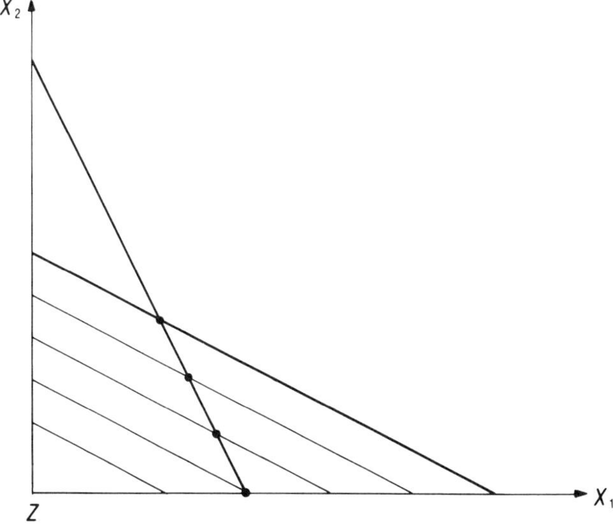

Fig. 4-10. Graphical representation of decreasing the available capital.

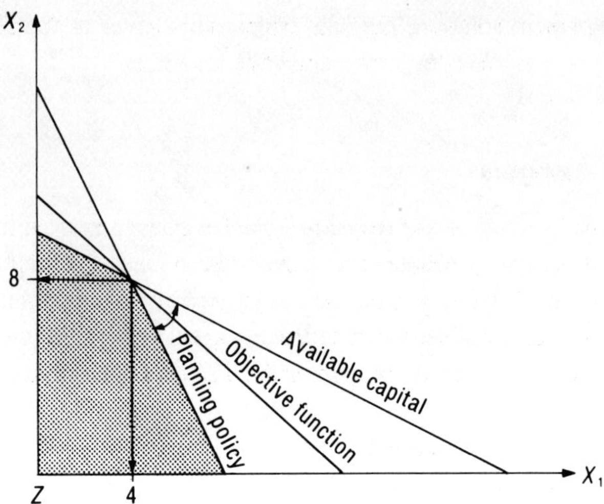

Fig. 4-11. Graphical representation of feasible solution space, with the objective function for the optimum solution showing the range of slopes of the objective function for which the decisions at the optimum solution remain the same.

Just as the coefficients in the columns provide tradeoff information from which we can compute the range of the effects, so do the coefficients in the rows provide such information. Let us restate the final tableau:

	X_1	X_2	S_1	S_2	
X_2	0	1	2/270	− 1/180	8
X_1	1	0	− 1/270	1/90	4
			28/270	4/45	272

The second row states the tradeoffs for the coefficients of X_1 in the objective, and the effect on the objective of a unit increase in these coefficients can be calculated. Considering just X_1, we can extract the appropriate parts of the tableau to produce the following data:

	S_1	S_2	
X_1	− 1/270	1/90	4
Z	28/270	4/45	272
new $Z = Z + 1X_1$	27/270	1/10	276

Thus, a unit increase in the coefficient of X_1 in the objective at the optimum solution allows the value of the objective to go from 272 to 276, with adjustments in the coefficients for S_1 and S_2.

We can now ask how much the coefficient of X_1 in the objective can change before X_1 moves out of the solution (thereby *destabilizing* the solution). Looking at the new objective function row, we can see that the coefficient for S_1 has decreased. If that coefficient becomes negative, we know that another iteration of the tableau is required, and we move to another vertex. Therefore, the upper bound for the coefficient of X_1 occurs when $S_1 = 0$—that is, just before it goes negative. The S_1 column contains the information needed to carry out this calculation:

$$U_1(-1/270) + 28/270 = 0$$

$$U_1 = 28$$

Thus, the upper bound for the coefficient of X_1 in the objective is given (in thousands of dollars) by

$$20 + 28 = 48$$

In figure 4-11, this is equivalent to the objective function line's becoming coincident with the planning policy constraint line.

In a similar fashion, we can find the lower bound by noting that a unit decrease in this coefficient decreases the coefficient of S_2:

	S_1	S_2	
X_1	$-1/270$	$1/90$	4
Z	$28/270$	$4/45$	272
new $Z = Z + 1X_1$	$29/270$	$7/90$	268

The lower bound can be determined from the S_2 column:

$$-L_1(1/90) + 4/45 = 0$$

$$L_1 = 8$$

Thus, the lower bound for the coefficient of X_1 in the objective is given (in thousands of dollars) by

$$20 - 8 = 12$$

In figure 4-11, this is equivalent to the objective function line's becoming coincident with the available capital constraint line.

The optimum solution remains stable, provided that any change in the coefficient of X_1 remains in the range \$12–\$28. In a similar fashion, we can find the range for the coefficient of X_2 to be \$10–\$40.

This information, along with the sensitivity information, is of importance to designers because it provides additional knowledge about the environment at the optimum and provides numerical support for the decisions.

NONLINEAR PROGRAMMING USING LINEAR PROGRAMMING

Not all that many design decision problems can be formulated as linear programming problems—either because the objective function is nonlinear or because the constraints are nonlinear (or both)—and no nonlinear programming method equivalent to the simplex method exists for the solution of nonlinear programming problems. Because of the efficacy of the simplex method, various approaches have been developed to allow problems formulated as nonlinear programming problems to be converted into one or more linear programming problems. Many approaches to the solution of nonlinear programming problems have been developed besides the ones we will be describing.

Piecewise-Linear Objective Functions

Often we find problems in which the returns in the objective function do not remain constant for all values of the decision variables. For example, although the sale price of an apartment may remain the same irrespective of whether it is the first or hundredth apartment sold, the unit selling costs vary as apartments are sold (often, to cite just one variable, the cost of holding unsold apartments is factored into the selling costs); therefore, the return is no longer constant. We might find the following situation:

Type of Apartment	*Number Sold*	*Sale Price*	*Capital Cost*	*Selling Cost*	*Profit*
1-bedroom	1 to 100	\$110,000	\$80,000	\$3,000	\$27,000
1-bedroom	100 to 200	\$110,000	\$80,000	\$5,000	\$25,000
2-bedroom	1 to 50	\$190,000	\$150,000	\$4,000	\$36,000
2-bedroom	51 to 100	\$190,000	\$180,000	\$7,000	\$33,000

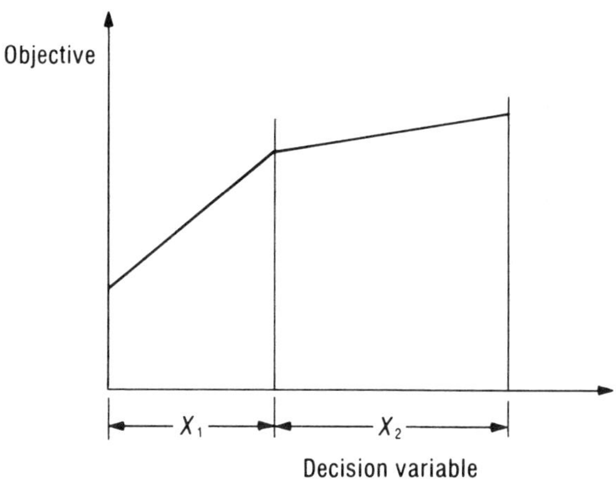

Fig. 4-12. Piecewise-linear objective function.

How can we formulate this as a linear programming problem? If we use four decision variables instead of two, we effectively are modeling the objective function as a series of linear relations, as in figure 4-12:

Name and Range	*Variable*
1-bedroom, 1 to 100	X_1
1-bedroom, 101 to 200	X_2
2-bedroom, 1 to 50	X_3
2-bedroom, 51 to 100	X_4

The maximizing objective in this case becomes (in thousands of dollars):

$$27X_1 + 25X_2 + 25X_2 + 36X_3 + 33X_4$$

In order to isolate these variables, we need to place constraints on them:

$$X_1 \leqslant 100$$

$$X_3 \leqslant 50$$

This will force X_2 into consideration when the number of 1-bedroom apartments becomes greater than 100. Such an artifice will only work if the contribution to the objective of X_1 is greater than that of X_2 and if the contribution of X_3 is greater than that of X_4, since X_1 and X_3 must be consumed before X_2 and X_4 are. This implies that the piecewise-linear objective function must be concave downward when being maximized, as in figure 4-12. From here on, it becomes a standard linear programming problem.

Sequential Linear Programming

Since the simplex method for solving linear programming problems is so powerful, a number of techniques for solving nonlinear programming problems are based on converting them to linear programming problems.

Consider a nonlinear programming problem with nonlinear constraints and a nonlinear objective, represented graphically in figure 4-13. An examination of figure 4-13 indicates that the feasible solution space is not convex. Further, it is unlikely that the solution will lie at the intersection of constraints. We can convert the problem into a linear programming problem by approximating the constraints and the objective as linear functions. If we select an initial feasible set of values for the decision variables, various methods are available for directly determining these linear approximations. Probably the best known of these is the Taylor series; however, it is beyond the scope of this book to explore this method in detail. Books that do provide such treatment are cited at the end of this

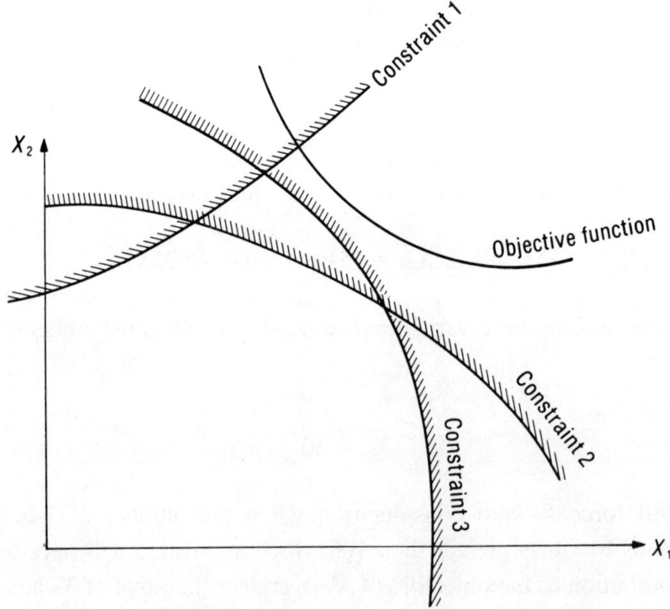

Fig. 4-13. Graphical representation of a nonlinear programming problem.

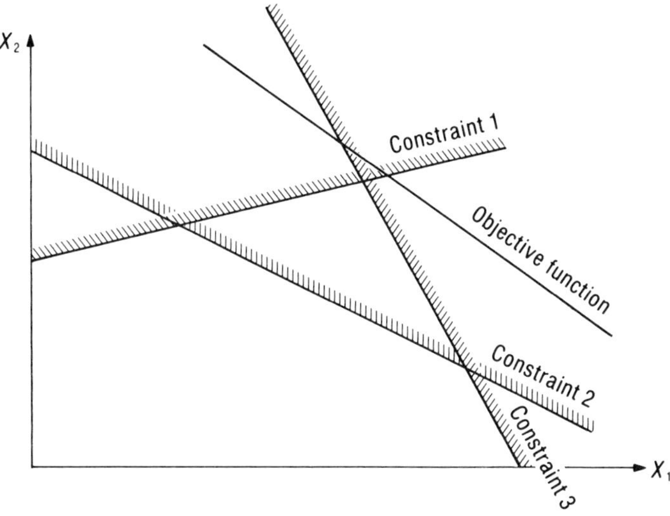

Fig. 4-14. Linear programming approximation of the nonlinear programming problem shown in figure 4-13.

chapter. Figure 4-14 shows this approximation as a linear programming model when the initial feasible decision values are $X_1 = X'_1$ and $X_2 = X'_2$.

The reason we have to select an initial solution is to provide a base for the determination of the tangents of the constraints and of the objective—for that is what the linear approximations are. We can now solve this linear programming problem and use the new values of X_1 and X_2, together with this linear program's optimum, as the initial values in the original nonlinear programming problem to determine a new set of tangents and, hence, a new linear programming problem. We end up solving a sequence of linear programs that will converge to a solution (or a good approximation of the solution) to the nonlinear problem.

Consider the dimensionless apartment shown in figure 4-15. The cost

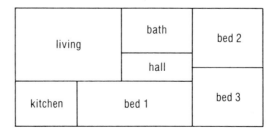

living
bath
hall
bed 2
kitchen
bed 1
bed 3

Fig. 4-15. Dimensionless floor plan of a three-bedroom apartment.

of the kitchen and bathroom are both double the cost of all the other rooms. The objective is to find the length and width of each room that will minimize the overall cost of the apartment, subject to the following restrictions (again, dimensions are expressed in 300-mm (1-ft) units):

Room	*Min Length (units)*	*Max Length (units)*	*Min Width (units)*	*Max Width (units)*	*Min Area (sq units)*	*Max Area (sq units)*	*Max Proportion (ratio)*
living	8	20	8	20	120	300	1.5
kitchen	6	18	6	18	50	120	
bath	5.5	5.5	8.5	8.5			
hall	0	15	3.5	6	0	72	
bed1	10	17	10	17	100	180	1.5
bed2	9	20	9	20	100	180	1.5
bed3	8	18	8	18	100	180	1.5

Further, there must be space—say, 3.0 units—for a doorway in the walls connecting bed2 and bed3 to the hall, and all rooms are rectangular (as is the entire plan).

This design decision problem can be formulated as a nonlinear programming problem as follows. The *decision variables* are given in the following table (*length* is defined as the horizontal dimension, and *width* as the vertical dimension in figure 4-15):

Room	*Length/Width*	*Label*
living	length	X_1
bath	width	X_2
hall	width	X_3
kitchen	length	X_4
kitchen	width	X_5
hall	length	X_6
bed1	length	X_7
bed2	length	X_8
bed2	width	X_9
bed3	width	X_{10}

Although at first there appear to be fourteen decision variables (namely, the length and the width of each room), some of these are computable from others and therefore are dependent variables. The problem can be formulated quite differently. The *objective function* can now be written as

$$Z = \min (X_1X_2 + X_1X_3 + 2X_4X_5 + 2X_6X_2 + X_6X_3 + X_7X_5 + X_8X_9 + X_8X_{10})$$

subject to the following *constraints:*

X_1	$\leqslant$	20	
X_1	$\geqslant$	8	
$(X_2 + X_3)$	$\leqslant$	20	
$(X_2 + X_3)$	$\geqslant$	8	living
$X_1X_2 + X_1X_3$	$\leqslant$	300	
$X_1X_2 + X_1X_3$	$\geqslant$	120	
$X_1/(X_2 + X_3)$	$\leqslant$	1.5	
X_4	$\leqslant$	18	
X_4	$\geqslant$	6	
X_5	$\leqslant$	18	kitchen
X_5	$\geqslant$	6	
X_4X_5	$\leqslant$	120	
X_4X_5	$\geqslant$	50	
X_6	$\leqslant$	5.5	
X_6	$\geqslant$	5.5	bath
X_2	$\leqslant$	8.5	
X_2	$\geqslant$	8.5	
X_6	$\leqslant$	15	
X_6	$\geqslant$	0	
X_3	$\leqslant$	6	hall
X_3	$\geqslant$	3.5	
X_6X_3	$\leqslant$	72	
X_6X_3	$\geqslant$	0	
X_7	$\leqslant$	17	
X_7	$\geqslant$	10	
X_5	$\leqslant$	17	
X_5	$\geqslant$	10	bed1
X_7X_5	$\leqslant$	180	
X_7X_5	$\geqslant$	100	
X_7/X_5	$\leqslant$	1.5	

$$
\begin{aligned}
X_8 &\leqslant 20 \\
X_8 &\geqslant 9 \\
X_9 &\leqslant 20 \\
X_9 &\geqslant 9 \qquad \text{bed2} \\
X_8 X_9 &\leqslant 180 \\
X_8 X_9 &\geqslant 100 \\
X_8 / X_9 &\leqslant 1.5
\end{aligned}
$$

$$
\begin{aligned}
X_8 &\leqslant 18 \\
X_8 &\geqslant 8 \\
X_{10} &\leqslant 18 \\
X_{10} &\geqslant 8 \qquad \text{bed3} \\
X_8 X_{10} &\leqslant 180 \\
X_8 X_{10} &\geqslant 100 \\
X_8 / X_{10} &\leqslant 1.5
\end{aligned}
$$

$$
\begin{aligned}
X_9 - X_2 &= 3 \\
X_{10} - X_5 &= 10
\end{aligned} \qquad \text{doorway}
$$

$$
\begin{aligned}
X_1 + X_6 - X_4 - X_7 &= 0 \\
X_2 + X_3 + X_5 - X_9 - X_{10} &= 0
\end{aligned} \qquad \text{wall alignments}
$$

This list contains redundant constraints.

At one stage during the linearization process, the current solution is given by

$$
\begin{aligned}
X_1 &= 11.25 \\
X_2 &= 8.50 \\
X_3 &= 6.00 \\
X_4 &= 6.50 \\
X_5 &= 9.75 \\
X_6 &= 5.50 \\
X_7 &= 10.26 \\
X_8 &= 10.25 \\
X_9 &= 11.50 \\
X_{10} &= 12.75
\end{aligned}
$$

and the approximate linear model for this solution is

$$Z = \min(14.50X_1 + 16.75X_2 + 19.75X_3 + 23.24X_4 + 23.00X_5 + 9.75X_6 + 24.25X_7 + 10.00X_8 + 10.25X_9 + 22.25X_{10})$$

subject to

$$\begin{aligned}
X_2 &\geqslant 8.5 \\
X_2 &\leqslant 8.5 \\
X_6 &\geqslant 5.5 \\
X_6 &\leqslant 5.5 \\
14.50X_2 + 11.25X_2 + 11.25X_3 &\leqslant 463.12 \\
14.50X_1 + 11.25X_2 + 11.25X_3 &\geqslant 283.12 \\
9.75X_4 + 6.49X_5 &\leqslant 183.26 \\
9.75X_4 + 6.49X_5 &\geqslant 113.26 \\
5.50X_3 + 6.00X_6 &\leqslant 105.00 \\
10.26X_5 + 9.75X_7 &\leqslant 280.06 \\
10.26X_5 + 9.75X_7 &\geqslant 200.06 \\
11.50X_8 + 10.25X_9 &\leqslant 297.88 \\
11.50X_8 + 10.25X_9 &\geqslant 217.88 \\
12.75X_{10} + 10.25X_8 &\leqslant 316.94 \\
12.75X_{10} + 10.25X_8 &\geqslant 236.94 \\
X_1 - 1.5X_2 - 1.5X_3 &\leqslant 0 \\
X_7 - 1.5X_5 &\leqslant 0 \\
X_8 - 1.5X_9 &\leqslant 0 \\
X_8 - 1.5X_{10} &\leqslant 0 \\
X_9 - X_2 &= 3.00 \\
X_{10} - X_5 &= 3.00 \\
X_1 + X_6 - X_4 - X_7 &= 0 \\
X_2 + X_3 + X_5 - X_9 - X_{10} &= 0
\end{aligned}$$

The final solution is given by the following table of values:

Room	*Length*	*Width*
living	10.50	14.50
bath	5.50	8.50
hall	5.50	6.00
kitchen	5.95	9.95
bed1	10.05	9.95
bed2	8.95	11.50
bed3	8.95	12.95

The minimum cost is 715.98 cost units.

Finding a set of initial feasible decisions may not always be straightforward. Numerical vagaries sometimes prevent this method from converging to the optimum solution quickly. While the simplex method performs uniformly well on any problem, the sequential linear programming method for the solution of nonlinear programming problems carries no such guarantee. Many techniques unrelated to linear programming have also been developed to solve nonlinear programming problems.

SCOPE OF LINEAR PROGRAMMING

Linear programming is the mathematical programming method, par excellence. As long as its requirements are satisfied, it guarantees to find the optimum solution in a finite number of tableaux. The final tableau of the simplex method is rich in postoptimality information about the solution, providing both sensitivity and stability information in a quantifiable form. Furthermore, many computer programs that use the simplex method are available. It can be used quite effectively as the basis of a method for the solution of nonlinear programming problems.

In order for a problem to be solvable by the linear programming method, the following two requirements of a problem formulation must be satisfied: the variables must all be continuous; and all relationships that describe the problem must be linear. As we saw in the preceding section, one of the fundamental concerns in architecture—area—is represented as a nonlinear expression. In general, the number of design decision problems in architecture and building that satisfy both of these requirements is not as large as the number of problems that do not. Chapter 5 describes a method that does not rely on these requirements.

FURTHER READING

Two good introductory texts on linear programming that do not demand mathematical sophistication are:

Hughes, A.J., and Grawiog, D.E. 1973. *Linear Programming: An Emphasis on Decision Making*. Reading, MA: Addison-Wesley.

Lev, B., and Weiss, H.J. 1982. *Introduction to Mathematical Programming*. New York: North-Holland.

A more formal and detailed treatment of linear and nonlinear programming can be found in:

Beightler, C.S.; Phillips, D.T.; and Wilde, D.J. 1979. *Foundations of Optimization*. 2d ed. Englewood Cliffs, NJ: Prentice-Hall.

Nonlinear programming methods, including those based on linear programming, are well described in:

Bazaara, M.S., and Shetley, C.M. 1979. *Nonlinear Programming*. New York: Wiley.

Himmelblau, D.M. 1972. *Applied Nonlinear Programming*. New York: McGraw-Hill.

Works that describe the use of linear and nonlinear programming in design decision problems include:

Aguilar, R.J., and Hand, J.E. 1968. A generalized linear model for optimization of architectural planning. *Proceedings of the 1968 Spring Joint Computer Conference,* pp. 81–88.

Brotchie, J.F., and Linzey, P.T. 1971. A model for integrated building design. *Building Science* 6:89–96.

Dudnik, E.E. 1977. Uncertainty and the design of building subsystems—a linear programming approach. *Building and Environment* 12:111–16.

Gordon R.E. 1969. A linear programming model for multi-zone unit space allocation. *Heat, Piping and Air Conditioning* 14(11):123–28.

Mitchell, W.J.; Steadman, J.P.; and Liggett, R.S. 1976. Synthesis and optimization of small rectangular floor plans. *Environment and Planning B* 3:37–70.

CHAPTER 5

DESIGN USING DYNAMIC PROGRAMMING

We have seen in chapter 3 that differential calculus offers a direct and elegant solution to the optimization of a small class of continuous and differentiable functions within a closed region, and in chapter 4 that linear programming is a highly developed and efficient procedure for the optimization of continuous linear objective functions that are subject to linear constraints. Given such good optimization techniques, it is regrettable that few important problems from architecture and building design fit into either of these classes.

The ideal optimization technique for architecture and building would handle problems with data that are discrete, nonlinear, discontinuous, and/or stochastic; unfortunately, neither classical calculus nor linear programming matches this specification. Dynamic programming is important because it can handle problems with all of these characteristics. Moreover, it always yields a global optimum and can operate with highly complex problems of suitable form. If we could always use it, we could write down the algorithm and close the book here. The key, though, is the requirement for suitable form. Dynamic programming requires that a problem be organized in a rather special serial form that is rarely obvious at first inspection and in some instances may not even be possible.

Dynamic programming has no general solution algorithms comparable to the differentiation procedure of differential calculus or the simplex method of linear programming. Instead, there is only a principle of optimality and a set of techniques that may help to put it into effect. Rather than being the passive applicator of a well-known algorithm, the designer hoping to use dynamic programming must make use of creative ingenuity to structure the problem so that the power of the concept can be brought to bear. This is a considerable intellectual challenge; dynamic programming is high in logic and low in mathematics, and the clear-thinking designer with a grasp of the logic of the situation can succeed where the pure mathematician may fail to see the overall structure for the component equations.

The idea that the ease with which a problem can be solved—and whether it can be solved at all—depends on its *formulation* has made Edward de Bono and his "lateral thinking" famous. De Bono adduces the tennis game problem, a classic example of the benefits of lateral thinking. You are required to organize a rather large tennis tournament that has 319 entries. Tennis tournaments have a pyramidal structure with a final, semifinals, quarterfinals, and so on, down to the first round of the pyramid. Clearly, some byes from the first round to the second round will be needed to make this structure work. How many matches, in total, do you need to schedule?

Try out your mental arithmetic before continuing.

There are two ways of solving this problem, and it is worth exploring both of them. The first way is to solve the winners problem. If you win a match in a tennis tournament you go on to the next round. We have 1 winner from the final, 2 from the semifinals, 4 from the quarterfinals, and then 8, 16, 32, 64, 128, and 256 winners from each of the previous rounds. But, 256 winners means $256 \times 2 = 512$ players, and we only have 319 entrants, so this round needs to include some byes. If we let X be the number of first round matches and Y be the number of first-round byes, all we need to do is solve the following pair of simultaneous equations:

$$2X + Y = 319 \text{ (two players for each match and one for each bye)}$$

$$X + Y = 256 \text{ (players needed for the next round)}$$

Then we simply add up $X + 128 + 64 + 32 + 16 + 8 + 4 + 2 + 1$ to get the total number of matches. It is not difficult, but a sheet of paper helps.

Now consider the alternative losers problem. If you lose a match in a tennis tournament, you get knocked out. Put another way, players get knocked out at the rate of one per match. Indeed, only one player does not lose a match, and that is the champion. If there are 319 entrants, there must be 318 losers; hence 318 games.

Given a bit of lateral thinking, the mental arithmetic is not just easier, it is trivial. What is more, we now have a field solution: the number of matches in a tennis tournament is $X - 1$, where X is the number of players; and we can solve a 3-player problem, a 73-player problem, and even a grand 5,673-player problem with equal ease.

Richard Bellman, the inventor of dynamic programming, formulated the principle of optimality, which has something of the same elegance and utility that de Bono's lateral thinking ideas possess. Bellman stated the following intuitively obvious principle:

> an optimal set of decisions has the property that whatever the first decision is, the remaining decisions must be optimal with respect to the outcome which results from the first decision.

This is indeed intuitively obvious, although perhaps not at first reading. Such language needs thinking about. The principle has been restated by Rutherford Aris in rather more straightforward terms:

> if you don't do the best you can with what you happen to have got, you will never do the best you might have done with what you should have had.

To see what this means for problem solving, let us tackle some design problems. Since the essence of dynamic programming is logic and not mathematics, it is better to demonstrate the power of the principle of optimality by example than by equations.

PROBLEM: FINDING A SHORTEST ROUTE

In the annals of operations research, there is a recurring problem known as the shortest path problem. This comes in many guises: the paths may be roads between towns, railways between junctions, or cable routes between floor ducts in a building. The aim, though, is always to find the shortest path through a network. We shall take a very simple example.

You are appointed to supervise construction of a house in the country at *K*, a site that can be reached from the towns of *H*, *I*, and *J*. Your office is at *A*, and it is not immediately clear whether the best way to reach *K* is to set out toward *B*, *C*, or *D*, towns that are each well connected with *E*, *F*, and *G*, and through them to *H*, *I*, and *J*. The distances involved are shown diagrammatically in figure 5-1. (We shall use kilometers (km) as our unit of distance; 1 km = 0.62 miles.) Since you are not being paid for traveling time, it is important to find the shortest route. How can you be sure you have the shortest route with the least possible effort?

A heuristic designer might approach the problem as follows. We have three towns to get through: *D* is closer than *B* or *C*, so we shall go there

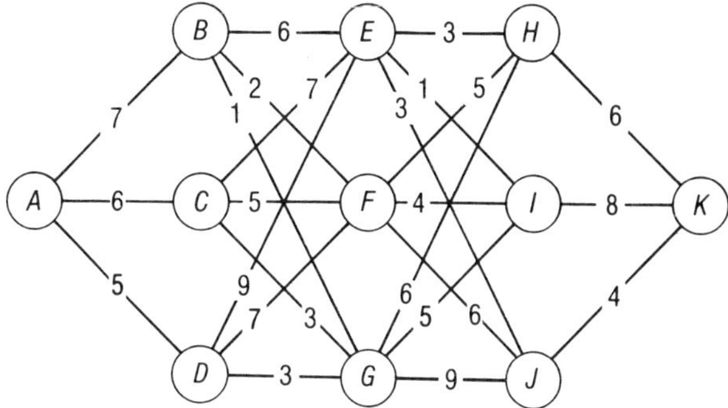

Fig. 5-1. Network diagram showing the distances for various routes between locations *A* and *K*.

first, and the distance traveled is 5 km; from *D*, *G* is closer than *E* or *F*, so we shall go there next, and the distance traveled is 5 + 3 = 8 km; similarly to *I*, with the total distance traveled now 12 km; then to *K*, to make a total distance of 21 km. A methodical designer might enumerate all the feasible route combinations from *A* to *H* (in fact, twenty-seven routes) and choose the shortest—a slow but sure approach.

A lateral thinking designer remembers Aris's restatement of the principle of optimality: "If we do not do the best we can with what we happen to have, we will never do the best we might have done with what we should have had." Let us imagine we have got somehow to *H*. If we cannot even work out the shortest route from *H* to *K*, we shall certainly be incapable of working out the shortest route from *A* to *K*.

In fact there is only one route from *H* to *K*, but that does not alter the argument. *If* the best route *does* happen to pass through *H* (or *I*, or *J*), we can see the best route from then on (fig. 5-2(a)). So far so good, but rather trivial. Now let us consider the previous set of three towns. *If* the best route *does* happen to pass through *E*, the best route from then on will clearly be that with the smallest sum of the distances *E* to *H* plus *H* to the end, *E* to *I* plus *I* to the end, and *E* to *J* plus *J* to the end. If we happen to be at *E*, the best policy turns out to be to head for *J*, and there are 3 + 4 = 7 km to go (fig. 5-2(b)). If we happen to be at *F*, the best policy is also to head for *J*, and there are 6 + 4 = 10 km left. Similarly, if we happen to be at *G* the best policy is to go to *H* and there are 6 + 6 = 12 km left. Rather than calculate total distances from start to finish, we are working out the part distances between the finish and various towns that *might* prove to be on the best route to the finish.

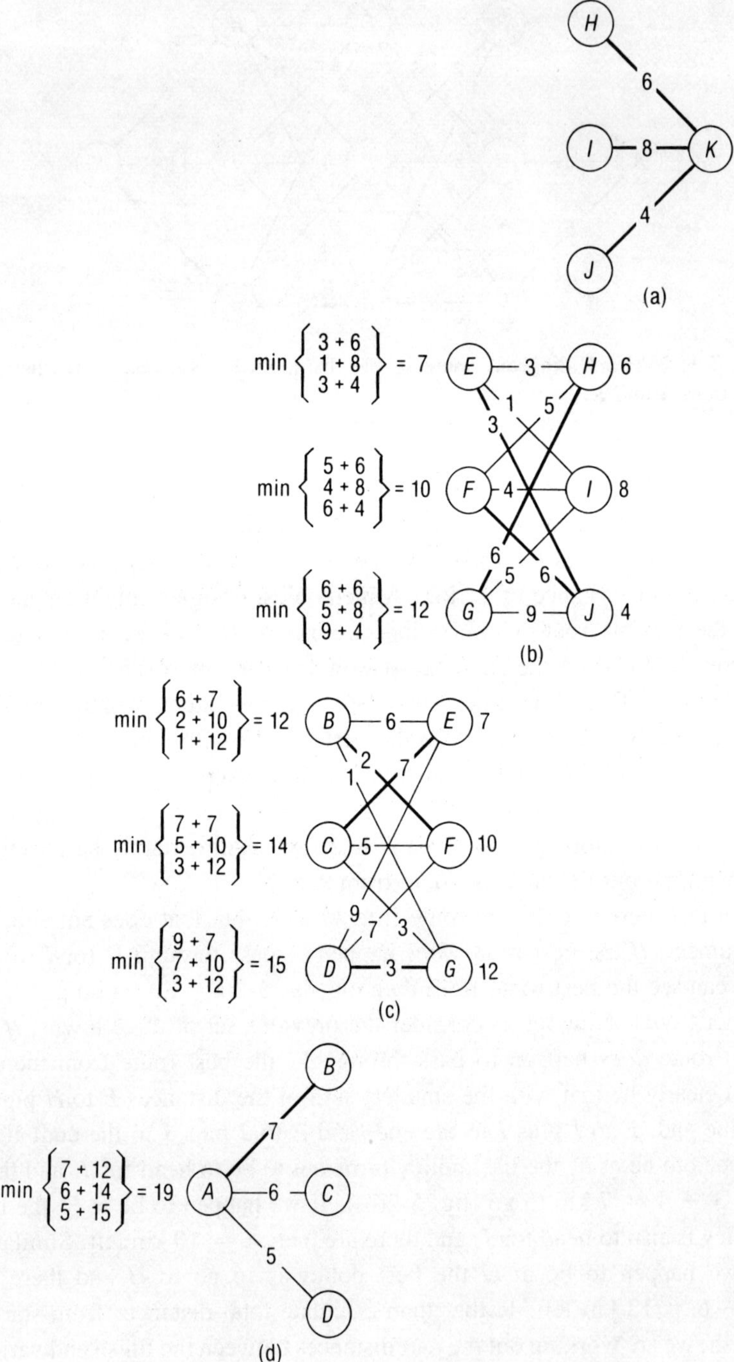

Fig. 5-2. Optimal subpolicies for a shortest-route problem.

Why this is a good idea begins to show up when we think about the best route to *K* if we happen to be at *B*. We already know the best routes and the shortest distances from *E, F,* and *G* to *K,* so all we need to work out now is the smallest sum of the distance from *B* to *E* or *F* or *G* and the relevant shortest distance from those towns to the end. In fact the best policy is to drive to *F* (fig. 5-2(c)), and there are 12 km left. Similar best policies and shortest distances can be worked out for *C* and *D*. The important point is that we only need to know which town to head for next and the total distance from our present position; having got to that next town, we have already worked out the rest of the problem. For our starting point at *A,* we carry out similar calculations for the towns of *B, C,* and *D;* we find that the best plan is to go first to *B,* and the shortest total distance is 19 km (fig. 5-2(d)). Tracing back, we find that from *B* we should head for *F;* from *F* to *J;* and from *J* to *K*.

Counting the number of calculations we have had to carry out, we find that we have made twenty-one additions (an addition here being a summing of two numbers) and fourteen comparisons (again of pairs of numbers). If instead we had enumerated all the possible routes from *A* to *K* and compared the results to find the shortest, we would have to do seventy-one additions and twenty-six comparisons.

How is this apparently magical work reduction achieved? It will become clearer with further examples, but consider how the problem was approached. The total problem was divided into a number of stages. At each stage we considered the possible states of our being in one of the alternative towns through which the shortest route might pass. Instead of looking immediately for the optimal route policy from start to end, we looked for optimal subpolicies in each of these possible states. Remember these terms (*stages, states,* and *optimal subpolicies*); they will be used again.

Before we turn to another problem, two points are worth mentioning. Suppose that, instead of starting out from your office at *A,* one day you find yourself talking to another client in the town of *D* just before you are due at a site meeting at *K*. Do you need to carry out a new dynamic programming optimization to find the shortest route from *D* to *K?* The answer, of course, is no: as part of the solution of the *A*-to-*K* problem, we have already solved the *D*-to-*K* problem (from figure 5-2, the shortest route is through *G* and *H*). In fact we solved the problems of the shortest routes from *B, C, D, E, F, G, H, I,* and *J* to *K* (some of them admittedly trivial), all in the course of solving the *A*-to-*K* problem. The notion of solving a series of problems within the solution of the principal problem, called *invariant imbedding,* is an important and useful characteristic of dynamic programming. The second point to note is that in this problem we could have inverted the whole solution approach. Instead of working backward from *K* to *A* we could equally well have worked forward from *A* to *K,* looking first at the shortest way of getting from *B* or *C* or *D,* then at the shortest way of getting to *E* or *F* or *G,* and so on. We would, of course, have ended up with the same result. Try solving the problem in this forward direction.

PROBLEM: DESIGNING TRADITIONAL CONCRETE FORMWORK

Wet concrete slabs that are cast in situ need to be supported by a formwork construction while the concrete sets and hardens. The four main components of traditional horizontal formwork are plywood sheets, timber joists, timber bearers, and adjustable tubular steel props (fig. 5-3). Almost invariably, the sheets, joists, and bearers are precut to size, and a contractor

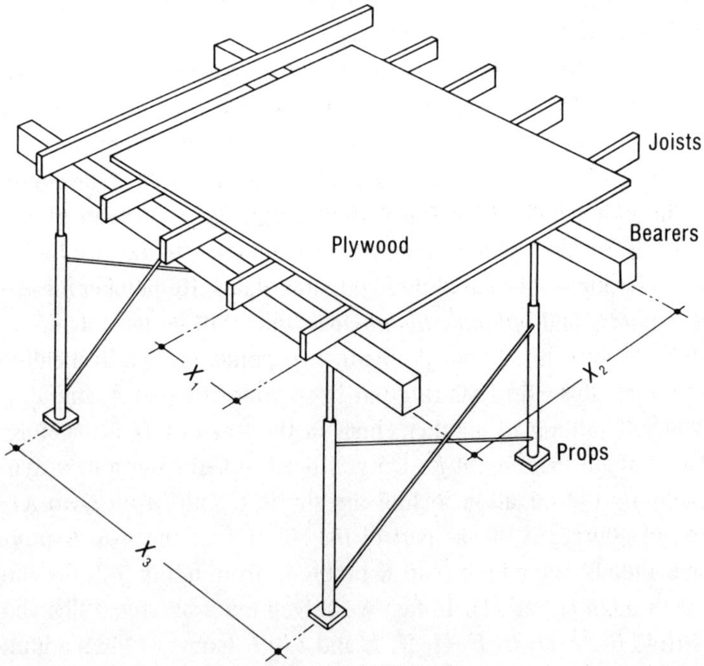

Fig. 5-3. Traditional concrete formwork: plywood sheeting on joists spanning between bearers supported by adjustable steel props.

normally designs the system by a priori deciding on the spans and selecting the minimum component sizes which satisfy the design criteria for each component. This will not necessarily produce the optimum design. For a particular job with long spans of flat concrete floor slabs, you are asked to produce a least-cost design.

Since formwork contributes a substantial percentage of the cost of finished concrete structures, real gains can be made in optimizing its design. The problem is to determine the component sizes (from a discrete available range) and the component spans in order to minimize the aggregate cost of the sheets, joists, bearers, and props, where these costs take labor into account.

It would be very advantageous to break this formwork system into smaller subsystems that could be optimized individually. Plywood sheeting is expensive, and the cost of plywood can be minimized by using sheets 9 mm ($^3/_8$ inch) thick. But sheets this thin will only span (say) 400 mm (16 inches) without excessive deflection, so the cost of close-spaced joists might then become excessive. Hence, we cannot optimize one component in isolation. If we want to break the problem down into subproblems or stages, we need to be more subtle in going about it.

Because the mass of the formwork components is small in comparison with the mass of the concrete supported, it can reasonably be ignored in designing the structure. (In chapter 6, we shall examine the effect of taking these self-weights into account on the solution of this problem.) Since the load per unit area is fixed, we can identify the following relationships:

1. The choice of sheet thickness depends on sheet span, X_1 (fig. 5-3).
2. The choice of joist size depends on joist spacing, X_1, and joist span, X_2.
3. The choice of bearer size depends on bearer spacing, X_2, and bearer span, X_3.
4. The number of props also depends on X_2 and X_3.

If we were solving this problem by exhaustively enumerating all possibilities, we would try every combination of feasible values for X_1, X_2, and X_3 and work out the cost of each combination. To keep things simple, we shall just take three values for X_1, six values for X_2, and seven values for X_3 (fig. 5-4), making $3 \times 6 \times 7 = 126$ span combinations to calculate and compare. To ensure we cover all possibilities we could set these spans up as a tree (fig. 5-5).

	Size mm	Size in.	Span mm	Span in.	Cost/m² of Form Work
Plywood:	9	3/8	400	14	\$10
	13	1/2	600	24	\$15
	18	3/4	900	36	\$20
Joists:	50 × 50	2 × 2	Depends on Spacing		
	75 × 50	3 × 2			
	100 × 50	4 × 2			
	125 × 50	5 × 2			
	150 × 50	6 × 2			
Bearers:	150 × 50	6 × 2			
	150 × 75	6 × 3			
	175 × 50	7 × 2			
	175 × 75	7 × 3			
	200 × 75	8 × 3			
	225 × 75	9 × 3			

Objective: Minimize plywood cost & joist cost & bearer cost & prop cost

Fig. 5-4. Feasible spans for different sizes of plywood, joists, and bearers.

Since (from relationship 1 above) the design of the sheet depends only on its span, one way of organizing these calculations is to consider and cost all the possible plywood sheet spans before turning to the joists. Let these costs be c_1, c_2, and c_3, all measured in dollars per unit of sheet. Moreover, since (from relationship 2 above) the design of the joist depends only on its span and on the span of the sheet, we could similarly design the joists for each combination of joist span and sheet span before turning to the bearers. The necessary thicknesses and costs for the plywood are already calculated; all we need to do is calculate the joist size to carry the imposed load, given values for joist span and joist spacing, and add the joist cost (again in terms of dollars per unit area of formwork) to the cost of the plywood sheeting.

At this point let us pause and take stock. We have calculated for each joist span, X_2, three different combined costs of joists plus sheets, depending on the choice of sheet span, X_1. We know that the size of the bearers is affected by the joist span, X_2, but not by the sheet span, X_1. This is the time for some lateral thinking. Clearly, for each joist span there will be a choice of sheet span that results in the cheapest combined cost of joist plus sheet. Therefore, if that particular joist span turns up in the optimal design, it must be in conjunction with the said sheet span. Furthermore, when we start to combine each bearer span value with each

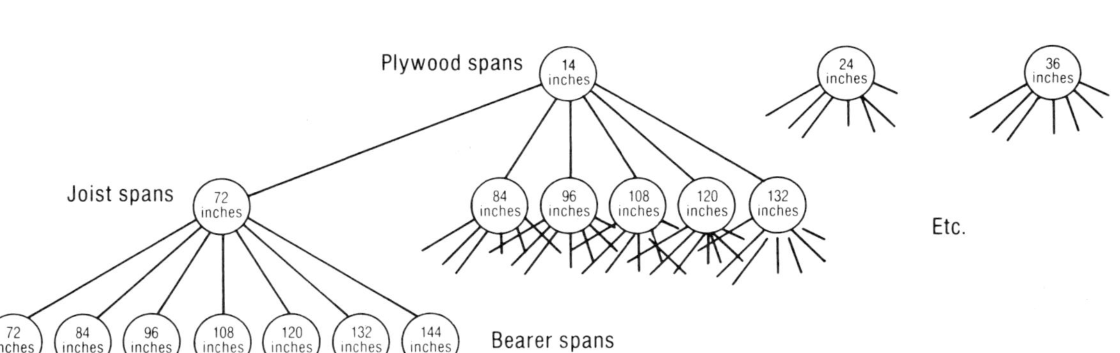

Fig. 5-5. Combinations of plywood, joist, and bearer spans, expressed as a tree of possibilities. The figures given are in inches; metric conversion is as follows: 14 in., 400 mm.; 24 in., 600 mm.; 36 in., 900 mm.; 72 in., 1,800 mm.; 84 in., 2,100 mm.; 96 in., 2,400 mm.; 108 in., 2,700 mm.; 120 in., 3,000 mm.; 132 in., 3,300 mm.; 144 in., 3,600 mm.

joist span value to see which works out cheapest, we need not combine each value of sheet span but only the best choice given the joist span. Remember again Aris's restatement of the principle of optimality: "If we do not do the best we can with what we happen to have, we will never do the best we might have done with what we should have had." If we cannot do the best we can with any feasible joist span, we will certainly be incapable of doing the best possible with the whole structural system.

This becomes clearer if we reorganize the tree structure of figure 5-5 into the network of figure 5-6 (note the similarities between this network and the distance diagram in figure 5-1). First we find the least cost (in

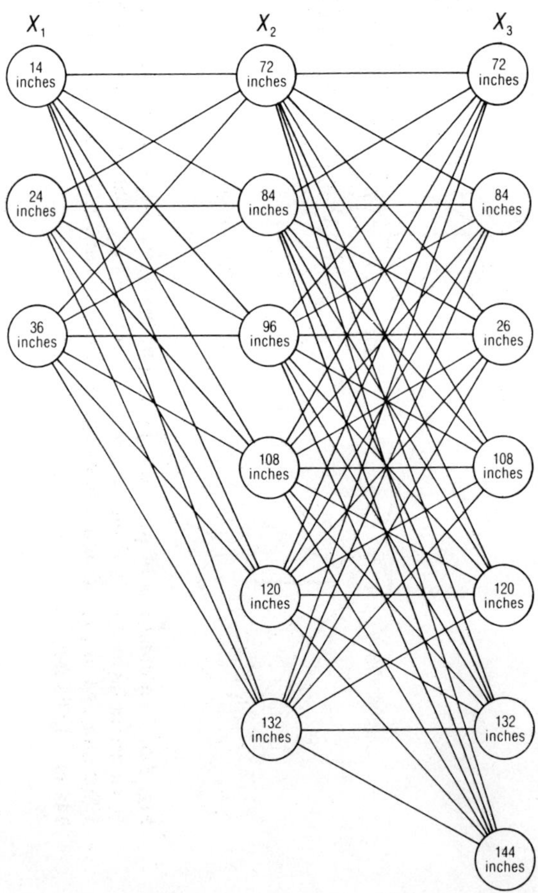

Fig. 5-6. Tree of possibilities for plywood, joist, and bearer spans, redrawn as a network. The figures given are in inches; for metric conversions, see figure 5-5.

dollars per unit area) and the corresponding solution (in terms of plywood thickness) for each feasible plywood sheet span. Then we find the total cost of each feasible combination of joist and sheet span, and identify the least cost (in dollars per unit area) and the corresponding solution (now in terms of plywood thickness, plywood sheet span—that is, the joist centers—and joist size) for each feasible joist span. We do not need to recalculate anything about the plywood sheet, since we have that from the first stage. Then we find the total cost (plywood plus joists plus bearers plus posts) for each feasible combination of joist and bearer span, knowing already the part cost for the joist and sheet part of the structure. Finally we choose the total structural system (now in terms of bearer size, bearer span, and posts) that costs the least. Instead of 126 combinations of exhaustive enumeration, we in fact need to do $(3 \times 6) + (6 \times 7) = 60$ combinations, using the principle of optimality.

Now let us review how the problem was approached. The total problem was divided into a number of stages, each of which added a component to the structural system: first, the plywood sheet; next, the joists; and finally, the bearers plus posts. At each stage we considered the possible states of each of the feasible spans, assuming that component to be the span used in the optimal solution. Instead of looking immediately for an optimal design policy for the whole structural system, we looked for optimal subpolicies, given each of these possible states.

We were able to impose this structure for two reasons. First, decisions on bearer span do not invalidate our earlier choice of a best plywood sheet span for each joist span, so the sheet/joist/bearer problem can legitimately be disaggregated into a series made up of a sheet only problem, a sheet/joist problem, and a sheet-plus-joist/bearer problem that can be solved sequentially. Second, the basic objective of the design is to minimize the sum of a series of discrete component costs, so the objective is separable into additive parts related to the serial structure we imposed. These characteristics—a serial problem structure composed of stages and states, with a separable objective function—are the fundamentals of dynamic programming optimization.

At the end of our discussion of the shortest route problem, we noted that a number of other problems were embedded within the principal problem (*invariant imbedding*) and that the problem could equally well be solved forward or backward. Do the same notions apply to this formwork problem? Certainly there is some invariant imbedding. If instead of the range of bearer spans listed in figure 5-4, for example, we find that the only available bearers on site are 2,400 mm (8 ft) or 3,000 mm (10 ft) long, this more restricted problem has been solved within the original problem. On the other hand, we cannot invert the solution procedure and work backward: to size the bearers (and hence find the cost) for a particular bearer span, we need to know the bearer spacing; and this, as we have seen, depends on the joist design. This time we have to work in the particular order beginning with plywood sheeting, then adding joists, and finally adding bearers and props.

SOME SYMBOLS AND TERMINOLOGY

To solve a problem by dynamic programming, we need to be able to transform it into a series of subproblems that can be solved sequentially. This transformation must be *invariant*—meaning that the transformed version must have the same feasible solutions and the same performances as the original problem. If the transformation cannot be made, the problem cannot be solved by dynamic programming. Each subproblem is a stage in the solution of the total problem. We shall now put these stages, states, and so on, into mathematical form, using conventional terminology.

We divided the concrete formwork problem in the preceding section into three stages: a plywood sheet problem, a plywood sheet/joist problem, and a sheet-plus-joist/bearer problem. Each stage corresponded to the addition of another component to the structural system. In dynamic programming terminology, we can define a *stage variable* as the structural component, which in the formwork example has three values (plywood sheet, joist, and bearer). We shall denote a stage by n; in the formwork example, $n = 1, 2, 3$, corresponding to the three added components.

At each stage we considered the possible states of each one of the feasible spans, assuming that component to be the span used in the optimal solution. In dynamic programming, we speak of input states to and output states from a stage. An *input state* describes the state of the system before the operation of the stage, and an *output state* describes the state of the system after that stage. Thus, in the formwork problem, an input state to stage 2 is a set of feasible plywood spans (and each plywood span will have an associated plywood thickness chosen to minimize cost), while the output state is a set of feasible joist spans (where each joist span implies not only an associated joist depth but also a corresponding plywood span and plywood thickness, all selected to minimize cost). Hence, the output state provides all the information about design variables that is necessary for the next stage. We call a variable whose value provides this information a *state variable,* and we denote the output states from stage n by X_n.

At each stage we make some design decisions about the added structural component and about its relationships to the part-design before that component was added, in order to minimize the total cost for the set of components considered thus far. The variables we can control as design decisions are known as *decision variables,* and the decision variables at stage n are denoted by D_n. The additional cost of the parts of the system designed at stage n is known as a *stage return* (this is a general term in dynamic programming for something that measures the effectiveness or utility of a stage), and it is denoted by r_n.

In stage 1 of the formwork problem, we considered three feasible states for the span of a plywood sheet structural subsystem. For each of these states, we made a decision about plywood thickness in order to minimize the cost of plywood in association with that span. In dynamic programming terminology, we were faced with the following variables:

1. No *input states,* since this was the first stage
2. *Output states,* X_1 (plywood spans), with three state values—400 mm (16 inches), 450 mm (18 inches), and 600 mm (24 inches)
3. *Decisions,* D_1 (on plywood thickness), with three decision values—9 mm ($^3/_8$ inch), 13 mm ($^1/_2$ inch), and 18 mm ($^3/_4$ inch)
4. *Stage returns,* r_1 (cost of plywood in dollars per unit area), which were a function of the decisions and output states; that is, $r_1 = r_1 (X_1, D_1)$

The aim of the stage is to find the optimal return for each value of the output state by controlling the decision variables—in this case, to find the lowest cost of plywood for each plywood span by controlling the plywood sheets. The optimal return here will be a vector of three values; one for each state value. Denoting $f_1(X_1)$ as the optimal return as a function of the output states at stage 1, we have

$$f_1 (X_1) = \underset{D_1}{\text{opt}} [r_1 (X_1, D_1)] \qquad (5.1)$$

This means that, for each value of the state variable, the optimal return lies among the stage returns (which in turn is a function of the state variable and the decisions) and is achieved by controlling the decisions.

Now let us turn to stage 2 of this formwork problem, where we add joists to the structural system. We have previously defined the following variables:

1. *Input states,* X_1 (plywood spans), with three state values—400 mm (16 inches), 450 mm (18 inches), and 600 mm (24 inches)
2. *Output states,* X_2 (joist spans), with six state values—1,800 mm (6 ft), 2,100 mm (7 ft), 2,400 mm (8 ft), 2,700 mm (9 ft), 3,000 mm (10 ft), and 3,300 mm (11 ft)

Clearly, one decision variable is joist depth, since we can choose a joist depth in order to minimize the cost of the system for each joist span value. The choice of joist depth, though, depends not only on the joist span but also on the joist centers—that is, on the plywood spans that are the input states to the stage. Since we can choose a plywood span to go with any joist span, we in fact have two decision variables and can identify the following values:

3. *Decisions,* D_2, on joist depths, with five decision values—50 mm (2 inches), 75 mm (3 inches), 100 mm (4 inches), 125 mm (5 inches), and 150 mm (6 inches)—and on plywood spans, with three decision values—400 mm (16 inches), 450 mm (18 inches), and 600 mm (24 inches)

Finally, we have the following stage return variable:

4. *Stage returns* (cost of joists, in dollars per unit area of formwork), which are a function of the decisions and output states, in the form $r_2 = r_2(X_2, D_2)$.

As for stage 1, the optimal return will be a vector of values: one for each state value. This time, though, we are interested in the *lowest total cost* for joists and plywood for each joist span—that is, the optimal return for the first two stages. If we denote $f_2(X_2)$ as the optimal return at stage 2 as a function of the output state at stage 2, we have

$$f_2\,(X_2) = \underset{D_2}{\text{opt}}\,[r_2\,(X_2, D_2) + f_1\,(X_1)] \tag{5.2}$$

This means that for each value of the state variable, the optimal return lies among the sums of the stage returns and the optimal returns for stage 1 and is achieved by controlling the decisions.

By now it should be fairly clear that, at stage 3, we have the following variables:

1. *Input states,* X_2 (joist spans), with six state values—1,800 mm (6 ft), 2,100 mm (7 ft), 2,400 mm (8 ft), 2,700 mm (9 ft), 3,000 mm (10 ft), and 3,300 mm (11 ft)
2. *Output states,* X_3 (bearer spans), with seven state values—1,800 mm (6 ft), 2,100 mm (7 ft), 2,400 mm (8 ft), 2,700 mm (9 ft), 3,000 mm (10 ft), 3,300 mm (11 ft), and 3,600 mm (12 ft)
3. *Decisions,* D_3, on bearer depths, with four values—150 mm (6 inches), 175 mm (7 inches), 200 mm (8 inches), and 225 mm (9 inches)—on bearer widths, with two values—50 mm (2 inches) and 75 mm (3 inches)—and on joist spans, with six values—1,800 mm (6 ft), 2,100 mm (7 ft), 2,400 mm (8 ft), 2,700 mm (9 ft), 3,000 mm (10 ft), 3,300 mm (11 ft), and 3,600 mm (12 ft)
4. *Stage returns,* r_3 (cost of bearers and props, in dollars per unit area of formwork), where $r_3 = r_3(X_3, D_3)$

The optimal return at stage 3 will be given by

$$f_3(X_3) = \underset{D_3}{\text{opt}} \, [r_3(X_3, D_3) + f_2(X_2)] \tag{5.3}$$

which identifies the optimal return for each value of the output states to stage 3—the final stage. All that remains is to choose the lowest value from among those listed for this vector. If we let X^* be the optimal output state (the particular bearer span corresponding to the lowest total cost) and we let f^* (X^*) be the lowest total cost, we can say

$$f^*(X^*) = \underset{X_3}{\text{opt}} \, f_3(X_3) \tag{5.4}$$

In this section, we have restated the concrete formwork problem in terms of accepted dynamic programming terminology. In the next section, we shall explore the mathematics of dynamic programming in more general and formal terms.

MATHEMATICAL FORAY

Consider the nth of a series of N stages in a dynamic programming problem formulation. There are five principal components (fig. 5-7):

1. An *input state*, X_{n-1}, that gives all relevant information about inputs to the stage
2. An *output state*, X_n, that gives all relevant information about outputs from the stage
3. A *decision variable*, D_n, that controls the operation of the stage
4. A *stage return*, r_n, a scalar variable that measures the effectiveness or utility of the stage as a single-value function of inputs, decisions, and outputs; that is,

$$r_n = r_n(X_{n-1}, D_n, X_n) \tag{5.5}$$

5. A *stage transformation*, t_n, a single-value transformation that expresses each component of the output state as a function of the input state and decisions; that is,

$$X_n = t_n(X_{n-1}, D_n) \tag{5.6}$$

In equation 5.6, the symbol t is used abstractly to represent the transformations that yield all components of the output state. In practice, this transformation may be as simple as a one-line equation, or it may involve looking up a table or a set of tables, or it may itself be a quite complex mathematical model. Conceptually, at least, we can invert this transformation, giving us

$$X_{n-1} = t'(X_n, D_n) \tag{5.7}$$

where t' is an inversion of t_n that allows us to express X_{n-1} in terms of X_n. Substituting equation 5.7 in equation 5.5, we get

$$r_n = r_n(t'(X_n, D_n), D_n, X_n) \tag{5.8}$$

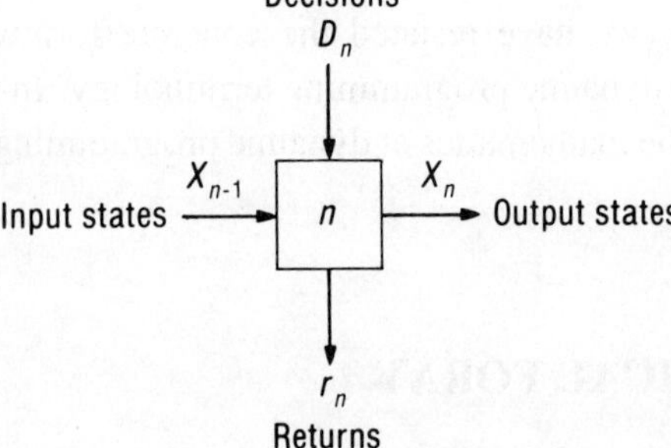

Fig. 5-7. The *n*th stage of a dynamic programming problem formulation.

or more simply (since r_n and t' are both representing functions),

$$r_n = r_n(X_n, D_n). \tag{5.9}$$

If X_n and D_n are both scalars, the dimensionality of the optimization is one state variable and one decision variable. Generally, however, there will be more than one state variable and more than one decision variable, and the dimensionality will be given by an ordered pair of numbers (S,Q), where S is the number of state variables, and Q is the number of decision variables. The dimensionality of a problem can vary from stage to stage.

The one-stage optimization problem is to find the optimal stage return as a function of the output state. Denoting $f(X_n)$ as the optimal stage return and $D_n{}^* = D_n(X_n)$ as the optimal decision policy (that is, the optimal set of values for the decision variables), we get

$$f(X_n) = r_n(X_n,D_n{}^*) = \underset{D_n}{\text{opt}}\, [r_n(X_n,D_n)] \tag{5.10}$$

In an ordinary optimization problem, the optimal return is a value. Here, the optimal return $f(X_n)$ is a vector (a sequence of values): one for each value of the output state. The idea of determining optimal returns as vectors is a key to dynamic programming.

A serial multistage system consists of a set of stages joined together in a series so that the output of one stage becomes the input to the next (fig. 5-8). Thus, the input state, X_{n-1}, to stage n is the output state from the

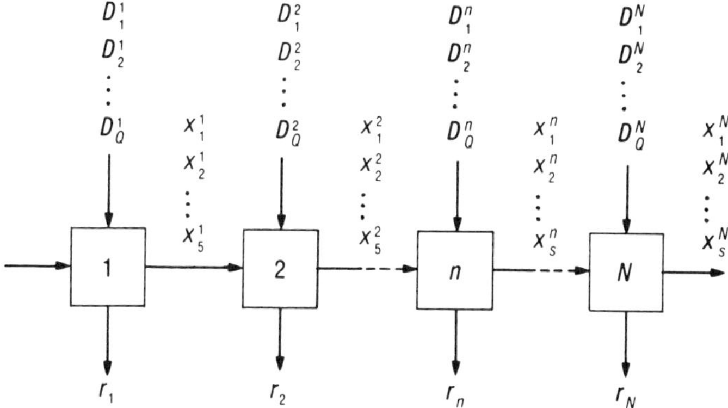

Fig. 5-8. Example of a serial multistage system. The stages are joined together so that the output from one stage becomes the input to the next stage. Here, there are Q decisions and S output states at each stage; Q and S can have different values at different stages.

previous stage, $n - 1$. The state variables describe the state of the system at each stage; if there are S state variables, each able to take M values, there will be MS possible states for the system.

A problem must satisfy two conditions in order for the logic of this decomposition into sequential stages to be valid:

1. The objective function must be separable so that it can be divided into a series of discrete stage returns. The simplest form is additive, although some other forms are possible.
2. It must be possible to organize the problem in the required serial structure in such a way that later decisions do not invalidate earlier ones. This is only true if the return to any stage is a monotonically nondecreasing function of the return to earlier stages.

These are known formally as conditions of *separability* and *monotonicity*. It may be possible to relax the conditions by using additional stage variables or by delaying the choice of input states over a number of stages; the necessary techniques for relaxing them will be introduced in chapter 6.

Computational aspects of dynamic programming involve the iterative solution of recursive equations that represent this sequential decision process. If $f_n(X_n)$ denotes the optimal n-stage return (that is, the return from all stages up to stage n), the general recursion equations applying at each stage can readily be developed.

We can restate equation 5.10 with the inclusion of **O**, an operator that guarantees separability. Typically, this operator is addition (Σ) but it need not be. So equation 5.10 becomes

$$f_n(X_n) = \underset{D_i}{\text{opt}} \left[\overset{n}{\underset{i=1}{\mathbf{O}}} r_i(X_i, D_i) \right] i = 1, \ldots, n \tag{5.11}$$

where

$X_n = (X_1, X_2, \ldots, X_S)_n$	is the S state variables that define the state of the system at stage n
$D_n = (D_1, D_2, \ldots, D_Q)_n$	is the Q decision variables that control the operation of stage n
r_n	is the return at stage n
$\mathbf{o}, \mathbf{o} \in \mathbf{O}$	is a composition operator that stipulates separability

Since the operator is separable, we can move the nth operation outside the brackets and restate equation 5.11 as

$$f_n(X_n) = \underset{D_n}{\text{opt}} \left[\underset{D_i}{\text{opt}} \left[\overset{n-1}{\underset{i=1}{\mathbf{O}}} r_i(X_i,D_i)\right]\right] \quad i = 1, \ldots, n-1 \tag{5.12}$$

that is,

$$f_n(X_n) = \underset{D_n}{\text{opt}} \left[r_n(X_n,D_n) \mathbf{\ o\ } \underset{D_i}{\text{opt}} \left[\overset{n-1}{\underset{i=1}{\mathbf{O}}} r_i(X_iD_i)\right]\right] \quad i = 1, \ldots, n-1 \tag{5.13}$$

From equation 5.11, we have

$$f_{n-1}(X_{n-1}) = \underset{D_i}{\text{opt}} \left[\overset{n-1}{\underset{i=1}{\mathbf{O}}} r_i(X_i, D_i)\right] \quad i = 1, \ldots, n-1 \tag{5.14}$$

Hence, substituting for $\underset{D_i}{\text{opt}} \left[\overset{n-1}{\underset{i=1}{\mathbf{O}}} r_i(X_i, D_i)\right]$, from equation 5.14 into equation 5.13, we get

$$f_n(X_n) = \underset{\mathbf{D}_n}{\text{opt}}\ r_n(X_n,D_n) \mathbf{\ o\ } f_{n-1}(X_{n-1})] \tag{5.15}$$

which is the fundamental recursive equation describing the conceptual structure of dynamic programming.

The optimal return, or performance, of the system is given by

$$f_N(X^*_N) = \underset{X_N}{\text{opt}}\ f_N(X_N) \tag{5.16}$$

in other words, the optimal Nth stage return in an N-stage series associated with one of the final states. For computation, all that needs to be stored, beyond the two stages concerned in the recursion equation, is the optimal decision vector and input state for each feasible value of the state variables at every stage. The set of decisions and values leading to the optimal total return can then be recovered on completion of the procedure.

The power of dynamic programming can be seen by comparing the number of computations it requires with the number required by exhaustive enumeration (often the only alternative). If there are M values for the state variables in each stage and a corresponding number of decisions in a N-

stage problem, exhaustive enumeration would require $(N - 1)M^{N+1}$ additions. To choose the optimum from these requires $M^{N+1} - 1$ comparisons; hence, the total amount of computation required using exhaustive enumeration is expressed by $NM^{N+1} - 1$.

Dynamic programming requires $(N - 1)^2$ additions. There are $M(M - 1)$ comparisons needed for each stage and an additional $M - 1$ for the last stage making a total of $NM(M - 1) + (M - 1)$. Hence, the total amount of computation required using dynamic programming is expressed by $(2N - 1)M^2 - (N - 1)(M - 1)$.

We can see that, as the number of values of the state variables increases, the amount of computation required increases exponentially. This is called the *curse of dimensionality*. As the number of stages increases, however, the amount of computation required only increases linearly. This gives us a strategy to guide our formulation of dynamic programming problems: if there is a choice, it is always better to have more stages than more state values.

We can now illustrate the power of dynamic programming. If we have a design problem formulated with fifty stages and ten states per stage, the amount of computation required to determine the optimal decisions by exhaustively enumerating all possible decisions is approximately 5×10^{52} additions and comparisons. A computer that can perform 1 million such computations per second would take more time than the universe is known to have been in existence to find the optimal solution. Using dynamic programming, the same computer would find the optimal solution in less than 1 second.

SOLUTION PROCEDURES

As with most skills, the trick of transforming a design optimization problem into a form that can be tackled by dynamic programming gets easier with experience. Certain recognizable characteristics suggest that dynamic programming can work in a particular case. After identifying the exogenous and endogenous variables, we must study the objective function. Can it be separated into meaningful components that are added together (or subtracted or multiplied) to give the same result? Then we must study the endogenous variables. Can decisions be made about some of them, without knowing values for all the others? Does this suggest some order for a series of linked subproblems that can be solved sequentially? Fundamentally, can suitable stage and state variables be identified, and can the problem be transformed into the required serial structure in such a way that later decisions do not invalidate earlier ones? There is no algorithm for this transformation; it depends on the problem solver's skill and usually requires several attempts before a successful formulation is found. Remember, too, that there is no guarantee of success; as is the case with calculus and linear programming, not every design problem is amenable to solution by dynamic programming.

Once this transformation is achieved, things get easier. Our next step is to clarify the problem, using a stage/state diagram like the one shown in figure 5-6. Then we simply cycle through the stages and states, finding the optimal return and decisions for each of these states at each stage. At this point, for each state, we have an individual optimization problem within an optimization problem. In the concrete formwork problem, we did not discuss how this would be carried out. Since the number of states and decision values was small, the easiest way would be to try out all the decision possibilities and compare the results. Indeed, in the great majority of dynamic programming design problems of interest to us, this subsidiary optimization is carried out by exhaustive comparison. There is, though, no restriction here; any optimization technique (exhaustive enumeration, calculus, linear programming, dynamic programming itself, or any other method) can be used to make these decisions.

We must, however, keep a record of the optimal return and the optimal decisions. When we finish the last state of the last stage, we compare the total returns associated with each of the last states and identify the optimal one—giving us the lowest cost, shortest distance, or whatever the optimization criterion might be. In design, this optimal value is of little use unless we know how it is achieved and what set of decisions produced it. The optimal decisions for this final state will indicate the input state from the next-to-last stage, so we can look at the optimal decisions noted for that state. In this way, we can trace back through all the stages to identify the optimal set of decisions (or *optimal policy*) that produced the optimal solution. Flow charts for the complete optimization and traceback procedures are given in figure 5-9, where it is assumed that the subsidiary optimization at each state is done by exhaustive search.

The next part of this chapter contains two more examples involving applications of dynamic programming to architecture and building problems. Work through these examples first; then reread the two sections you have just finished. With a wider set of examples in mind, you will find that some of the subtleties of the technique become clearer.

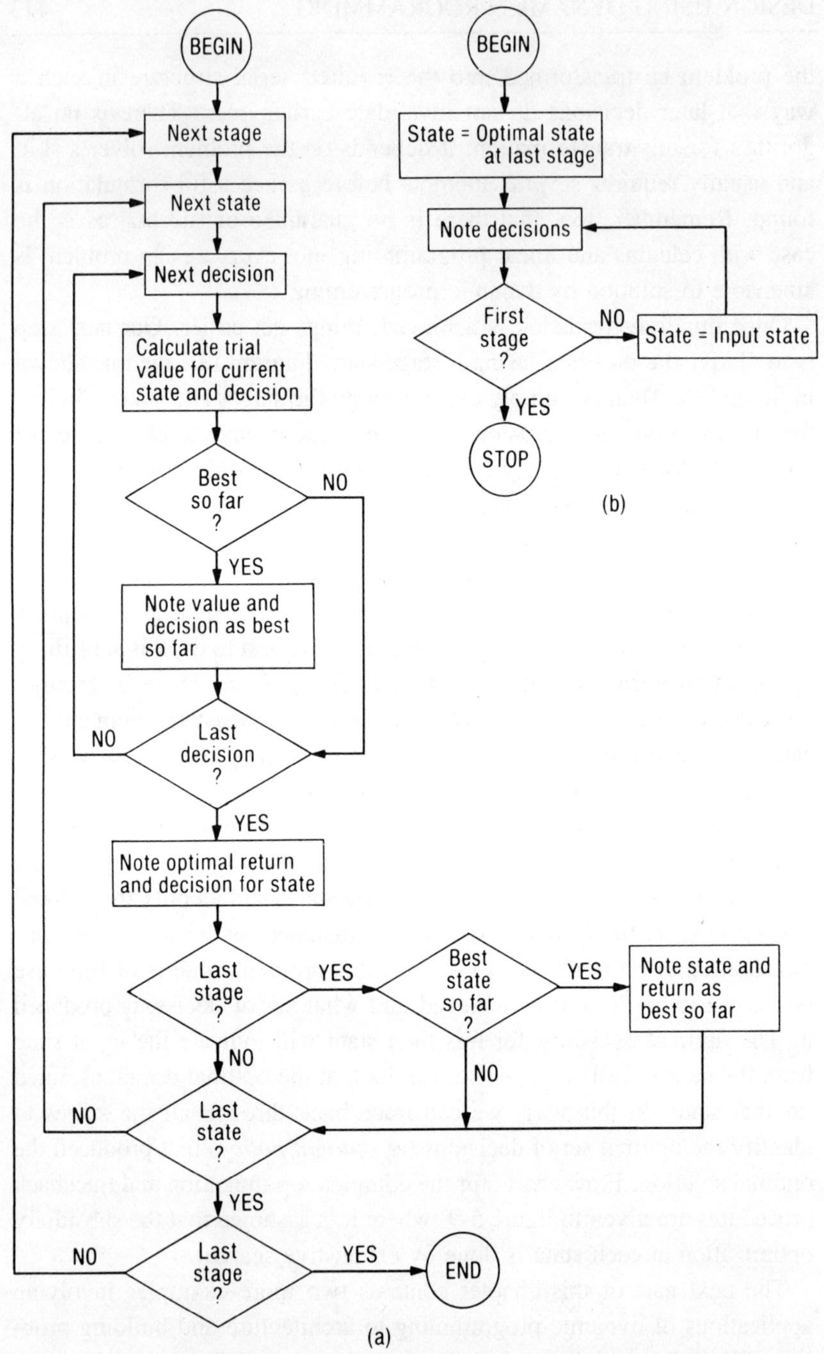

Fig. 5-9. Flow charts showing the procedures for (a) finding an optimal solution (return and final state) for a stage/state dynamic programming problem and (b) tracing back to find the optimal set of decisions, given an optimal final state.

PROBLEM: ECONOMIC FEASIBILITY STUDY

Description

Your clients have an option on a large urban site in an expanding town; they urgently need some information on the financial feasibility of development. They envisage a mixed project of housing, retail, and office areas and know of a hotel chain interested in leasing a hotel on part of the site. From previous experience, they can estimate rental income as a function of floor areas devoted to these different activities. You have calculated building and other development costs on the same basis and have related these through projected interest rates to produce a table of expected annual profit against gross floor area (allowing for services, elevators, and so on) for each development type (fig. 5-10). Planning regulations restrict the total floor area of the complex to 7 units (we shall keep these unspecified; you can think of them as 10,000s of square meters or 100,000s of square feet). Your problem now is to advise your clients on the mix of development that will maximize the return and therefore be most likely to ensure economic viability.

Formulation

As usual, the solution to this problem is not immediately apparent. In fact, it is one of an important group of dynamic programming problems,

	Returns ($100,000s)			
Area	Housing	Retail	Office	Hotel
0	0	0	0	0
1	2	6	1	8
2	4	9	1	12
3	6	9	2	20
4	8	10	3	16
5	10	11	15	12
6	12	12	12	10
7	14	13	20	4

Fig. 5-10. Tableau of returns (annual profit) against decisions (areas allocated) for areas of 0 to 7 units allocated to four activities.

called *tableau allocation problems,* where a fixed resource (in this case floor area) must be allocated among several competing demands (in this case, housing, retail, office, and hotel developments) in order to maximize some return.

We shall define the following terms:

1. *Stage variable*—the development type, T_n (n = 1, 4), with four values (housing, retail, office, and hotel) that refer to the development type added at stage n
2. *State variable*—the floor area, A_j (j = 1, 7), with seven values (0, 1, 2, 3, 4, 5, 6, and 7) that indicate the area allocated to all development types included up to the nth stage
3. *Decisions*—decisions, $D_{j,n}$, on the floor area to be allocated to the nth development type, given an available area of A_j
4. *Stage return—the return,* $r_{j,n}$, achieved by including the nth development type, depending on the decision, $D_{i,n}$, on the area to be allocated to that development type (this is the information contained in figure 5-10)

As for our other problems, we can represent this formulation as a network stage/state diagram (fig. 5-11). The optimal subpolicy to the ith state at the nth stage is the best possible way of allocating an area A_i among the first n development types in order to maximize the return. For example, the optimal subpolicy to state 5 at stage 3 is the best possible way of distributing 5 units of area among the development types of housing, retail, and office uses. The optimal return will be the return given by this optimal subpolicy. When we get to state 7 at stage 4 we will have the optimal way of allocating 7 units among all four uses, and the return obtained by so doing will be the solution to our problem.

Solution

In this formulation, we shall commence by determining the optimal ways of developing only housing on the site (stage 1). Then we shall determine the optimal ways of adding retail to this partially developed site, knowing that we already have the best ways of developing housing. This will give us the best ways of developing housing and retail. Since we do not know (at this stage) which of the possible states will be in the optimal solution, we need to keep them all. Next, we shall find the optimal ways of adding offices to this partially developed site, knowing that we already have the

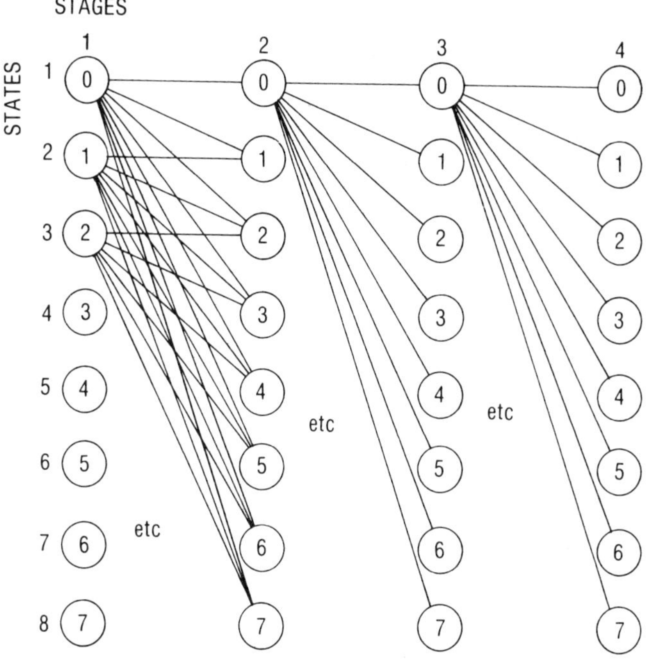

Fig. 5-11. The space allocations problem expressed as a network, illustrating a dynamic programming problem formulation with four stages and eight possible states at each stage. The links show the possible links between states at different stages. For a state of "3 units allocated" at stage 2, for example, the possible input stages from stage 1 are 0, 1,000, 2,000, or 3 units allocated (the balance being made up from the area allocated at stage 2). The remaining output states from stage 1 (4,000, 5,000, 6,000, and 7 units) are not valid input states to the state of "3 units allocated" at stage 2 because no decisions are available that take away area at a stage.

best ways of developing housing and retail; we will not have to recalculate this because the previous stage will contain just this information. Finally, we shall find the optimal ways of adding the hotel to this partially developed site, knowing that we already have the best ways of developing housing, retail, and offices. This final stage can be examined to locate the optimal solution in terms of the optimal value of the objective function, and the optimal decisions can be traced backward from this.

We already have a table of the stage returns (fig. 5-10). To solve the problem, we shall use two new tables—one for the optimal return to any state, and one for the optimal decision at any state.

At stage 1, there is no choice of decisions; the optimal way to allocate A_j among housing alone is to allocate it all to housing. Consequently, column 1 of the optimal returns table is the same as column 1 of the stage returns table, and column 1 of the decisions table reflects this.

Stage 1 Optimal Returns Table (in $100,000s)

Area	*Housing*
0	**0**
1	**2**
2	**4**
3	**6**
4	**8**
5	**10**
6	**12**
7	**14**

Stage 1 Optimal Decisions Table

Area		*Housing*
0		**0**
1		**1**
2		**2**
3		**3**
4		**4**
5		**5**
6		**6**
7		**7**

At stage 2, though, decisions must be made. We shall work through the states one by one. The optimal return from allocating 0 units is $0. In allocating 1 unit, we have the following choice:

Housing	*Retail*	*Return (in $100,000s)*	
0	1	0 + 6 = 6	optimal subpolicy
1	0	2 + 0 = 2	

The optimal subpolicy is to allocate 1 unit to retail use; we write *6* in the optimal return table and *1* (meaning 1 unit allocated to the development type being added at this stage) in the decision table. In allocating 2 units, we have the following choice:

Housing	*Retail*	*Return (in $100,000s)*	
0	2	0 + 9 = 9	optimal subpolicy
1	1	2 + 6 = 8	
2	0	4 + 0 = 4	

The optimal subpolicy is to allocate all of the 2 units to retail use; we write *9* in the optimal return table and *2* in the decision table. Similarly, in allocating 3 units between housing and retail use, we have the following choice:

Housing	*Retail*	*Return (in $100,000s)*	
0	3	0 + 9 = 9	
1	2	2 + 9 = 11	optimal subpolicy
2	1	4 + 6 = 10	
3	0	6 + 0 = 6	

In line with the optimal subpolicy, we write *11* in the optimal return table and *2* in the decision table. (We can work out later that having 2 units of retail means that we must have 1 unit of housing to make up the 3 units.) We do the same for the other possible states of 4, 5, 6, and 7 units allocated between housing and retail. (Calculate these yourself to check.) For 7 units, for example, we have the following choice:

Housing	*Retail*	*Return (in $100,000s)*	
0	7	0 + 13 = 13	
1	6	2 + 12 = 14	
2	5	4 + 11 = 15	
3	4	6 + 10 = 16	
4	3	8 + 9 = 17	
5	2	10 + 9 = 19	optimal subpolicy
6	1	12 + 6 = 18	
7	0	14 + 0 = 14	

Therefore, we write *19* in the optimal returns table and *2* in the optimal decisions table:

Stage 2 Optimal Returns Table (in $100,000s)

Area	*Housing*	***Housing + Retail***
0	0	**0**
1	2	**6**
2	4	**9**
3	6	**11**
4	8	**13**
5	10	**15**
6	12	**17**
7	14	**19**

Stage 2 Optimal Decisions Table

Area	*Housing*	***Housing + Retail***
0	0	**0**
1	1	**1**
2	2	**2**
3	3	**2**
4	4	**2**
5	5	**2**
6	6	**2**
7	7	**2**

At stage 3, we consider the states of 0, 1, 2, 3, . . . , 7 units to be allocated between offices (the new use added at stage 3) and [housing + retail] use (the latter bracketed together). We can consider [housing + retail] as a single entity because we have now sorted out the best way of allocating between these two any area left over after office use. To calculate optimal returns, we need to work with column 2 of the optimal returns table (which gives us the combined housing and retail returns) and column 3 of the stage returns table (which gives us the office returns).

As we did for stage 2, we work through the stage 3 states one by one. The optimal return from allocating 0 units is $0. In allocating 1, 2, 3, and 7 units, the following choices are available to us:

Allocation	*[Housing and Retail]*	*Office*	*Returns (in $100,000s)*	
1 unit	0	1	0 + 1 = 1	
	1	0	6 + 0 = 6	optimal subpolicy
2 units	0	2	0 + 1 = 1	
	1	1	6 + 1 = 7	
	2	0	9 + 0 = 9	optimal subpolicy
3 units	0	3	0 + 2 = 2	
	1	2	6 + 1 = 7	
	2	1	9 + 1 = 10	
	3	0	11 + 0 = 11	optimal subpolicy
.	.	.	.	
.	.	.	.	
.	.	.	.	
7 units	0	7	0 + 20 = 20	
	1	6	6 + 12 = 18	
	2	5	9 + 15 = 24	optimal subpolicy
	3	4	11 + 3 = 14	
	4	3	13 + 2 = 15	
	5	2	15 + 1 = 16	
	6	1	17 + 1 = 18	
	7	0	19 + 0 = 19	

We write the respective optimal returns and optimal decisions in the appropriate tables (for 4, 5, and 6 units as well as for the areas shown above), completing stage 3:

Stage 3 Optimal Returns Table (in $100,000s)

Area	*Housing*	*Housing + Retail*	***Housing + Retail + Offices***
0	0	0	**0**
1	2	6	**6**
2	4	9	**9**
3	6	11	**11**
4	8	13	**13**
5	10	15	**15**
6	12	17	**21**
7	14	19	**24**

Stage 3 Optimal Returns Table (in $100,000s)

Area	*Housing*	*Housing + Retail*	***Housing + Retail + Offices***
0	0	0	**0**
1	1	1	**0**
2	2	2	**0**
3	3	2	**0**
4	4	2	**0**
5	5	2	**5** or **0**
6	6	2	**5**
7	7	2	**5**

At stage 4, we add hotel use to our consideration. Strictly, we are only interested in the state of 7 units to be allocated between hotel use and [housing + retail + office] use (bracketed together as a composite entity), since we know from the definition of the problem that we have exactly 7 units to allocate. It may, however, prove better to leave some of the available site area undeveloped (see, for example, the set of stage returns for this final hotel stage when too large a hotel gives less return than one of optimal size). Moreover, it may be useful to solve the 1, 2, 3, . . . , 6 units problems, as well as the 7 units problem, so that we know what to do if planning regulations should change or if part of the site should cease to be available. As a result, in the optimal returns and decisions tables, we complete the whole of the last column and not just the bottom row. The calculation procedure is exactly the same as for stage 3—this time taking column 3 of the optimal returns table (which gives us the combined housing, retail, and office returns) and column 4 of the stage returns table (which gives us the hotel returns). Check some of the calculations yourself. Figure 5-12 shows the completed final optimal returns table, while figure 5-13 shows the completed final optimal decisions table.

In this case the optimal return is given when the final state is 7 units, indicating that it is best to use the whole available floor area. The optimal final stage decision is 3 units of hotel, so there must be 7 − 3 = 4 units of [housing, retail, and office]. If we look at the state of 4 units allocated between [housing and retail] and offices at stage 3, we find that the optimal stage 3 decision was 0 units of office, hence 4 − 0 = 4 units of [housing and retail]. Next, looking at the state of 4 units allocated between housing and retail at stage 2, we find that the optimal stage 2 decision was 2 units

Optimal return ($100,000s)

Area	Housing	Housing & Retail	Housing & Retail & Office	Housing & Retail & Office & Hotel
0	0	0	0	0
1	2	6	6	8
2	4	9	9	14
3	6	11	11	20
4	8	13	13	26
5	10	15	15	29
6	12	17	21	31
7	14	19	24	33

Fig. 5-12. Tableau of optimal returns for the space allocation problem.

of retail area, hence 4 − 2 = 2 units of housing. The optimal policy, then, is

2 units housing, 2 units retail, 0 office space, and 3 units hotel

which gives an optimal annual return of $3,300,000. Looking down the other final states, we can find the optimal return for smaller floor areas and trace back the associated optimal decisions in the same way. More-

Optimal decision

Area	Housing	Retail	Office	Hotel
0	0	0	0	0
1	1	1	0	1
2	2	2	0	1
3	3	2	0	3
4	4	2	0	3
5	5	2	5/0	3
6	6	2	5	3
7	7	2	5	3

Fig. 5-13. Tableau of optimal decisions for the space allocation problem.

over, if the hotel chain should pull out of the project, we have the optimal return for using the entire site for housing, retail, and office with no hotel (the last row of the third column of the returns table). In fact, we have solutions to a whole range of problems that may (or may not!) prove to be useful. What, for example, is the best policy if the client only purchases part of the site so that we can build 4 units of floor space, and the hotel chain pulls out? We already know the answer (from the returns and decisions tables)—another example of invariant imbedding in dynamic programming.

PROBLEM: DESIGNING ELEVATOR BANKING SYSTEMS

Description

In modern tall buildings, the amount of space taken up by the vertical transportation system can become exceedingly large, and the time required to fill the upper floors with their working population can become excessively long. To reduce both, the total number of elevator cars is commonly divided into groups. Each group, called a bank, serves the ground floor and a common set of upper floors, called a zone (fig. 5-14). Elevator banking allows more usable area on the floors above the elevator shafts for the lower rise zones and also (and most important) speeds up the vertical communications between the ground floor and the rest of the building.

Suppose that your clients with the large urban site (in the previous problem) are also constructing a 51-floor office building in the city center. One of the outstanding problems is to decide on the best elevator banking policy. You, of course, are expected to provide the answer.

The building is intended to hold (by floor) the following working population:

Floor	*People per Floor*
2–13	270
14	0
15	270
16–26	210
27–38	205
39	0
40–51	185

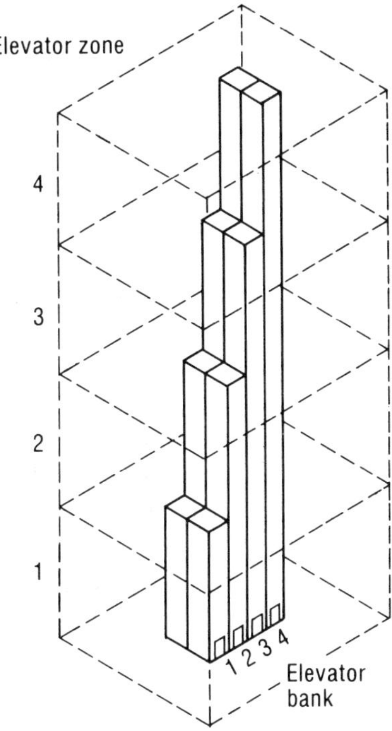

Fig. 5-14. Elevator banking in a multistory building. Each bank of elevators serves a particular zone of floors.

Floors 14 and 39 contain only mechanical equipment. The building is intended to have thirty-two elevator cars, with the following maximum velocities and capacities:

Number of Cars	*Maximum Velocity*	*Capacity (passengers)*
8	2.5 m/s (500 ft/min)	21
8	4.0 m/s (800 ft/min)	21
8	6.0 m/s (1,200 ft/min)	19
8	7.0 m/s (1,400 ft/min)	19

Formulation

The major objective in determining a banking policy is to design a system with the best possible passenger-carrying capability in the morning rush hour, when virtually all passenger traffic is in the up direction, originating at the main floor. A reasonable measure of performance, then, is the time required to fill the building completely. Obviously, this will happen when the filling times for the rises served by each bank are as equal as possible.

The filling time for a bank will be a function of the following factors:

1. The capacity of the cars in the bank, c
2. Their maximum velocity, v
3. Their acceleration, a
4. Their door operation time
5. The time required to load and unload passengers
6. Floor heights
7. The number of floors served, m

We need first to calculate the time it takes for a car to make a round trip from the main floor through a series of upward stops, and back down again. In the morning peak arrival period cars will be close to full when they leave the main floor, and interfloor and downward (exiting) traffic will be so small that it can be ignored. The number of upper floor stops per round trip can be approximated as the following binomial random variable with expectation:

$$m - m(1 - 1/m)^c \tag{5.17}$$

This binomial variable assumes that each passenger is equally likely to get off at any of the m floors, independent of the actions of any other passenger (here we shall simply accept the expression as a useful mathematical model and get on with the formulation). The time, t, for an elevator car to travel s meters—starting and finishing at rest—can be calculated exactly or can be approximated by simple equations of motion. If $s \leqslant (v^2/a)$,

$$t = 2\sqrt{(s/a)} \tag{5.18}$$

Otherwise,

$$t = 2v/a + (s - v^2/a)/v \tag{5.19}$$

Door operation times can be obtained from manufacturer's data, and the time required to load and unload a given number of passengers can be measured at a comparable installation.

In order to generalize our formulation, let N denote the number of banks of cars, and let H be the highest floor of the building; therefore, the elevators serve floors 2 to H (floor 1 being the main floor), and there are

$H - 1$ floors to be served. In our dynamic programming formulation, we shall define the following terms:

1. *Stage variable*—the number of elevator banks, n ($n = 1, N$); thus, at stage 1 we consider one bank, at stage 2 we consider two banks, and so on.
2. *State variable*—the highest floors served by the n banks, X_n; in general, we shall find (for each stage n) the optimal way for the first n banks to serve floors 2, 3, . . . , X_n for values of X_n from $n + 1$ to H.
3. *Decisions*—D_n on the floors to be alloted to the nth elevator bank, given a highest floor of X_n.
4. *Stage return*—the filling time, r_n, required for the nth bank to fill up to the highest floor, X_n; that is, $r_n = r_n(X_n)$.

The idea of the formulation is to let bank n serve floors ($X_{n-1} + 1$, $X_{n-1} + 2$, . . . ,X_n) and to require banks 1, 2, . . . $n - 1$ to serve floors 2, 3, . . . , X_{n-1} optimally. For each state X_n ($n + 1 < X_n < H$), we choose a value of X_{n-1} such that the maximum filling time for any bank is minimized. The optimal return $f_n(X_n)$ to any stage will therefore be a minimax expression given by

$$f_n(X_n) = \min_{n \leq X_{n-1} \leq X_n} \max[r_n(X_n), f_{n-1}(X_{n-1})] \qquad (5.20)$$

Conceptually, $f_n(X_n)$ is the best the system can do if banks 1, 2, . . . , n serve floors 2, 3, . . . , X_n. If we start with one bank and continue adding one bank at each stage for N stages, we shall find out what we want to know: the best the system can do when all N banks serve all of the floors (2, 3, . . . , H).

At stage 1 we have only one bank available for the assignment, and there is no choice of policy; one bank must serve all of the floors (2, 3, . . . , H), and the maximum filling time is the only filling time:

$$f_1(X_1) = r_1(X_1) \qquad (5.21)$$

At stage 2, banks 1 and 2 can be assigned. For each state X_2 ($3 < X_2 < H$), consider assigning bank 2 to floors 3, 4, . . . , X_2. The maximum of the two filling times is

$$\max[f_1(X_1), r_2(X_2)] \qquad (5.22)$$

where $f_1(X_1)$ is the time required for bank 1 to fill floors 2, 3, . . . , X_1 and $r_2(X_2)$ is the time required for bank 2 to fill floors $X_1 + 1, X_1 + 2, \ldots,$ X_2. We wish to choose X_1 such that equation 5.20 is minimized. Hence,

$$f_2(X_2) = \min_{2 \leq X_1 \leq X_2} \max[f_1(X)_1, r_2(X_2)] \qquad (5.23)$$

For the general n-stage problem, consider (for each state X_n) assigning bank n to floors $X_{n-1}, X_{n-1} + 1, \ldots, X_n$. This implies that banks 1, 2, . . . , $n - 1$ must serve floors 2, 3, . . . , X_{n-1} optimally. The important point is that we already know how to do this from the $(n - 1)$-stage problem. Indeed, the dynamic programming problem is completely specified by equations 5.20 and 5.21 above. Solution of these recursive equations for $n = 1, 2, \ldots, N$ and $X_n = n + 1, n + 2, \ldots, H$ will yield $f_N(X_N)$—the minimum filling time for N banks to serve X_N floors. We are interested in $f_N(X_N)$ when $X_N = H$. Having found this minimum filling time, we need to work backward in the usual way to find the input state to each state on the optimal policy, and thence establish the banking policy that provides the best performance.

Solution

To use the solution method just described, we need to establish in advance the number of banks and the division of the available cars into the banks—ordered so that bank 1 serves the lowest floors, bank 2 is alloted to the second group, and so on. Only iterative application of the algorithm will give more design information on the effect of different numbers of banks or different configurations of cars per bank. Returning to our original problem of a 51-story building with thirty-two elevator cars, we shall assume that we have eight banks of four cars each. Unlike the site feasibility study problem, this problem can only be solved in a reasonable amount of time by means of a computer program. Fortunately, our design problem turns out to be exactly the same as an example quoted and solved by Powell, and the optimal banking policy is shown in figure 5-15. In a design situation, we probably would want to rerun the algorithm with a number of other car configurations to show how the passenger carrying capability varied.

Before continuing, let us compare this problem with the site feasibility problem in the preceding section. Both are allocation problems, although of very different types. In the former case, we allocated floor areas to

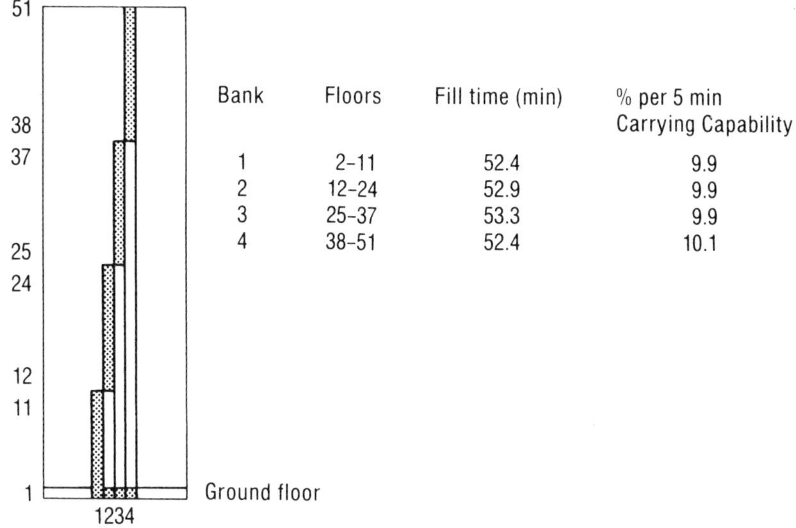

Bank	Floors	Fill time (min)	% per 5 min Carrying Capability
1	2-11	52.4	9.9
2	12-24	52.9	9.9
3	25-37	53.3	9.9
4	38-51	52.4	10.1

Fig. 5-15. Optimal solution to the elevator banking problem.

uses; in this case, we allocate floors to elevator banks. Look, too, at the similarities (and any differences) in the way the stage returns, the optimal returns to the stages, and the decisions are established, and consider what other problems (differing building heights, different numbers of elevator banks and elevators) have their solutions embedded within the 51-floor, 32-elevator and 8-elevator-bank problem solution. In this case, the embedded solutions are not particularly useful, given our original problem specification.

POSTOPTIMALITY ANALYSIS

We want here to put in a brief note about postoptimality analysis—a subject that will be considered at greater length in chapter 6. As has been mentioned, the sensitivity and stability of an optimal solution are of particular interest to designers. *Sensitivity* indicates the degree to which an optimal performance is affected by changes in the problem environment; *stability* indicates the range of changes in the problem environment for which the decisions that make up a solution remain constant. Information necessarily generated as part of the dynamic programming optimization procedure can provide some data on the sensitivity and stability of the optimal solution.

Consider the optimal returns table of the site feasibility problem (fig.

5-12). We can see directly that the optimal return is fairly insensitive with respect to floor area; if we are forced to accept a design change that reduces floor area from 7 units to 6 units, our annual return reduces from $3,300,000 to $3,100,000—only a 6 percent reduction accompanying a 14 percent reduction in floor area. But our anticipated return is considerably more sensitive with respect to design changes about development type; if the hotel chain should pull out of the project, our annual return drops from $3,300,000 to $2,400,000—perhaps no longer enough to justify financing the scheme. Such information is vital to decision makers.

Now assume that we want to build our 7 units of development, but Murphy's law tells us that optimal solutions never work out. Can we establish a second-best policy and return, or even a third-best? Without more work we cannot do so, but we can get an approximation—or more accurately, a lower bound to it. To arrive at our optimal return ($3,300,000 for 7 units) we had to calculate every combination of allocating that space between [housing + retail + office] uses and hotel uses. The following calculations were involved:

[Housing + Retail + Office]	*Hotel*	*Returns (in $100,000s)*	
0	7	4	
1	6	16	
2	5	21	
3	4	27	3rd best policy
4	3	33	optimal policy
5	2	27	3rd best policy
6	1	29	2nd best policy
7	0	24	

We can see that $2,900,000 is a lower bound to the second-best return and that the policy associated with it is 1 unit of hotel space and 6 units of other development. Interestingly, this return is less than the return from only developing 6 units of space altogether (fig. 5-12), and so that may be another option. The reason the former is only a lower bound is that, way back in the calculations, it may have been better as a second-best policy to make some different distribution of space between, say, the housing and retail areas than between the hotel and the rest. We do not retain such information unless we have made special provisions to this end. The necessary steps for preserving information of this type are explained in chapter 6.

SCOPE OF DYNAMIC PROGRAMMING

We close this chapter with a review of the scope, advantages, and disadvantages of dynamic programming as a design optimization technique. The fundamental prerequisite for using dynamic programming is that the design problem be separable into a series of subproblems that can be solved sequentially. This transformation must be invariant so that the transformed version has the same feasible solutions and the same performances as the original problem. There is no standard form for such programming, and the required transformation is rarely apparent at first sight. Each type of problem needs to be explored anew. Moreover, the transformation has to satisfy some rather rigorous requirements of separability and monotonicity—meaning that the objective function for the optimization must be divisible into discrete stage returns that can be associated with each subproblem, and that the series of subproblems must be organized in such a way that later decisions do not invalidate earlier ones. The four examples we have described at length give an idea of this transformation process.

We have also mentioned one other problem associated with the use of dynamic programming; the curse of dimensionality. In all of our examples so far, the output states and returns have been vectors; that is, the states of the systems modeled have always been representable as a value for a single variable (values for town name, timber span, floor area, and floor story, in the four examples). In many problems, however, we shall find that the state of the system can only be adequately described by values for two, three, four, or even more variables. If we need twenty feasible values for floor area to describe the range of alternative states of a system at some stage, we are faced with 20 output states. If we need not only twenty values for floor area, but also twenty values for aspect ratio, twenty values for orientation, and twenty values for floor story to describe the range of alternative states of some system, we are faced with 160,000 output states. The amount of computation required rises exponentially with the number of state variables. That is the curse of dimensionality, and in dynamic programming it can be a fearsome curse.

The news, though, is not all bad, and dynamic programming has some powerful advantages to set against these disadvantages. It will handle problems with nonlinear, discontinuous, and discrete variables, which means that it will handle a whole range of problems in architecture and building design that are outside the scope of alternative methods. It guarantees a global optimum and, as we saw in the last section, can provide near-optimum solutions. The characteristic of invariant embedding means that whole classes of problems can sometimes be solved in one execution of the optimization procedure. Constraints on design variables generally make the computation easier instead of harder (as in linear programming and most other optimization techniques). And finally—but by no means least important—once the principles of dynamic programming have been grasped, the procedure is conceptually quite easy to understand and relatively easy to embody in computer programs. For all these reasons, we have found dynamic programming to be a particularly useful method of design optimization in architecture and building. In chapters 6 and 7 we shall extend its usefulness and demonstrate some more complex applications of it.

FURTHER READING

A complete discussion of dynamic programming optimization can be found in:

Nemhauser, G.L. 1966. *Introduction to Dynamic Programming*. New York: Wiley.

A good text that addresses formulation issues is:

Dreyfus, S.E., and Law, A.M. 1977. *The Art and Theory of Dynamic Programming*. New York: Academic Press.

Richard Bellman's two books on dynamic programming require a reasonable degree of mathematical sophistication of the reader, but they do contain the ideas and words of the person who originally conceived the optimality principle:

Bellman, R.E. 1957. *Dynamic Programming*. Princeton: Princeton University Press.

Bellman, R.E., and Dreyfus S.E. 1962. *Applied Dynamic Programming*. Princeton: Princeton University Press.

De Bono's book is:

De Bono, E. 1970. *Lateral Thinking: A Textbook of Creativity*. London: Ward Lock.

The concrete formwork problem described in this chapter is drawn from:

Gero, J.S., and Kaneshalingham, K. 1978. A method for the optimum design of traditional formwork. *Engineering Optimization* 3(4):249–51.

The elevator banking system problem is drawn from:

Powell, B.A. 1971. Optimal elevator banking under heavy up-traffic. *Transportation Science* 5(2):109–21.

Examples of the use of dynamic programming in design decision problems can be found in:

Gero, J.S. 1976. Dynamic programming in the CAD of buildings. In *CAD76,* ed. D.R. Smith and C.W. Jones, pp. 31–37. Guildford, England: IPC Science and Technology Press.

———. 1977. A note on "Synthesis and Optimization of Small Rectangular Floor Plans." *Environment and Planning B* 4:81–88.

———. 1978. Computer aided dimensioning of architectural plans (using dynamic programming). In *CAD78,* ed. A. Pipes, pp. 482–94. Guildford, England: IPC Science and Technology Press.

Gero, J.S., and Dudnik, E.E. 1978. Uncertainty and the design of building systems—a dynamic programming approach. *Building and Environment* 13:147–52.

Radford, A.D., and Gero, J.S. 1979. On the design of windows. *Environment and Planning B* 6(1):41–45.

———. 1979. Optimization for information in integrated environmental design. In *PArC79,* pp. 447–56. Berlin: AMK.

Rosenman, M.A., and Gero, J.S. 1985. A system for integrated optimal design. *Design Optimization,* ed. J.S. Gero, pp. 259–94. New York: Academic Press.

PART 3

DYNAMIC PROGRAMMING IN DESIGN

We devote a whole part of this book to dynamic programming because it has properties that make it particularly appropriate for the kinds of problems with which design is concerned. It can handle discrete variables and nonlinear objectives, and it is efficient with constraints. Its formalism of stages and states matches the notions of stages and states in the design process, which we described in part 1. But dynamic programming is not a panacea. The conditions of separability and monotonicity restrict its range of application, and the absence of a standard methodology means that deeper thought about the structure of each separate problem is required of the user than is sometimes necessary with other methods. In this part, we explore dynamic programming a little further, introduce some computational refinements that expand its applicability to a much wider range of problems, and describe some case studies of its use in more detail than we have used in previous illustrative examples.

In chapter 6 we develop ways of relaxing the necessity for the rigid serial structure we saw in chapter 5. We show how a graphical representation of a design problem can be operated on to produce the sequential form necessary for dynamic programming. We also show how the amount of useful information generated for the design can be enhanced by adding techniques for postoptimal sensitivity and stability analysis; this materially increases the value of the dynamic programming method. To demonstrate the increased applicability and utility that are achieved through these techniques and to assist you in gaining experience in problem formulation, we devote chapter 7 to a detailed presentation of some design examples.

Since this part is concerned with development rather than with the introduction of new concepts, you may wish to skip over some of it at first reading if you find the going hard.

CHAPTER 6

ADVANCED DYNAMIC PROGRAMMING

In chapter 5, we stated that dynamic programming is a particularly useful technique for design applications, but one need not work long with dynamic programming to realize that the basic form of the technique (as described in the last chapter) requires some elaboration in order to handle many of the kinds of problems that we would like to work with, and in order to get out of the technique all of the information that we would like to extract. In this chapter we look at some more advanced elaborations of the technique. First, we shall describe some conditions under which problems that cannot be formulated in strictly serial form can still be handled by the technique, and we shall detail the methods involved. Then we shall extend the discussion of postoptimality analysis that we initiated in chapter 5, with a view to explaining some techniques for generating sensitivity and stability information.

NONSERIAL DYNAMIC PROGRAMMING

The requirements that a problem must satisfy in order to be solvable using dynamic programming all relate to the user's ability to decompose the problem into sequential stages. These requirements manifest themselves as separability and monotonicity conditions. Many building design problems, however, prima facie fail to satisfy the separability requirements. Thus, a need exists for *nonserial dynamic programming* formulations to handle such problems as cases in which the output states of one stage are connected not only to the adjacent stage but also to other stages. This occurs, for example, when the roof of a building subsystem is logically related directly to both the walls (which support it) and the foundations (which have to be termite-proofed if the roof is made of timber).

In addition, nonserial formulations can be used to transmit information between stages—information that would not be transmitted by the normal sequential paths. Such secondary paths can be used to transmit information that is dimensionally inhomogeneous with the information transmitted along the primary paths.

Feedforward Nonserial Dynamic Programming

From chapter 5, we know that the general recursion equations for dynamic programming take the form

$$f_1(X_1) = \underset{D_1}{\text{opt}}\,[r_1(X_1,D_1)] \tag{6.1}$$

and

$$f_n(X_n) = \underset{D_n}{\text{opt}}\,[r_n(X_n,D_n)\ \mathbf{o}\ f_{n-1}(X_{n-1})] \quad n = 2, \ldots, N \tag{6.2}$$

where

X_n = a particular state variable at stage n
r_n = the return associated with stage n
D_n = a decision variable that can be manipulated to optimize the objective
$f_n(X_n)$ = the optimal return to stage n
o = a composition operator that stipulates separability

A *feedforward nonserial system* consists of a staged serial system with a diverging branch at one stage that converges with the main system at a later stage. The transformations and returns consist of the following types:

1. The usual serial ones for all stages other than the stages at which divergence or convergence takes place
2. The diverging stage transformations and returns at the diverging stage
3. The converging stage transformations and returns at the converging stage

G. L. Nemhauser, in his book *Introduction to Dynamic Programming*, has developed the pertinent relations for the general case. Here we develop the relations for the situation in which the returns are separable into two types: those associated with the path going from a state in one stage to a state in another stage; and those associated with the state itself. In this treatment, the composition operator is strictly addition.

Let $P_{n-1} = [p^j{}_{n-1}]$ be the return for the path going from the state X in the stage n to state j in stage $n - 1$; and let $N_n = \{n_n\}$ be the return for the state X in stage n. Hence, equations 6.1 and 6.2 can be rewritten as

$$f_1(X_1) = \{n_1\} \tag{6.3}$$

and

$$f_n(X_n) = \underset{j}{\text{opt}}\ [(\{n_n\} + [p^j{}_{n-1}]) + f_{n-1}(X_{n-1})] \tag{6.4}$$

The optimal decisions can be determined using a traceback procedure. This serial formulation can readily be interpreted graphically.

Consider the system shown in figure 6-1, consisting of three stages with three states in each stage plus a feedforward loop between stages 1 and 3. This could be represented as

$$\{n_1\}[p_1{}^j]\{n_2\}[p_2{}^j]\{n_3\}$$

$$\underbrace{\qquad\qquad [p_{s13}] \qquad\qquad}$$

where $p_{s13} = [p^j{}_{s13}]$, the return for the path in the feedforward loop going from state j in stage 1 to state X in stage 3.

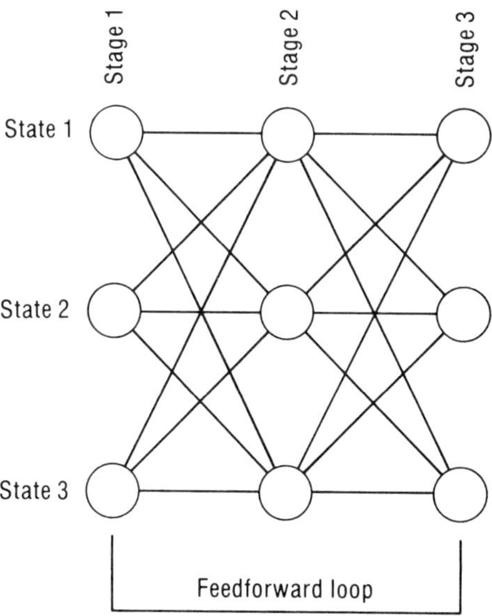

Fig. 6-1. Three-stage sequential system with one feedforward loop.

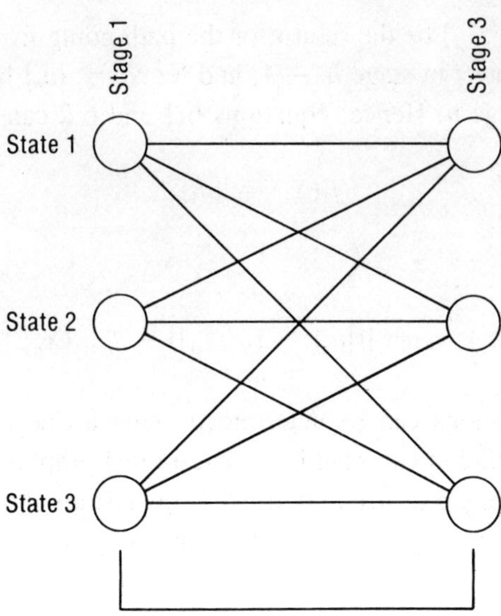

Fig. 6-2. Sequential system shown in figure 6-1, after condensation.

In order for us to be able to solve this problem by dynamic programming, there can only be one independent path from stage to stage. Achieving this one way involves condensing the independent paths into one so that the serial nature of the formulation is preserved. In the example in figure 6-1, the primary paths may be condensed between stages 1 and 3 to produce an equivalent path return from stage 1 to stage 3, shown in figure 6-2.

Let $P_{p13} = [p^j{}_{p13}]$ be the optimal return for the primary path going from state j in stage 1 to state X in stage 3; and let $P_{e13} = [p^j{}_{e13}]$ be the optimal return for the equivalent path going from state j in stage 1 to state X in stage 3. That is,

$$P_{e13} = P_{s13} + P_{p13}$$

The result after condensation can now be represented as

$$\{n_1\}[p^j{}_{e13}]\{n_3\}$$

which can be solved by the serial formulation of equations 6.3 and 6.4.

The general formulation for a dynamic program with nested feedforward loops can now be outlined in the following steps:

1. Formulate the problem with primary and secondary paths (fig. 6- 3(a)).

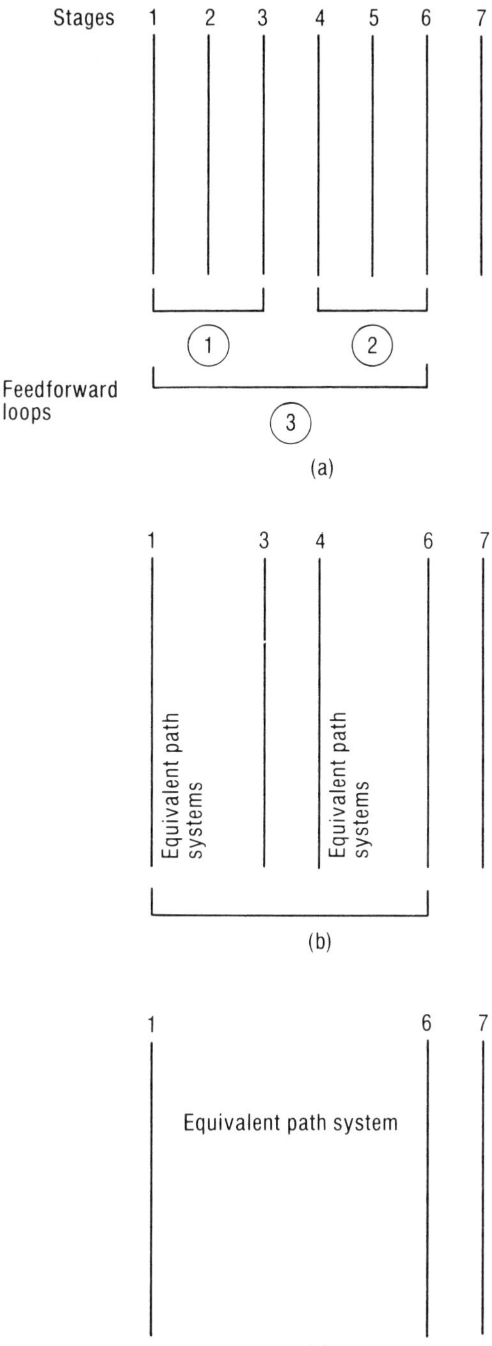

Fig. 6-3. Seven-stage sequential system with secondary paths (nested feedforward loops): (a) the original system; (b) the system after two condensations; and (c) the system after all feedforward loops have been absorbed.

2. Condense all primary paths that are completely encompassed by feedforward (secondary) loops, and replace them with the equivalent path (fig. 6-3(b)).
3. Repeat step 2 until all feedforward loops are absorbed (fig. 6-3(c)).
4. Solve the resulting problem (fig. 6-3(c)) as a serial dynamic program to obtain the optimal decisions and the optimal return.

Problem: Designing an Elementary Structural System

Description

Design the most economical raised platform to support a uniform load of 9,600 N/m^2 (200 lb/ft^2) of horizontal projection. The structural system consists of the following components: a rectangular surface 9 m (30 ft) long and 6 m (20 ft) wide; four columns each 12 m (40 ft) in length, braced as required; and an appropriate foundation to transfer all forces safely to the ground.

Formulation

The problem is shown diagrammatically in figure 6-4. There are seven platform types, three column types, and three foundation types (table 6-1).

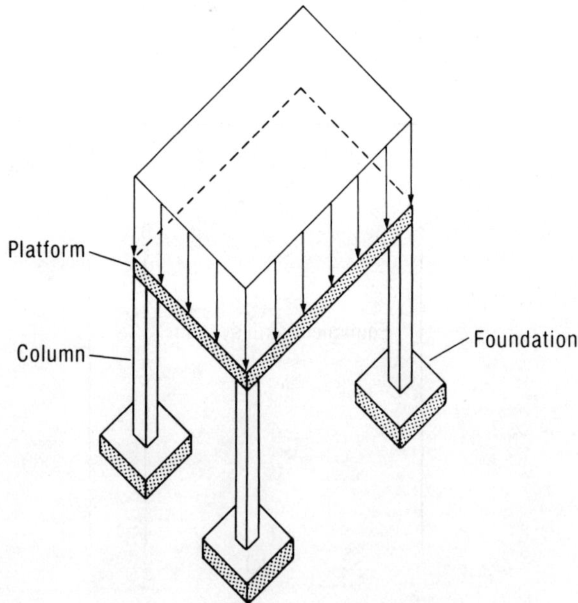

Fig. 6-4. Diagrammatic representation of an elementary structural design problem.

Table 6-1. Elementary structural system design.

	STAGES		
States	*Platforms*	*Columns*	*Foundations*
1	solid one-way concrete slab	reinforced concrete tied	spread footings
2	one-way concrete pan joist	reinforced concrete spiral	drilled concrete piles
3	solid two-way concrete slab	structural steel	driven steel piles
4	concrete waffle slab		
5	steel beams and steel deck		
6	steel bar joists		
7	steel beams and composite concrete deck		

This system is represented graphically in figure 6-5. In this formulation, costs (rather than weight) constitute the state variable. The node costs for the columns and foundations are based on the cost of one of the elements, which is designed to carry a load of 59,000 kg (130,000 lb). The path costs are estimates of whatever additional costs would be incurred as a result of using a particular column with a particular foundation in the design. The size of the foundation varies with (among other things) the type of platform used. This information can be conveyed as a cost in a feedforward or secondary loop from stage 1 to stage 3.

Solution

The following matrices are present:

$$\{n_1\} = \begin{bmatrix} 1{,}100 \\ 1{,}650 \\ 1{,}300 \\ 1{,}800 \\ 3{,}000 \\ 2{,}400 \\ 2{,}000 \end{bmatrix} \qquad [p_1{}^j] = \begin{bmatrix} 1{,}765 & 2{,}350 & 1{,}865 \\ 710 & 1{,}080 & 745 \\ 1{,}070 & 1{,}560 & 1{,}165 \\ 450 & 720 & 450 \\ 50 & 80 & 50 \\ 100 & 160 & 100 \\ 500 & 800 & 500 \end{bmatrix} \qquad \{n_2\} = \begin{bmatrix} 1{,}400 \\ 140 \\ 4{,}000 \end{bmatrix}$$

$$[p_2^{\,j}] \qquad \{n_3\}$$

$$\begin{bmatrix} 350 & 375 & 290 \\ 190 & 300 & 250 \\ 90 & 150 & 180 \end{bmatrix} \qquad \begin{bmatrix} 400 \\ 600 \\ 600 \end{bmatrix}$$

$$[p^{j}_{s13}]$$

$$\begin{bmatrix} 1{,}050 & 675 & 485 \\ 450 & 225 & 150 \\ 650 & 375 & 280 \\ 280 & 125 & 60 \\ 0 & 0 & 0 \\ 0 & 50 & 310 \\ 300 & 150 & 90 \end{bmatrix}$$

Thus,

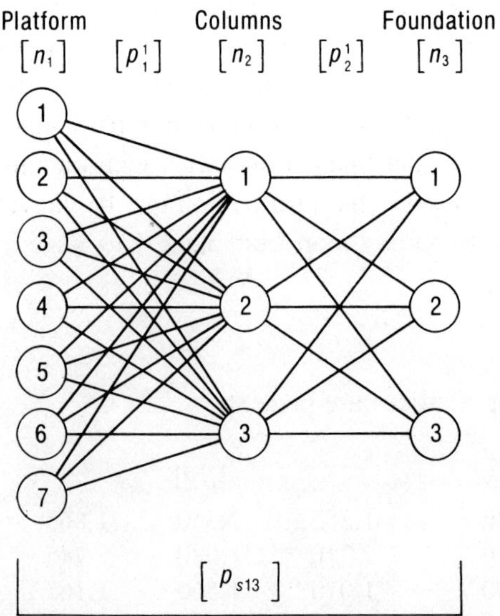

Fig. 6-5. Graphical representation of the same elementary structural design problem, in feedforward nonserial form.

$$[p^j_{p13}] = \begin{bmatrix} 3,515 & 3,540 & 3,455 \\ 2,460 & 2,485 & 2,400 \\ 2,820 & 2,845 & 2,760 \\ 2,200 & 2,225 & 2,140 \\ 1,770 & 1,780 & 1,730 \\ 1,850 & 1,860 & 1,790 \\ 2,250 & 2,275 & 2,190 \end{bmatrix}$$

and

$$[p^j_{e13}] = \begin{bmatrix} 4,565 & 4,215 & 3,940 \\ 2,910 & 2,710 & 2,550 \\ 3,470 & 3,220 & 3,010 \\ 2,450 & 2,350 & 2,200 \\ 1,770 & 1,780 & 1,730 \\ 1,850 & 1,910 & 2,100 \\ 2,550 & 2,425 & 2,280 \end{bmatrix}$$

Thus,

$$f_n(X_n) = \begin{bmatrix} 5,640 \\ 4,800 \\ 4,910 \\ 4,600 \\ 5,170 \\ 4,650 \\ 4,880 \end{bmatrix}$$

The optimal return is \$4,600; and by tracing back, we can identify the following optimal decisions:

Stage	*State*
platform	concrete waffle slab
columns	reinforced concrete tied
foundations	driven steel piles

We describe a more extensive case study using nested loops in chapter 7.

Delayed Decisions

Feedforward loops of the kind described in the earlier section on feedforward nonserial dynamic programming may be independent or nested, but they may not cross each other. It does not matter how long the feedforward loops are. In other problems, these loops do cross each other.

Consider the general problem in which the decisions for a stage can only be made (if ever) at a later stage, when additional information is available—a situation that can be represented by intersecting feedback loops (fig. 6-6). If the number of stages over which the decisions must be delayed is small, the problem may be solvable by the method of *delayed decisions,* in which all possible decision options at some stage n are provisionally accepted and carried forward until some late stage $n + q$ when the decision can be made about which options to eliminate on grounds of nonoptimality.

If q is the number of stages forward at which the decisions for a particular stage can actually be made, we can rewrite equation 6.2 as

$$f_n(X_n) = \underset{D_{n,n+q}}{\text{opt}} \; (r_n(X_n) \; \mathbf{o} \; f_{n-1}(X_{n-1})) \; n = 2, \ldots, N \qquad (6.5)$$

where $n + q$ is the stage at which the decision D_n is made.

In a computer implementation, the difficulty this produces relates to storage; until a decision can be made, every possible value for it must be retained. Consequently, a large number of input and output states is associated with each state variable. When $q = 0$, the analysis is one of classical dynamic programming. When q is large, the quantity of information to be carried becomes very great and analysis becomes infeasible.

An example of the use of delayed decisions in producing design information for an external lighting problem is described in chapter 7. The method of delayed decisions only works in situations where the problem is well ordered and the feedback loops are consistently short. In the worst

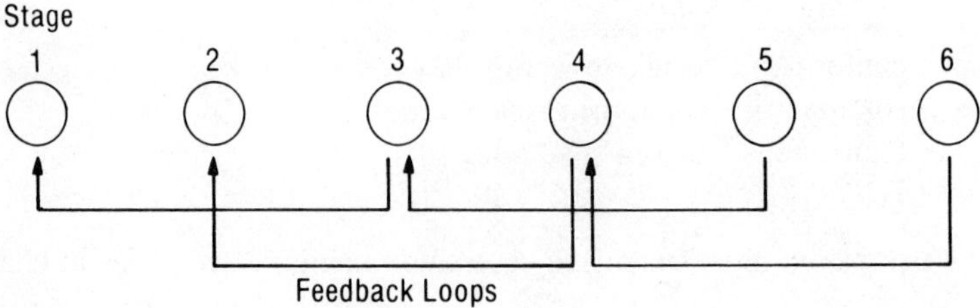

Fig. 6-6. Six-stage sequential system with intersecting feedback loops.

case of a feedback loop between last and first stages, the method degenerates into exhaustive enumeration. For the much more general problem of any number of intersecting feedback and feedforward loops over any number of stages, we need another, more general methodology. In fact, it is not possible to use dynamic programming to identify a guaranteed optimal solution in such cases; but it is possible to use *artificial intelligence* concepts, combined with dynamic programming, to find an approximation to the optimal solution.

ARTIFICIAL INTELLIGENCE APPROACHES

There exist artificial intelligence techniques for making a decision in the present by considering the effect of such a decision on the future. These techniques are widely used in games such as chess, where a present position is evaluated and then an estimate of the future position (resulting from a particular move) is made. A comparison of the scores is made among several moves, and the most favorable score is chosen.

If we look at the simple nonserial system shown in figure 6-7, we can see that at stage 2 we would like to make a decision about stage 1 but cannot do so because of the feedforward loop C_{13} from stage 1 to stage 3. Using the delayed decision technique, we would delay making a decision about stage 1 until stage 3. Using artificial intelligence techniques, we could evaluate the present situation, estimate future consequences of making a decision at the present time, and compare the total values—all before making a decision, in order to decide which option to choose. Let

N_m = the cost vector of the state variable X_m at stage m
C_{mn} = the cost matrix of the relationships between stages m and n
$PR_{m(m+1)}$ = the present return in going from stage m to stage $(m + 1)$
$FR_{m(m+1)}$ = the future expected return in going from stage m to stage $(m + 1)$
$ER_{m(m+1)}$ = the total expected return in going from stage m to stage $(m + 1)$

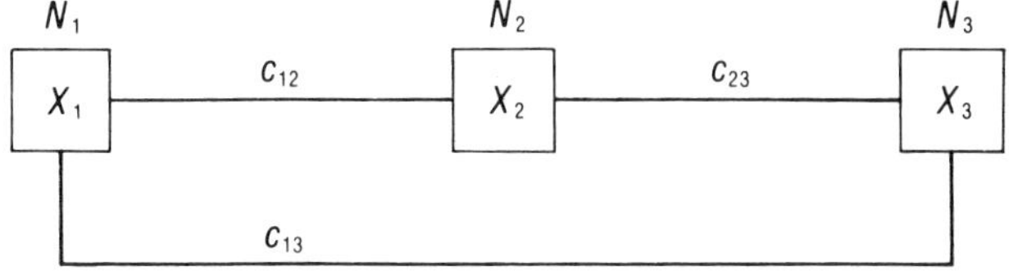

Fig. 6-7. Three-stage nonserial problem.

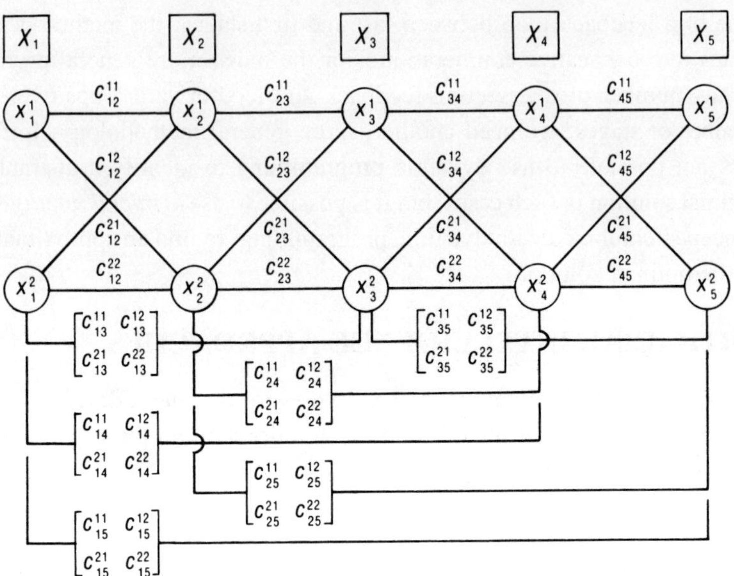

Fig. 6-8. Five-stage, fully connected system with two states per stage.

At stage 1, the returns are composed of the returns from stage 1 only. At stage 2 the present situation is composed of the return in going from stage 1 to stage 2:

$$PR_{12} = N_1 + C_{12} + N_2$$

The future consequence is composed of the return in going from stage 1 to stage 3:

$$FR_{12} = C_{13} + N_3$$

The total expected return is the sum of the present and future returns:

$$\begin{aligned} ER_{12} &= PR_{12} + FR_{12} \\ &= N_1 + C_{12} + N_2 + C_{13} + N_3 \end{aligned}$$

This expected return has to be calculated for each state in stage 2 in going from each state in stage 1—and taking into consideration each state in stage 3 connected to states in stage 1.

Let us examine the system described in graphic form in figure 6-8. It has only two states for each of its five stages. For the sake of simplicity, we shall disregard the node values (they in no way affect the method).

Using exhaustive enumeration or delayed decision dynamic programming for this problem, we would have to investigate $2^5 = 32$ separate paths: from path 1 1 1 1 1 through to path 2 2 2 2 2.

Heuristic Algorithms

Let us now look at two heuristic algorithms using artificial intelligence techniques and see if we can use them to solve the problem in figure 6-8. Consider the optimization problem as one of finding the minimum return (cost). First let us define some notation. Let

X_n = the state variable at stage n
x_n^i = the particular value, i, of the state variable at stage n
D_n = the decision variable at stage n
d_n^j = the particular value, j, of the decision variable at stage n, that is, the path from stage 1 to stage $n - 1$
D_n^* = the optimal decision for stage n
D_n^{j*} = the particular optimal decision for state j at stage n
C_{mn}^{ij} = the cost of the arc in going from state i at stage m to state j at state n
R_{ijk} = the three-stage return for states i, j, k in stages 1, 2, 3, respectively
ER_{ijk} = the three-stage expected return for states i, j, k in stages 1, 2, 3, respectively
ijk = the three-stage path through states i, j, k in stages 1, 2, 3, respectively

Algorithm One

The first algorithm (dynamic programming with feedforward intersection loops) considers, at each stage n, the returns of all arcs terminating at stage n (the present return) plus any future values (the future return) for feedforward loops from the preceding stage, $n - 1$, only, for which a decision is to be made. The algorithm then evaluates the expected return as the sum of the present return plus the minimum of the future returns, compares the expected returns, and selects the minimum—each state j at stage n.

STAGE 1

As with serial dynamic programming, there is no optimization at stage 1. The returns are equal to zero, and the decisions are the states themselves.

X_1	R_1	$D_1{}^*$
$x_1{}^1 = 1$	$R_1 = 0$	1
$x_1{}^2 = 2$	$R_2 = 0$	2

STAGE 2

The present return is obtained as is shown in the following table:

	D_2	
X_2	$d_2{}^1 = 1$	$d_2{}^2 = 2$
$x_2{}^1 = 1$	$R_{11} = R_1 + C_{12}{}^{11} + C_{11}{}^{12}$	$R_{21} = R_2 + C_{12}{}^{21} + C_{12}{}^{21}$
$x_2{}^2 = 2$	$R_{12} = R_1 + C_{12}{}^{12} + C_{12}{}^{12}$	$R_{22} = R_2 + C_{12}{}^{22} + C_{12}{}^{22}$

The future returns, from stage 1, are made up of the arcs (1,3), (1,4), and (1,5). Depending on whether we go through state 1 or 2 at stages 3, 4, and 5, the returns will be either $C_{13}{}^{11}$ or $C_{13}{}^{12}$, either $C_{14}{}^{11}$ or $C_{14}{}^{12}$, and either $C_{15}{}^{11}$ or $C_{15}{}^{12}$ for state 1 at stage 1; and they will be either $C_{13}{}^{21}$ or $C_{13}{}^{22}$, either $C_{14}{}^{21}$ or $C_{14}{}^{22}$, and either $C_{15}{}^{21}$ or $C_{15}{}^{22}$ for state 2 at stage 1.

In each case, we select the minimum future value—that is, $\min(C_{13}{}^{11}, C_{13}{}^{12})$ $\min(C_{13}{}^{21}, C_{13}{}^{22})$, and so on—so that the total expected return is as shown in the following table:

	D_2		
X_2	$d_2{}^1 = 1$	$d_2{}^2 = 1$	$D_2{}^*$
$x_2{}^1 = 1$	$ER_{11} = R_{11} + \min(C_{13}{}^{11}, C_{13}{}^{12})$ $+ \min(C_{14}{}^{11}, C_{14}{}^{12})$ $+ \min(C_{15}{}^{11}, C_{15}{}^{12})$	$ER_{21} = R_{21} + \min(C_{13}{}^{21}, C_{13}{}^{22})$ $+ \min(C_{15}{}^{21}, C_{15}{}^{12})$ $+ \min(C_{15}{}^{21}, C_{15}{}^{22})$	$D_2{}^{1*} = 2$
$x_2{}^2 = 2$	$ER_{12} = R_{12} + \min(C_{13}{}^{11}, C_{13}{}^{12})$ $+ \min(C_{14}{}^{11}, C_{14}{}^{12})$ $+ \min(C_{15}{}^{11}, C_{15}{}^{12})$	$ER_{22} = R_{22} + \min(C_{13}{}^{21}, C_{13}{}^{22})$ $+ \min(C_{14}{}^{21}, C_{14}{}^{22})$ $+ \min(C_{15}{}^{21})$	$D_2{}^{2*} = 2$

By selecting the minimum expected return for each state in stage 2 (in the same way as for serial dynamic programming), we make a decision about which state in stage 1 gives the minimum path to state j in stage 2, taking into consideration future path values that will be added in at later stages.

If, for example, for state 1 in stage 2 we find that $D_2^{1*} = d_2^2 = 2$, and for state 1 in stage 2 we find that $D_2^{2*} = d_2^2 = 2$, we now get a new set of data at stage 3.

STAGE 3

	D_3	
X_3	$d_3^1 = 21$	$d_3^2 = 22$
$x_3^1 = 1$	$R_{211} = R_{21} + C_{23}^{11} + C_{13}^{21}$	$R_{221} = R_{22} + C_{23}^{21} + C_{13}^{21}$
$x_3^2 = 2$	$R_{212} = R_{21} + C_{23}^{12} + C_{13}^{23}$	$R_{222} = R_{22} + C_{23}^{22} + C_{13}^{22}$

Again, adding in minimum future loops from stage 2 to obtain the expected return, we get

	D_3		
X_3	$d_3^1 = 1$	$d_3^2 = 2$	D_3^*
$x_3^1 = 1$	$ER_{211} = R_{211} + \min(C_{24}^{11}, C_{24}^{12}) + \min(C_{25}^{11}, C_{25}^{12})$	$ER_{221} = R_{221} + \min(C_{24}^{21}, C_{24}^{22}) + \min(C_{25}^{21}, C_{25}^{12})$	$D_3^{1*} = 2$
$x_3^2 = 3$	$ER_{212} = R_{212} + \min(C_{14}^{11}, C_{24}^{12}) + \min(C_{25}^{11}, C_{25}^{12})$	$ER_{222} = R_{22} + \min(C_{13}^{21}, C_{13}^{22}) + \min(C_{25}^{21}, C_{25}^{22})$	$D_3^{2*} = 2$

If, for example, we find that $D_3^{1*} = d_3^1 = 21$ and that $D_3^{2*} = d_3^2 = 22$, we now get a new set of data at stage 4.

STAGE 4

	D_4	
X_4	$d_4^1 = 211$	$d_4^2 = 222$
$x_4^1 = 1$	$R_{2111} = R_{211} + C_{34}^{11} + C_{24}^{11} + C_{14}^{21}$	$R_{2221} = R_{222} + C_{34}^{21} + C_{24}^{21} + C_{14}^{21}$
$x_4^2 = 2$	$R_{2112} = R_{211} + C_{34}^{12} + C_{24}^{12} + C_{14}^{22}$	$R_{2222} = R_{222} + C_{34}^{22} + C_{24}^{22} + C_{14}^{22}$

Adding the minimum future loops from stage 3 to obtain the expected return, we get

X_4	D_4: $d_4^1 = 221$	D_4: $d_4^2 = 222$	D_4^*
$x_4^1 = 1$	$ER_{2111} = R_{2111} + \min(C_{35}^{11}, C_{35}^{12})$	$ER_{2221} = R_{2221} + \min(C_{35}^{21}, C_{35}^{22})$	$D_4^{1*} = 222$
$x_4^2 = 2$	$ER_{2112} = R_{2112} + \min(C_{35}^{11}, C_{35}^{12})$	$ER_{2222} = R_{2222} + \min(C_{35}^{21}, C_{35}^{22})$	$D_4^{2*} = 211$

If, for example, we find that $D_4^{1*} = d_4^2 = 222$ and that $D_4^{2*} = d_4^1 = 211$, we now get a new set of data at stage 5.

STAGE 5

X_5	D_5: $d_5^1 = 2221$	D_5: $d_5^2 = 2112$	D_5^*
$x_5^1 = 1$	$R_{22211} = R_{2221} + C_{45}^{11} + C_{35}^{21} + C_{25}^{21} + C_{15}^{21}$	$R_{21121} = R_{2112} + C_{45}^{21} + C_{35}^{11} + C_{25}^{11} + C_{15}^{21}$	$D_5^{1*} = 2221$
$x_5^2 = 2$	$R_{22212} = R_{2221} + C_{45}^{12} + C_{35}^{22} + C_{25}^{22} + C_{15}^{22}$	$R_{21122} = R_{2112} + C_{45}^{22} + C_{35}^{12} + C_{25}^{12} + C_{15}^{22}$	$D_5^{2*} = 2112$

At the final stage, the minimum is selected in the usual way.

Note that in the above problem exhaustive enumeration would evaluate all thirty-two possible paths, with 128 computations, whereas delayed decision would evaluate all thirty-two paths, with 63 computations. This algorithm evaluates only four paths out of the thirty-two, with 32 functional evaluations (16 for the future costs). In the above problem, this represents 96 computations and would seem not to give any advantage over the other methods. This, however, is due to the low number of states per stage in the example. In general, the saving in computation is of the same order as for serial dynamic programming, although the computations themselves are more elaborate. For a fully connected problem of n stages and m states per stage, the algorithm evaluates km^2 complete paths with $km^2(n - 1)$

functional evaluations, where k is the number of decisions kept; these figures stand as against m^n total paths and $\Sigma_{j=1^n} = m^j$ functional evaluations for delayed-decision dynamic programming, and m^n total paths and $m^n(n - 1)$ functional evaluations for exhaustive enumeration and nonserial dynamic programming.

For a fully connected problem of thirty stages, table 6-2 compares the number of paths evaluated and the number of functional evaluations for different numbers of states.

It can easily be seen that, for problems of this type of the order of ten stages and ten (or more) states per stage, the other three methods are out of the question as a result of both storage and time considerations.

It should be noted that, at a particular stage n when the question of which state in stage $n - 1$ should be taken is decided, the algorithm only considers future costs (feedforward loops) from stage $n - 1$. No consideration is given to the interaction between these costs and costs from stages previous to (or later than) the state chosen in the future stage. For this reason, the estimation function of the algorithm is only approximate, and there is no guarantee that a state chosen (a decision made) will not prove later to be extraneous to the optimal policy. The algorithm does, however, give an indication of the promise of a particular state. It is therefore quite feasible to keep more than one promising state (or path)—for example, the ten most promising states. Note that this would have the effect of increasing one's search only by a factor of ten. For larger problems, even more alternatives can be kept. If we consider this method as being analogous to a search through a decision tree, keeping promising states corresponds to widening our search through the tree.

Algorithm Two

The second algorithm is similar to the first, in that it evaluates an expected return as the sum of the present and future values. In its evaluation of future returns, however, it takes into consideration the interconnections from all stages prior to stage n—that is, stages 1 to $n - 1$.

STAGE 1

Stage 1 is the same for this algorithm as for the first algorithm.

STAGE 2

Since the only previous stage is stage 1, the calculations at stage 2 will be the same in this case as before.

Table 6-2. Comparison of the number of computations required for the various methods, for a fully connected problem of thirty stages.

	NO. OF STATES PER STAGE					
	2		*10*		*20*	
	No. of paths evaluated	*No. of functional evaluations*	*No. of paths evaluated*	*No. of functional evaluations*	*No. of paths evaluated*	*No. of functional evaluations*
Exhaustive enumeration and nonserial dynamic programming	1.1×10^{9}	3.20×10^{10}	9.3×10^{20}	2.70×10^{22}	1.07×10^{30}	3.11×10^{40}
Delayed decision	1.1×10^{9}	2.15×10^{9}	9.3×10^{20}	1.11×10^{30}	1.07×10^{30}	3.11×10^{39}
Heuristic method - K†	$4K$	$1.16K \times 10^{2}$	$1.0K \times 10^{2}$	$2.90K \times 10^{3}$	$4.00K \times 10^{2}$	$1.16K \times 10^{4}$

†K is the number of decisions kept.

STAGE 3

	D_3	
X_3	$d_3{}^1 = 21$	$d_3{}^2 = 22$
$x_3{}^1 = 1$	$R_{211} = R_{21} + C_{23}{}^{11} + C_{13}{}^{21}$	$R_{221} = R_{22} + C_{23}{}^{21} + C_{13}{}^{21}$
$x_3{}^2 = 2$	$R_{212} = R_{21} + C_{23}{}^{12} + C_{13}{}^{23}$	$R_{222} = R_{22} + C_{23}{}^{22} + C_{13}{}^{22}$

Adding in minimum future paths from stages 1 and 2, we get

	D_3	
X_3	$d_3{}^1 = 21$	$d_3{}^2 = 22$
$x_3{}^1 = 1$	$ER_{211} = R_{211} + \min[(C_{14}{}^{21} + C_{24}{}^{11}), (C_{14}{}^{22} + C_{24}{}^{12})] + \min[(C_{15}{}^{21}\ C_{25}{}^{11}), (C_{15}{}^{22} + C_{25}{}^{12})]$	$ER_{221} = R_{221} + \min[(C_{14}{}^{21} + C_{24}{}^{21}), (C_{14}{}^{22} + C_{24}{}^{22})] + \min(C_{15}{}^{21} + C_{25}{}^{21}), (C_{15}{}^{22} + C_{25}{}^{22})]$
$x_3{}^2 = 2$	$ER_{212} = R_{212} + \min[(C_{14}{}^{21} + C_{24}{}^{11}), (C_{14}{}^{22} + C_{24}{}^{12})] + \min(C_{15}{}^{21} + C_{25}{}^{11}), (C_{15}{}^{22} + C_{25}{}^{12})]$	$ER_{222} = R_{222} + \min[(C_{14}{}^{21} + C_{24}{}^{21}), (C_{14}{}^{22} + C_{24}{}^{22})] + \min[(C_{15}{}^{21} + C_{25}{}^{21}), (C_{15}{}^{22} + C_{25}{}^{22})]$

If (as for the first algorithm) we get $D_3{}^{1*} = d_3{}^1 = 21$ and $D_3{}^{2*} = d_3{}^2 = 22$, then at stage 4 we get a new set of data.

STAGE 4

	D_4	
X_4	$d_4{}^1 = 211$	$d_4{}^2 = 222$
$x_4{}^1 = 1$	$R_{2111} = R_{211} + C_{34}{}^{11} + C_{24}{}^{11} + C_{14}{}^{21}$	$R_{2221} = R_{222} + C_{34}{}^{21} + C_{24}{}^{21} + C_{14}{}^{21}$
$x_4{}^2 = 2$	$R_{2112} = R_{211} + C_{34}{}^{12} + C_{24}{}^{12} + C_{14}{}^{22}$	$R_{2222} = R_{222} + C_{34}{}^{22} + C_{24}{}^{22} + C_{14}{}^{22}$

Adding in minimum future paths from stages 1 and 2, we get

X_4	D_4	
	$d_4^1 = 211$	$d_4^2 = 222$
$x_4^1 = 1$	$ER_{2111} = R_{2111} + \min[(C_{15}^{21} + C_{25}^{11} + C_{35}^{11}), (C_{15}^{22} + C_{25}^{12} + C_{35}^{12})]$	$ER_{2221} = R_{2221} + \min[(C_{15}^{21} + C_{25}^{21} + C_{35}^{21}), (C_{15}^{22} + C_{25}^{22} + C_{35}^{22})]$
$x_4^2 = 2$	$ER_{2112} = R_{2112} + \min[(C_{15}^{12} + C_{25}^{11} + C_{35}^{11}), (C_{15}^{22} + C_{25}^{12} + C_{35}^{12})]$	$ER_{2222} = R_{2222} + \min[(C_{15}^{21} + C_{25}^{21} + C_{35}^{21}), (C_{15}^{22} + C_{25}^{22} + C_{35}^{22})]$

STAGE 5

Stage 5 of the second algorithm is the same as stage 5 of the first algorithm.

Note that, for both algorithms, the sum of the minimum future costs (the expected return component of the total expected return) is the same for all values of i for a given decision variable d_n^j. This saves a great amount of calculation, since it is only necessary to calculate the value of the estimated function for $i = 1$ and store it for $i = 2, 3, \ldots, I$.

Worked Example

Let us now examine a worked example, using the first algorithm. Take the system of figure 6-8, and put in numerical values to produce figure 6-9.

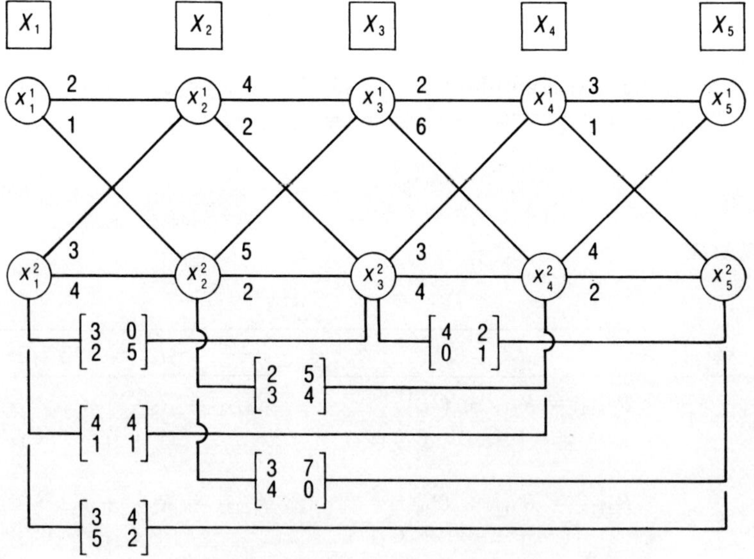

Fig. 6-9. System shown in figure 6-8, with numerical values.

Using exhaustive enumeration, we can determine that the optimal solution is path 1 2 2 1 2, with a value of 19 for the objective.

STAGE 1

$$X_1^1 = 1 \quad R_1 = 0 \quad D_1^{1*} = 1$$

$$X_1^2 = 2 \quad R_2 = 0 \quad D_1^{2*} = 2$$

STAGE 2

X_2	D_2: $d_2^1 = 1$	D_2: $d_2^2 = 2$	D_2^*
$x_2^1 = 1$	$R_{11} = 2$; $ER_{11} = 2 + \min(3,0) + \min(4,4) + \min(3,4) = 9$	$R_{21} = 3$; $ER_{21} = 3 + \min(2,5) + \min(1,1) + \min(5,2) = 8$	$D_2^{1*} = 2$
$x_2^2 = 2$	$R_{12} = 1$; $ER_{12} = 1 + 7 = 8$	$R_{22} = 4$; $ER_{22} = 4 + 5 = 9$	$D_2^{2*} = 1$

STAGE 3

X_3	D_3: $d_3^1 = 21$	D_3: $d_3^2 = 12$	D_3^*
$x_3^1 = 1$	$R_{211} = 3 + 4 + 2$; $ER_{211} = 9 + \min(2,5) + \min(3,2) = 13$	$R_{121} = 1 + 5 + 3$; $ER_{121} = 9 + \min(3,4) + \min(4,0) = 12$	$D_3^{1*} = 12$
$x_3^2 = 2$	$R_{212} = 3 + 2 + 5$; $ER_{212} = 10 + 4 = 14$	$R_{122} = 1 + 2 + 0$; $ER_{122} = 3 + 3 = 6$	$D_3^{2*} = 12$

STAGE 4

X_4	D_4: $d_4^1 = 121$	D_4: $d_4^2 = 122$	D_4^*
$x_4^1 = 1$	$R_{1211} = 9 + 2 + 3 + 4$; $ER_{1211} = 18 + \min(4,2) = 20$	$R_{1221} = 3 + 3 + 3 + 4$; $ER_{1221} = 13 + \min(0,1) = 13$	$D_4^{1*} = 122$
$x_4^2 = 2$	$R_{1212} = 9 + 6 + 4 + 4$; $ER_{1212} = 23 + 2 = 25$	$R_{1222} = 3 + 4 + 4 + 4$; $ER_{1222} = 15 + 0 = 15$	$D_4^{2*} = 122$

STAGE 5

	D_5		
X_5	$d_5^1 = 1221$	$d_5^2 = 1222$	D_5^*
$x_5^1 = 1$	$R_{12211} = 13 + 3 + 0 + 4 + 3 = 23$	$R_{12221} = 15 + 4 + 0 + 4 + 3 = 26$	$D_3^{1*} = 1221$
$x_5^2 = 2$	$R_{12212} = 13 + 1 + 1 + 0 + 4 = 19$*	$R_{12222} = 15 + 2 + 1 + 0 + 4 = 22$	$D_3^{2*} = 1221$

Both algorithms give the path 1 2 2 1 2 as the optimum path or policy, with the optimum objective of 19. In a small problem such as this, it is not necessary to keep more than the one decision, except where ties may occur. For larger problems, the second algorithm—because of its more accurate estimation function—would probably need to keep fewer decision variables in order to arrive at the optimal solution.

Efficacy of Artificial Intelligence Approaches

Both algorithms are capable of solving large, complex, nonserial problems of a general structure by using an estimation function to evaluate the likelihood of a particular branch's being part of the optimal policy. The use of this estimation function allows nonserial problems to be solved by a sequential decision process similar to that used in serial dynamic programming. It forms the basis of the A* algorithm used extensively in artificial intelligence search graphs.

In a practical problem, the order in which the subsystems are given is quite arbitrary. For example, a problem that is presented so as to appear nonserial might be restructured so as to appear as a serial problem. More generally, a restructuring of the order of elimination of the state variables (stages) is necessary in order to maximize the seriality of the elimination order. This minimizes the number of nonserial connections, which in turn minimizes the use of the heuristic evaluation function, the number of computations, and the possibility of error. Once an elimination order is obtained, using both a forward pass and a backward pass increases the accuracy of the solution obtained.

At this stage of development, one cannot be guaranteed of obtaining the global optimum; the solutions obtained even for quite large problems are well within reasonable margins of error, which would certainly be accepted for most practical problems. Both algorithms give a great reduction in computer time needed for their solution as against the delayed decision method.

The greatest advantage of these algorithms is not the reduction in computer time, however, but in their capability of solving large problems that cannot be handled by any other method. Larger and more complex problems can be solved by keeping more decisions—up to the storage capacity of the computer system. Thus, the accuracy of the solution is related to the capacity of the resources available, based on artificial intelligence approaches.

Algorithms provide a methodology for solving problems that, because of their size or structure, cannot be handled by more analytical methods. It is quite possible to conjecture that the part of a given problem that can be solved by a particular analytical method could be done so, after which the part that cannot could be solved by means of these or similar algorithms.

POSTOPTIMALITY ANALYSIS IN DYNAMIC PROGRAMMING

We have previously discussed the importance of postoptimality analysis in optimization in the context of design. If all that a designer gets from optimization is an optimal value and an optimal policy, he or she is left with many unanswered questions. Must the optimal policy be followed exactly, or may minor variations be made without significantly impairing the optimal performance? What if some part of the optimal policy becomes infeasible (perhaps because a construction material has become unavailable)? What if doubt arises about all the costs used in a cost optimization or about all the heat losses used in an energy optimization: does this make the whole policy wrong, or would minor variations still lead to the same (or a similar) optimal policy? What if the designer simply does not like the optimal solution for some reason not measured by the objective function: is there a second-best solution that is nearly as good and that does not arouse the designer's displeasure?

With dynamic programming, many such questions can be answered by a sensitivity and stability analysis, using only the information necessarily generated as part of the original optimization. We showed in chapter 5 how this analysis can be carried out taking as an example the problem of a site feasibility study described earlier in the chapter. This site feasibility study provides a good vehicle for exploring some ideas on postoptimality

Returns ($100,000s)

Area	Housing	Retail	Office	Hotel
0	0	0	0	0
1	2	6	1	8
2	4	9	1	12
3	6	9	2	20
4	8	10	3	16
5	10	11	15	12
6	12	12	12	10
7	14	13	20	4

Fig. 6-10. Tableau of returns (annual profit) against decisions (areas allocated) for areas of 0 to 7 units allocated to four activities.

analysis; in this chapter we shall take it further, embellishing it as necessary to demonstrate the major principles involved.

Last-stage Information

Let us look at the three best returns that emerged from our postoptimality analysis in chapter 5 and at the decisions that are associated with those policies. For the returns shown in figure 6-10, the following data are relevant:

		OPTIMAL POLICY			
Rank	*Optimal Return (in $100,000s)*	*Housing*	*Retail*	*Office*	*Hotel*
1	33	2	2	0	3
2	29	0	1	5	1
=3	27	1	2	0	4
=3	27	0	0	5	2

This ordering is based solely on the information we obtained at the final stage about ways of allocating 7 units of space. Specifically, this information is directed to identifying the best ways of sharing 7 units between a hotel and the combination [housing + retail + office] space, given that the way of sharing the space within the combination for any given floor area has already been fixed. The principle of optimality assures us that we have the best overall solution. We do not know, though, whether we have the second-best overall solution. This second-best choice may not be to have only 1 unit of hotel but to have (like the best choice) 3 units of hotel and to divide up the 4 units of [housing + retail + office] space in another (second-best) way. Normally, we do not have the information at the end of the optimization to find out whether or not that is the case.

Storing an Ordered Set of Solutions

The answer to this problem is simple, although it adds a lot to both computation and storage. Instead of just calculating and keeping the optimal return and decision for each state at each stage, we calculate and keep as many near-optimal returns and decisions as we need to give us the postoptimality information we seek.

Suppose we want to know the true first-, second-, and third-policies. In figure 6-11, we replace the single figure for optimal return for each state at each stage with three figures showing the three best returns; the dashes appear where only one or two subpolicies are feasible for that state. The first column (stage 1) is the same as the first column in figure 5-12; at the first stage, there is only one feasible decision for each state. The second column (stage 2) has one figure in the first row (there is only one feasible way of allocating 0 units between housing and retail uses: to have none of either), two figures in the second row (there are two feasible ways of sharing 1 unit in 1 unit lots between the two uses), and three figures for each of the other rows. The calculations are the same as in chapter 5; we are just keeping more information. The decision (how much area of retail space to include) is recorded in figure 6-12, and the input states are recorded in figure 6-13.

At stage 3, we have to do more work. To find the three best subpolicies at each state, we have to calculate for each state all the combinations of the return from that stage plus (in turn) the three best returns from each feasible input state—not just the optimal return for each input state. This is because two or three of the best policies at any state may well come through the same input state. We again record the three best decisions in figure 6-12 and the corresponding input states in figure 6-13. Now, though, we need to distinguish among different returns and policies associated with the same input state. We do that by adding a 1, 2, or 3 in parenthesis after the input state number.

Area		Housing	Housing & Retail	Housing & Retail & Office	Housing & Retail & Office & Hotel
0	1	0	0	0	0
	2	–	–	–	–
	3	–	–	–	–
1	1	2	6	6	8
	2	–	2	2	6
	3	–	–	1	2
2	1	4	9	9	14
	2	–	8	8	12
	3	–	4	6	10
3	1	6	11	11	20
	2	–	10	10	18
	3	–	9	10	17
4	1	8	13	13	26
	2	–	12	12	22
	3	–	11	12	21
5	1	10	15	15	29
	2	–	14	14	28
	3	–	13	14	26
6	1	12	17	21	31
	2	–	16	17	30
	3	–	15	17	25
7	1	14	19	24	33
	2	–	18	23	32
	3	–	17	19	32

Fig. 6-11. Tableau of the three best returns for the space allocation problem.

At stage 4, we repeat the same procedure. Where there are two equal third-best policies, we have recorded both. The three best returns and policies, then, are those shown in the following table:

		OPTIMAL POLICY *(in 100,000s of ft)*			
Rank	*Optimal Return (in $100,000s)*	*Housing*	*Retail*	*Office*	*Hotel*
1	33	2	2	0	3
=2	32	3	1	0	3
=2	32	1	2	1	3

Area		Housing	Retail	Office	Hotel
	1	0	0	0	0
0	2	–	–	–	–
	3	–	–	–	–
	1	1	1	0	1
1	2	–	0	0	0
	3	–	–	1	0
	1	2	2	0	1
2	2	–	1	0	2
	3	–	0	1	1
	1	3	2	0	3
3	2	–	1	0	1
	3	–	3	1	2
	1	4	2	0	3
4	2	–	1	0	3
	3	–	3	1	3 / 2
	1	5	2	5	3
5	2	–	1	0	3
	3	–	3	0 / 1	3
	1	6	2	5	3
6	2	–	1	5	3
	3	–	3	0	3
	1	7	2	5	3
7	2	–	1	5	3
	3	–	3	5 / 0	3

Fig. 6-12. Tableau of the three best decisions for the space allocation problem.

Thus, the three best policies all use 3 units of hotel, the second-best policy has a return very close to that of the optimal policy at $320,000—not the $290,000 of our approximate calculations, based on the information at the last stage from keeping only optimal decisions. Keeping this central information has caused us extra work; but if the work had been relegated to a computer program, the additional amount may not be significant. In the third case study described in chapter 7, not just the three best but the forty best returns and subpolicies are recorded at each stage. All of the embedded information is also available to us; this would enable us to

Area		–	Housing	Housing & Retail	Housing & Retail & Office
	1	–	–	–	–
0	2	–	–	–	–
	3	–	–	–	–
	1	–	0	1(1)	0
1	2	–	1	1(2)	1(1)
	3	–	–	0	1(2)
	1	–	0	2(1)	1(1)
2	2	–	1	2(2)	0
	3	–	2	1(1)	1(2)
	1	–	1	3(1)	0
3	2	–	2	3(2)	2(1)
	3	–	0	2(1)	1(1)
	1	–	2	4(1)	1(1)
4	2	–	3	4(2)	1(2)
	3	–	1	3(1)	1(3) / 2(1)
	1	–	3	0	2(1)
5	2	–	4	5(1)	2(2)
	3	–	2	5(2) / 4(1)	2(3)
	1	–	4	1(1)	3(1)
6	2	–	5	1(2)	3(2)
	3	–	3	6(1)	3(3)
	1	–	5	2(1)	4(1)
7	2	–	6	2(2)	4(2)
	3	–	4	2(3) / 7(1)	4(3)

Fig. 6-13. Tableau of input states associated with the decisions shown in figure 6-9.

identify the three best policies for any other hotel areas to be allocated and the three best policies for schemes without hotels or without hotels and offices.

This is much more information than we used to have, but it carries with it one potentially worrisome aspect. If all of the three best policies include 3 units of hotel space, that decision is quite stable and the return from it is clearly very attractive in comparison to other returns. But just how sensitive is our optimal return to the $200,000 figure associated with the decision specifying 3 units of hotel space in figure 6-10?

Sensitivity Analysis for Decision Returns

Let us look for the best policy and return that do not rely on our having 3 units of hotel. Here, it is easy: we just look down the list of optimal returns for other decisions at the final stage (in the table in the postoptimality analysis section of chapter 5) and find that the best alternative is $2,900,000 for a decision specifying 1 unit of hotel space. The policy that leads to this return was recorded at the beginning of this section. For our purposes, the best we can do without using 3 units of hotel is a return of $2,900,000—$400,000 less than we can expect with the use of 3 units of hotel. Put another way, our optimal policy remains optimal as long as the return on that decision is within $400,000 of the projected figure—that is, as long as the return is at least $2,000,000 − $400,000 = $1,600,000 (or within 20% of the projected figure). If our estimate is too low, that just increases the return on the policy.

What if the decision we are interested in is not at the final stage? We have probably thrown out the suboptimal decisions from any other stage, for economy of information storage. Nonetheless, we can always generate a new optimal return and policy that do not include a particular decision at any stage. We simply make certain that the decision will not be adopted, by replacing the stage return with a new return selected to ensure that it will not lie on any optimal policies or subpolicies. In our maximization problem, we give decision to be avoided a return of $-\infty$. For a minimization problem, we use $+\infty$. An algorithm for the process is shown in figure 6-14.

Sensitivity Analysis with Path Returns

In dynamic programming, we can distinguish between returns associated with decisions at stages and returns associated with combinations of states at different stages. In our site feasibility example, all of the returns are associated with the stage; but in the floor–ceiling system and hotel unit case studies we describe in chapter 7, there are two distinct sets of returns, associated with stages and with the paths between stages, respectively. An algorithm for decision sensitivity analysis with path (or arc) returns is shown in figure 6-15.

Sensitivity Analysis with Dispersed Return Components

Now consider a variation of our site feasibility problem. While keeping the same stages, states, and decisions, we shall now look at how the return

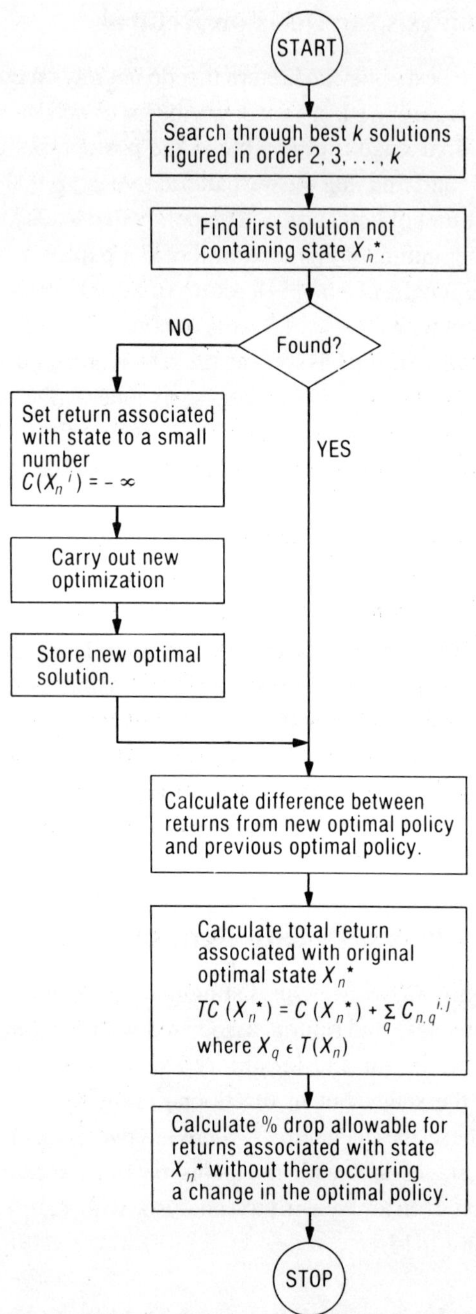

Fig. 6-14. Algorithm for finding the lower range of value associated with a state X_n* before another state replaces it in the optimal policy (maximization problem).

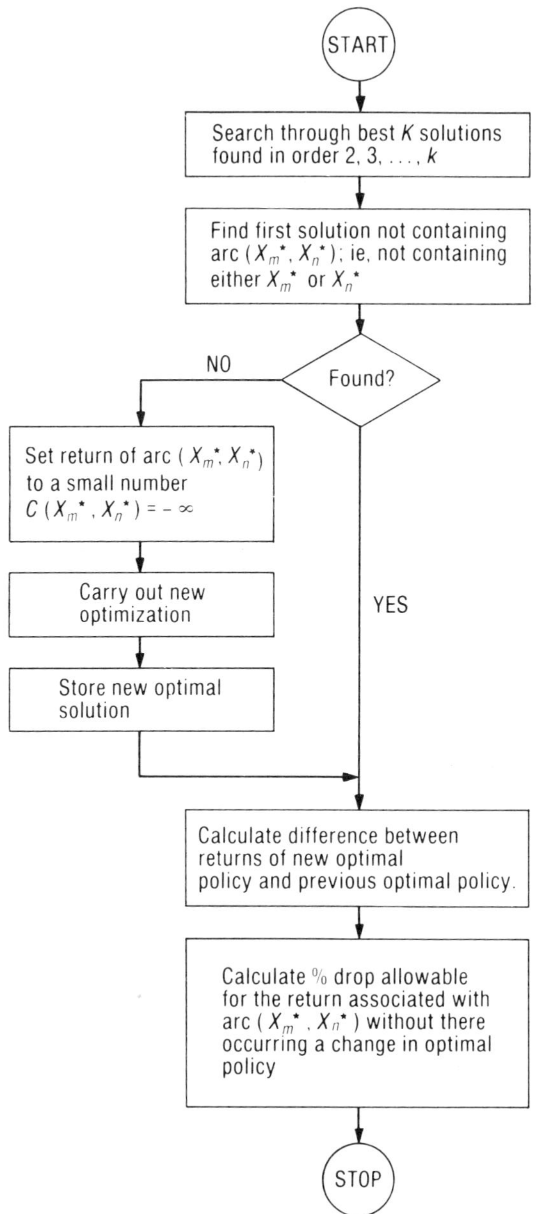

Fig. 6-15. Algorithm for finding the lower range of value associated with a path (arc) (X_m*, X_n*) before another arc replaces it in the optimal policy (maximization problem).

Returns ($100,000s)

Area	Housing	Retail	Office	Hotel
0	0 / 0	0 / 0	0 / 0	0 / 0
1	2 / 0	3 / 3	1 / 0	4 / 4
2	4 / 0	3 / 6	1 / 0	6 / 6
3	6 / 0	3 / 6	1 / 1	10 / 10
4	7 / 1	4 / 6	2 / 1	8 / 8
5	9 / 1	4 / 7	10 / 5	6 / 6
6	11 / 1	4 / 8	10 / 2	5 / 5
7	13 / 1	4 / 9	12 / 8	2 / 2

Fig. 6-16. Tableau of returns (annual profit, separated into rental return [top left triangles] and capital appreciation return [bottom right triangles]) against decisions (areas allocated) for areas of 0 to 7 units allocated to four activities.

is worked out. Assume that the returns shown in figure 6-10 are in fact each made up from two components: a rental return, and a capital appreciation return. Both are based on current forecasts of the future. Because we use the best available information, we assume that both are correct and give them equal weighting when adding them together. What, though, if our perception of the future is not quite right: if (for example) the rental market improves but the capital appreciation market does not, so that we should be giving more weight to the rental returns? How sensitive are our decisions to change in the relative importance of these two components?

In figure 6-16, we have split the site feasibility returns into the two components identified above. The top left triangle in each cell contains the rental return; the bottom right triangle contains the appreciation return. We calculate the returns as in the economic feasibility study problem in chapter 5 but this time we have the separate component returns as well as the total returns to consider.

For stage 2 we proceed with the following allocation data:

Allocation of 1 unit

No.	*Housing*	*Retail*	*Rental Return*	*Appreciation Return*	*Total Return (in $100,000s)*	
0	0	1	0 + 3 = 3	0 + 3 = 3	6	optimal subpolicy
1	1	0	2 + 0 = 2	0 + 0 = 0	2	

Allocation of 2 units

No.	*Housing*	*Retail*	*Rental Return*	*Appreciation Return*	*Total Return (in $100,000s)*	
0	0	2	0 + 3 = 3	0 + 6 = 6	9	Pareto optimal subpolicy
1	1	1	2 + 3 = 5	0 + 3 = 3	8	Pareto optimal subpolicy
2	2	0	4 + 0 = 4	0 + 0 = 0	4	

When we allocate 1 unit, solution 0 (we take our numbering from the area of housing) has the best rental, the best appreciation, and the best total return. Whatever relative weighting we apply to rental and appreciation returns, solution 0 is better than solution 1. When we allocate 2 units, though, the situation is rather different. Solution 0 is best in terms of its total return and appreciation return, but solution 1 has a better rental return. If we gave rental more weight in our decision making, at some point it would become the preferred option. Thinking back to the ideas about multiple objectives and the notion of domination that we described in chapter 1, we can say that solution 0 does not dominate solution 1 in all of the cost components, and so solution 1 is a *Pareto optimal* subpolicy.

Similarly, at the next level of units, we proceed with the following allocation data:

Allocation of 3 units

No.	*Housing*	*Retail*	*Rental Return*	*Appreciation Return*	*Total Return (in $100,000s)*	
0	0	3	0 + 3 = 3	0 + 6 = 6	9	
1	1	2	2 + 3 = 5	0 + 6 = 6	11	optimal subpolicy/ Pareto optimal policy
2	2	1	4 + 3 = 7	0 + 3 = 3	10	Pareto optimal policy
3	3	0	6 + 0 = 6	0 + 0 = 0	6	

And we continue in a like manner for all subsequent unit levels. Suppose that our problem is not to allocate 7 units among housing, retail, office, and hotel uses but just to allocate 7 units between housing and retail uses—a problem embedded within our original example. As before, we have the following data:

Allocation of 7 units

No.	*Housing*	*Retail*	*Rental Return*	*Appreciation Return*	*Total Return (in $100,000s)*	
0	0	7	0 + 4 = 4	0 + 9 = 9	13	Pareto optimal policy
1	1	6	2 + 4 = 6	0 + 8 = 8	14	Pareto optimal policy
2	2	5	4 + 4 = 8	0 + 7 = 7	15	
3	3	4	6 + 4 = 10	0 + 6 = 6	16	
4	4	3	7 + 3 = 10	1 + 6 = 7	17	
5	5	2	9 + 3 = 12	1 + 6 = 7	19	optimal policy/ Pareto optimal policy
6	6	1	11 + 3 = 14	1 + 3 = 4	18	Pareto optimal policy
7	7	0	13 + 0 = 13	1 + 0 = 1	14	

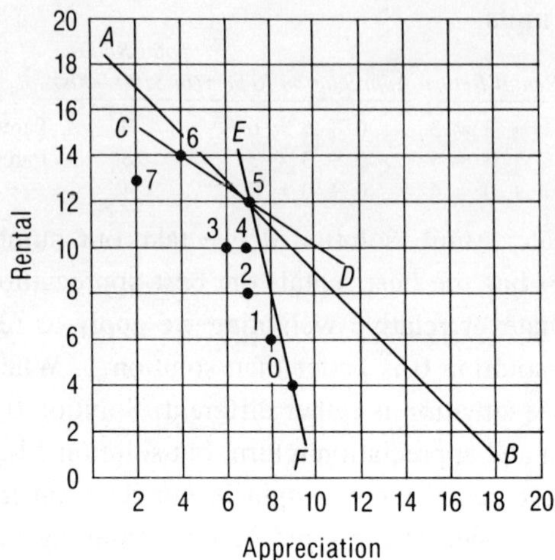

Fig. 6-17. Graph of rental return against appreciation return.

We shall plot these solutions on a graph of rental return against appreciation return (fig. 6-17). By the "northeast rule," the graph confirms that solutions 2, 3, 4, and 7 are dominated (solution 7 by solution 6; solutions 2, 3, and 4 by solution 5). Our implicit equal weighting of the costs means that an isopreference line will lie at 45° across the graph, and moving this out from the origin demonstrates that solution 5 on line *AB* is the optimal policy. If we consider the effect of increasing the relative weight given to the rental return, we see that solutions 6 and 5 are equal if the isopreference line *CD* is correct.

Given the component returns for these two solutions, we can calculate that the gradient of this line is $^3/_2$, meaning that the solutions are equal if weighting of the rental return is 1.5 times that of the appreciation return. Similarly, the isopreference line *EF* has a gradient of 4, meaning that solutions 5 and 0 are equal if the appreciation return is given a weighting 4 times that of the rental return. For the purposes of our postoptimality analysis, we are interested in the converse statement: our optimal policy (solution 5) remains the same between the extremes of rental return = 1.5 times appreciation return, and of appreciation return = 4 times rental return. These weights define the stability of the optimal policy. We can therefore be reasonably confident of the policy, even given some uncertainty about how rental and appreciation returns will fare relative to each other in the future.

Returning to our original problem and putting office and retail space back as options in our allocation problem, we go on to stage 3. We have the returns in figure 6-16. Our input states are not just the optimal policies to stage 2 (the policies that optimize the total return) but also the Pareto optimal policies for the component rental and appreciation returns. If we want to have all of this postoptimality information available to us at the end of the problem, we need to consider all of these subpolicies as input states—just as we considered the three best total return subpolicies in the last section. It can mean a great deal of computation and information storage.

We could continue this example by hand, but it gets a little tedious and it would be much easier to handle with a computer program. The writing of such a program we shall leave to the reader.

FURTHER READING

Good discussions on dynamic programming as a design tool can be found in:

Gero, J.S., ed. 1985. *Design Optimization*. New York: Academic Press.

Nonserial dynamic programming is discussed in:

Bertele, U., and Brioschi, F. 1972. *Nonserial Dynamic Programming*. New York: Academic Press.

Nemhauser, G.L. 1966. *Introduction to Dynamic Programming*. New York: Wiley.

Norman, J. 1972. *Heuristic Procedures in Dynamic Programming*. Manchester: Manchester University Press.

The material on feedforward dynamic programming is drawn from:

Gero, J.S.; Sheehan, P.J.; and Becker, J.M. 1978. Building design using feedforward nonserial dynamic programming. *Engineering Optimization* 3(4): 183–92.

The material on artificial intelligence approaches (including both of the algorithms used) is drawn from:

Rosenman, M.A., and Gero, J.S. 1980. Heuristic nonserial dynamic programming for large problems. *Engineering Optimization* 4(4): 167–78.

The material on postoptimality analysis is drawn from:

Rosenman, M.A.; Radford, A.D.; and Gero, J.S. 1980. Postoptimality analysis in dynamic programming. *Engineering Optimization* 4(4): 207–14.

Other works on advanced dynamic programming include:

Gero, J.S.; Radford, A.D.; and Cameron, J. 1979. Postoptimality analysis for multiattributive objective functions in dynamic programming. *Engineering Optimization* 4(2): 65–72.

Radford, A.D., and Gero, J.S. 1980. Quantized feedforward and feedback information for dynamic programming problems. *Engineering Optimization* 4(4): 227–28.

CHAPTER 7

DYNAMIC PROGRAMMING CASE STUDIES

In the last two chapters we have introduced the concepts of dynamic programming and developed a set of techniques that are particularly useful in design by optimization. It is time now to show how this set of techniques can be brought to bear on design problems that are more detailed and complex than the ones we have quoted so far. In this chapter we shall describe three such problems in some detail. In doing so, we want both to demonstrate the effectiveness and applicability of the methods we have described and to broaden our description of the way in which problems can be structured for solution by dynamic programming.

The three problems we have selected relate to the design of external lighting, the design of a major component of multistory buildings, and the problem of integrating components to provide a minimum-cost building. They cover a range of problem types and scales—from single component to whole building. More importantly, they are chosen because each example very clearly demonstrates one or more of the dynamic programming techniques we have described in chapters 5 and 6. The first example uses delayed decisions; the second uses nested loops; and the third example makes use of artificial intelligence concepts. In the second and third examples, we go on to demonstrate the use and utility of postoptimality analysis. In each case we separate description, prediction, and optimization models in the problem formulation.

While looking at these examples, bear in mind the object of the design exercise. Think about the kinds of information a designer would need in order to solve the stated problem, and how optimization can provide this information. Think about the solution in design terms—as the specification for a practical design policy, and not as an abstract mathematical statement. Consider, too, alternative approaches that do not use optimization: the use of simulation (for example), or design with no quantitative information at all. Are these reasonable options? Is the effort involved in optimization justified? These are the important issues. As always in this book, we shall concentrate on concepts and methodology in these examples and devote less space to the computations.

PROBLEM: DESIGNING EXTERNAL LIGHTING

You are commissioned to design a lighting scheme for a pedestrian mall in the historic town of Helzburg. To avoid erecting a multitude of lighting columns in an area of some architectural quality, you decide to suspend the luminaires from the center of wires strung across the mall from buildings on either side. There is a shortage of suitable anchorage points, however, and the wires cannot be regularly spaced. Furthermore, to make things really difficult, part of the mall should be brightly lit while other parts should have fairly low levels of lighting. The Helzburg Conservation Society is anxious that the lighting scheme should go ahead, but the town council is doubtful about carrying it out because of the cost. How do you select luminaire types and positions to provide the required distribution of illuminance at minimum cost?

The Description (Prediction) Model

We shall set out this problem in rather more formal terms than have been used in earlier examples. To measure illuminance, we need reference points; we shall use a regular series of such points along each side of the mall, defined by a regular, superimposed grid (fig. 7-1). To simplify the expression of the problem, we shall assume that the luminous intensity of the chosen light sources is equal in all directions; and because the dark red-brick Helzburg building façades are generally of low reflectance, we

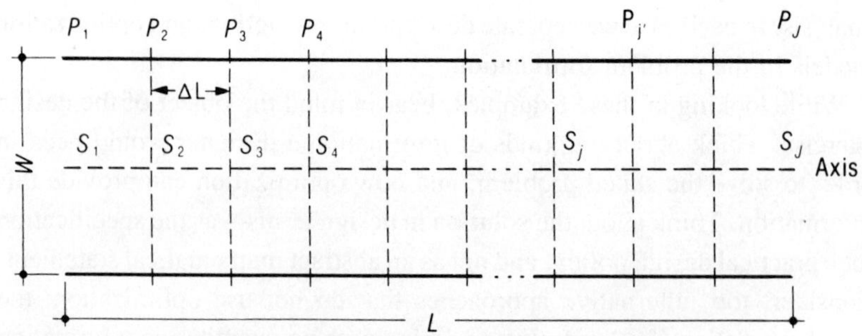

Fig. 7-1. Plan of the mall at Helzburg, with grid lines.

shall take no account of the reflected components of illumination. These assumptions simplify the methodology and avoid some very complicated calculations of light interreflections.

As usual, we shall begin by identifying the problem variables and categorizing them as either exogenous or endogenous. The notation we shall use includes the following *exogenous variables:*

1. Description of the mall (width, W, and length, L)
2. Mounting height, H, of the sources
3. Number of types of sources, T
4. Luminous intensity, I_t, of a single source, t, $t = 1, \ldots, T$
5. Cost, c_t, of a single source, t, $t = 1, \ldots, T$, including wiring, suspension cable, and installation

We also have the following *constraints* operating:

1. The number of sources must be less than or equal to a maximum number of sources, N.
2. The illuminance provided at a reference point j must be greater than or equal to a minimum illuminance, E_j (min), $j = 1, \ldots, J$.
3. The illuminance provided at a reference point, j, must be less than or equal to a maximum illuminance, E_j (max), $j = 1, \ldots, J$.

The design (or *endogenous*) variable we can control is simply: the type of source, t_k, at each possible source position, k, $k = 1, \ldots, k$.

For convenience, we shall use a grid of some small interval ΔL to combine the source point and reference point systems. We shall number the lines of this grid $1, 2, \ldots, J$, beginning at one end of the mall; that is, $(J - 1)\Delta L = L$ (fig. 7-1). Light sources will take positions at S_j on the centerline of this grid, and illuminances will be calculated at points, P_j, along the side of the grid. Some source positions will be infeasible because of the absence of anchorage points for the suspension wires.

Let E_{jk} be the illuminance provided at the reference points on grid j by a source on grid k. We shall later need this illuminance to be expressed as a function of the horizontal distance along the axis of the mall between j and k. Let this distance be y. By geometry, the direct distance, d, between source and reference point (fig. 7-2) is

$$d = (W^2/4 + y^2 + H^2)^{1/2} \tag{7.1}$$

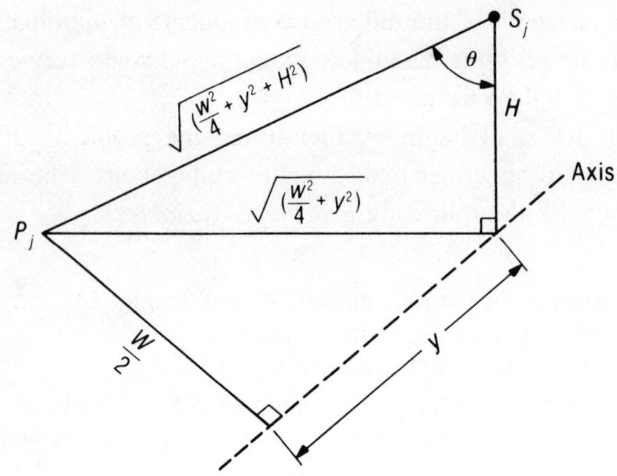

Fig. 7-2. Distance between light source and reference point.

The illuminance, E, produced on a horizontal surface is given by the following formula:

$$E = I/d^2 \cos\theta \tag{7.2}$$

In this equation, θ is the vertical angle shown in figure 7-2, and I is the luminous intensity of the source in that direction. If I is measured in candelas and d is measured in meters, E will be expressed in lux (if d is measured in feet, E will be expressed in foot-candles). We have

$$\cos\theta = H(W^2 + y^2 + H^2)^{-1/2} \tag{7.3}$$

So, substituting in equation 7.3, we get

$$E = IH(W^2 + y^2 + H^2)^{-3/2} \tag{7.4}$$

The distance y for any grids j and k will be given by $|j - k|\,\Delta L$. Substituting this value in equation 7.4, we get

$$E_{jk} = I_t H(W^2/4 + (|j - k|\Delta L)^2 + H^2)^{-3/2} \tag{7.5}$$

The Generation Model

Our generation model is produced simply by inserting in turn a feasible type of light source in one of the feasible light source positions. The order in which we choose to take light sources and positions is determined by the formulation of the problem for solution by dynamic programming, as described below.

The Optimization Model

We shall take the number of sources n, $n = 1, \ldots, N$, as the stage variable, and we shall take the type and position of the nth source as the state variable. At the first stage, we consider every possible state (type and position) for one source to illuminate one end of the mall, and then we calculate the resulting cost and illuminance. At the second stage, we consider every possible state for a second source, selecting (for each type and position of second source) the optimal type and position of a first source to go with it. We continue, adding one source at each stage. The optimal return is the minimum cost of light sources capable of satisfying the performance constraints.

At stage n, there are n sources, and we shall be working with the following terms:

1. *Input states*—the positions and types of an $(n - 1)$th source, together with an associated set of illuminances recording the illuminance produced by the first $n - 1$ sources at every reference point
2. *Output states*—the positions and types of an nth source together with an associated set of illuminances for the first n sources
3. *Decision*—simply the choice of input state for each output state
4. *Stage return*—the cost, c_n, of the nth source.

The *objective function* is to minimize the cost of providing illumination:

$$R = \min_{n,t} \sum_{i=1}^{n} (c_t)_i \tag{7.6}$$

In equation 7.6, n is the number of sources in the design proposal.

We can see from equation 7.2, that the illuminance due to a light source falls with the square of the distance from the source. The problem becomes amenable to dynamic programming if we ignore the effect of a source at reference points where the illuminance due to it falls below some minimum. We could define this value as a number of lux or as a proportion of the illuminance at a chosen reference point. Here, we shall define it as the proportion α of the illuminance given by a source of least-luminous intensity when measured at a reference point on the same grid line as the source. We shall call α the illuminance discount factor; the lower the value of α, the greater the degree of refinement of the solution (although computation will increase). If the sources are ordered so that I_1 is the highest luminous intensity and I_T is the lowest luminous intensity, the illuminance, E_d, below which the effect of a source is discounted will be given by

$$\text{discounted illuminance} = \alpha E_{jj}, \text{ for a luminaire } T \tag{7.7}$$

and the illuminance, E_{jk}, provided at a point j by a source at k will be ignored if

$$E_{jk} < \text{discounted illuminance} \tag{7.8}$$

We can then calculate a vector of illuminances, E_{jk}, $j = k, k \pm 1, \ldots, k \pm v_t$, that describes the illuminances resulting from a source of type t on grid k; v_t is the number of grid intervals over which that source has a lighting effect. The largest value of v_t will be v_1 (associated with the most powerful source, type 1). This means that if a source of type t is located at a distance of more than $(v_t + v_1)$ grid intervals from some other source, the two sources do not affect the same part of the mall, whatever other sources may lie between them (fig. 7-3). A decision to assign a certain source type to one of these source positions will therefore have no effect on the decision to assign a source type to the other source position. We shall express the distance or gap that is required for the sources to be independent in terms of the number of grid intervals, g, between the sources:

$$g_t = v_t + v_1, \ t = 1, \ldots, T \tag{7.9}$$

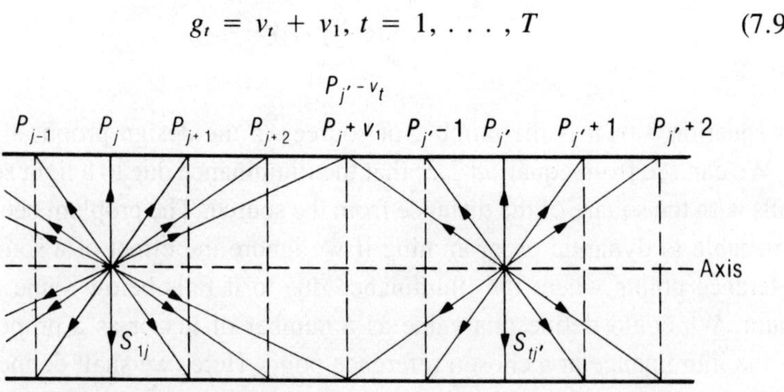

Fig. 7-3. Range of effect and independence of source $j' = j + (v_1 + t_t) = j + g_t$.

In this lighting problem, the general dynamic programming condition of separability between adjacent stages is not fulfilled: the light output from a source added at the nth stage affects the same part of the hall as a source added at the $(n - 1)$th stage. We have seen that only when a gap, g_t, exists between two sources is a decision on one of them not affected by a decision on the other. We overcome the problem by the method of delayed decisions (described in chapter 6). In this case, though, since the ability to make that decision depends not on the number of sources added but on their position and type, the stage at which a suspended decision can be made will vary with the decision path that is followed. If the source added at stage n is of type t on grid j, a decision can be made about any sources or grids $1, 2, \ldots, j - g_t$, whatever the stages at which those sources were added.

We shall position the sources and measure the illuminance produced, starting from one end of the mall so that the source added at a stage is always farther along the mall than any sources added at earlier stages. We can therefore check that the illuminance produced at any stage is greater than the minimum required at those reference points where the addition of sources in future stages (which must be farther up the mall) will have no effect. It is simple, too, to check that the illuminance at all reference points is less than the maximum illuminance allowed. Output states that fail to satisfy these constraints can be discarded.

The order in which the state variables are considered at any stage begins with the source type 1 of largest luminous intensity, I_1, taken in the available position closest to the starting end of the mall. At stage n, this will be the nth grid. We can make a decision for sources in positions 1 to $n - g_1$; that is, we can select the optimum input state, according to equation 6.5, from among all of the input states that follow an identical decision path through the stages after the stage in which the source on the $(n - g_1)$th grid was added.

Obviously, if at any stage the combination of a source added at grid j and some input state fails to satisfy a minimum illuminance constraint, a source of lower luminous intensity in combination with the same input state will also fail to satisfy that constraint. Likewise, if a source of largest luminous intensity added at grid j fails to satisfy a minimum illumination constraint, any source added at points $j + 1, \ldots, J$, farther up the mall will also fail to satisfy that constraint. Hence, if an input state, when combined with state variables source type $= t$ and grid $= j$, results in an output state that fails to satisfy the illumination constraint, it need not be considered with state variables source type $= t + 1, \ldots, T$, grid $= j$.

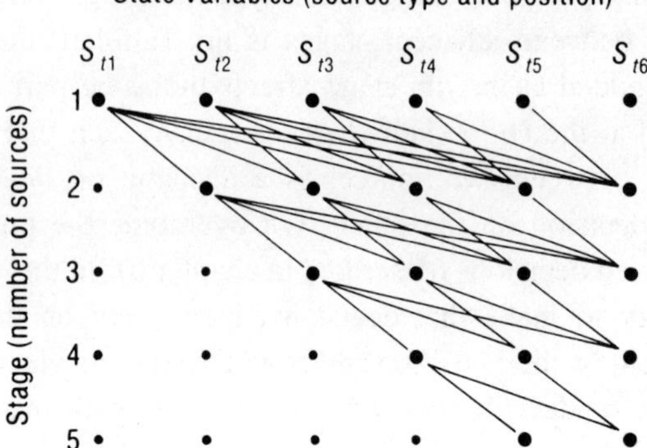

Fig. 7-4. Stage/state diagram for $N = 5$, $J = 6$, assuming all source points are feasible. The connecting lines between state variables in adjacent stages represent the decision paths. The second dimension of source type for each position is not shown.

Similarly, if an input state with the state variable source type = 1 results in an output state that fails to satisfy the constraint, it need not be considered with further state variables. When all input states are thus discounted, the analysis can continue to the next stage.

A diagrammatic representation of the problem is shown in figure 7-4. At stage 1, each source type, t, $t = 1, \ldots, T$, is placed in turn on the grid lines, k, $k = 1, \ldots, J$; and the corresponding cost, c_t, and set of illuminances, E_{jk}, $j = 1, \ldots, J$, are calculated. At stage n, the nth source is placed in turn on the remaining feasible grid lines, k, $k = n, \ldots, J$, and combined with input states taken from type and positions of the $(n - 1)$th source. The decision as to which of these possible output states is optimal must be suspended, as above. When all of the stages have been completed, the optimal policy of source types and positions can be found from the output states from any stage that are solutions and satisfy the constraints at every reference point. Clearly, if an output state from any stage is a solution, it is not included among the input states to the following stage. An algorithm for carrying out this procedure is shown in figure 7-5.

Results and Discussion

A computer program based on the algorithm given in figure 7-5 was written and used with the data shown in table 7-1 to produce the results illustrated in figure 7-6. Here, the illuminance at most reference points lies within

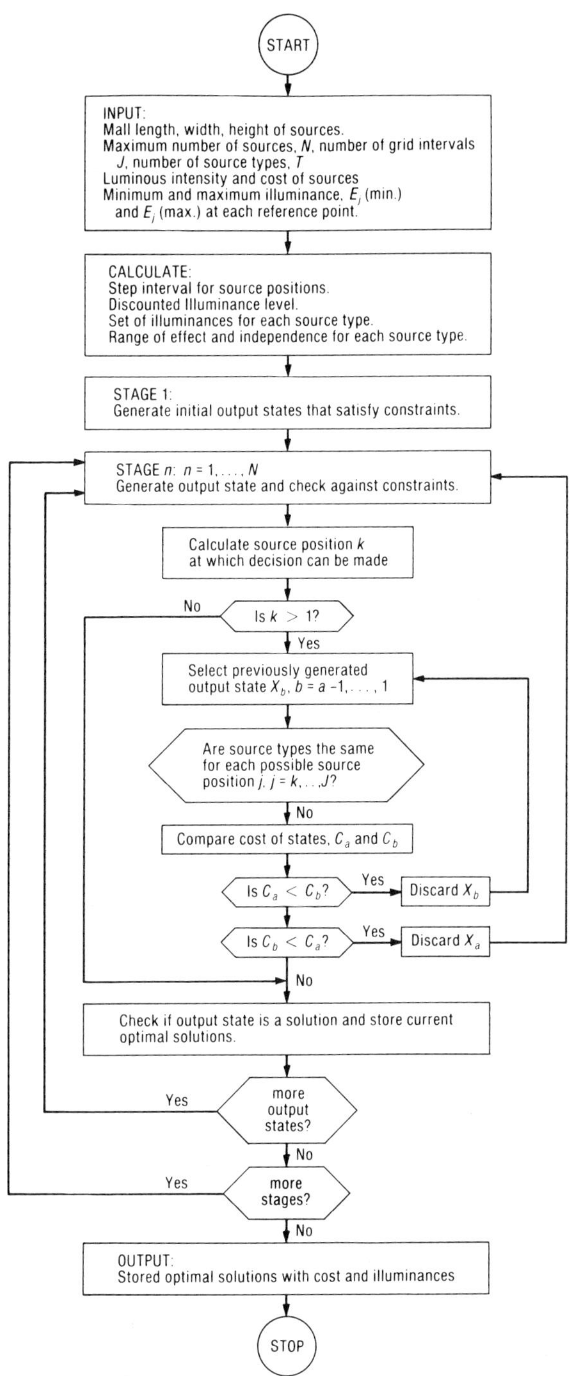

Fig. 7-5. Program flow chart with delayed decisions.

Table 7-1. Details of one section of the mall at Helzburg, with three possible light source types.

Mall length			30 meters (98 ft 6 ins)
Mall width			6 meters (19 ft 8 ins)
Source height			3 meters (9 ft 10 ins)
Maximum number of sources			8
Minimum illuminance required			300 lux (3,230 ft-candles)
		except at end of mall,	250 lux (2,690 ft-candles)
Maximum illuminance allowed			700 lux (7,532 ft-candles)
		except at beginning of mall,	500 lux (5,380 ft-candles)

Source type	1	2	3
Luminous intensity (candelas)	10,000	7,000	4,000
Cost (units)	9	7	5

the same minimum and maximum constraints. In fact, this was just one of many sets of results generated on the basis of different descriptions of the mall. The technique of delayed decisions proves to be computationally feasible for this well-conditioned backwardfeed dynamic program. It allows the problem formulation to satisfy the necessary separability con-

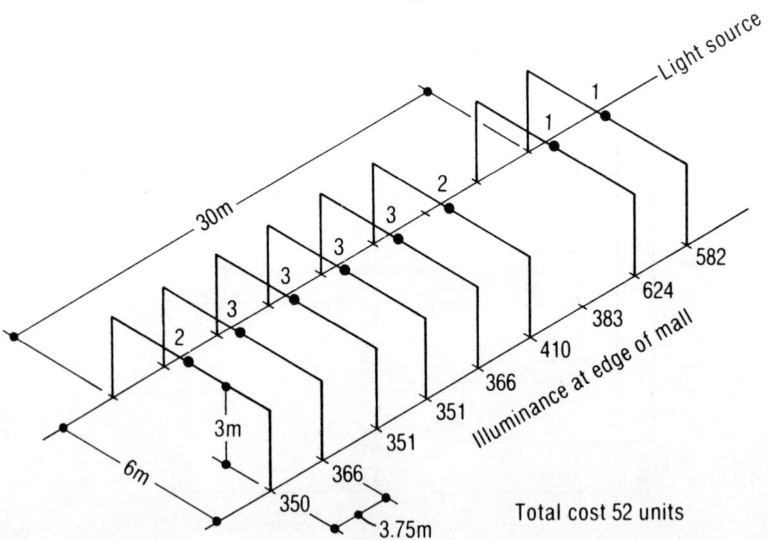

Fig. 7-6. Solution to the lighting problem for a section of the mall at Helzburg, with the given lighting levels and available lighting source types. There are other, equally optimal solutions. The computer program could, of course, be used with other configurations.

dition in a situation where the interrelationship of effects of decisions at sequential stages would otherwise make dynamic programming infeasible. It works here because of the well-conditioned nature of the problem: the feedback is constant at each stage and is of the same type throughout. The establishment of separability is, as we have seen, one of the keys to making dynamic programming work.

PROBLEM: DESIGNING THE FLOOR–CEILING SYSTEM IN A MULTISTORY BUILDING

In a multistory building, the floor–ceiling sandwich includes all the systems contained within the space defined by the ceiling below the space and the floor cover of the floor above it. This space could contain the following systems: structural; heat, ventilating, and air conditioning; electrical, and fire protection. Because of the complexity of interactions between these various subsystems, designers have treated each separately on the assumption that the optimum design is simply the sum of each system optimized separately. But this is not necessarily the case.

You are designing a multistory office building in which the outer core is structural and carries all the lateral loads as well as all the vertical loads that are not carried by the service core. The service core provides the vertical circulation paths for all the other systems. Thus, the floor–ceiling sandwich is concerned with horizontal distribution. This particular building is thirty stories high, with a plan as shown in figure 7-7; part of the design

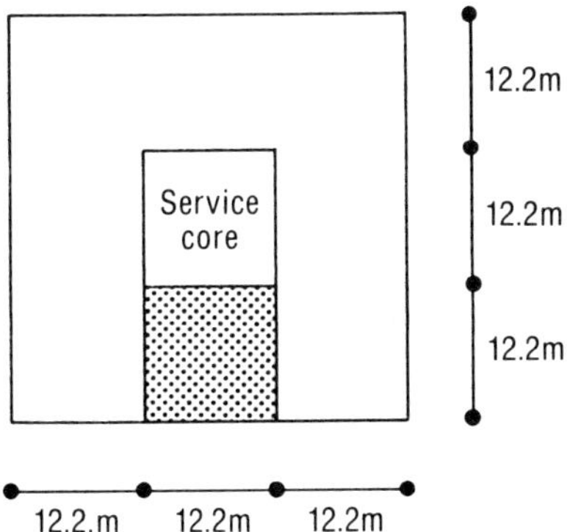

Fig. 7-7. Plan of a typical floor of the building for which the floor–ceiling sandwich is to be designed.

calls for column spacing of 6.1 meters (20 ft) around the periphery. As a result of symmetry, only a typical two-bay area needs to be considered.

The Description (Prediction) Model

We want to predict the cost of the floor–ceiling sandwich, and therefore we need to describe the construction in terms of the components that contribute to that cost. In doing so, we are interested not only in the direct cost of each component but also in the costs of using components in combination or association. For example, the cost of putting ducting in the building is influenced by the type of building frame and reinforcing we use. The ducting and building frame are component costs, whereas the cost of fitting the ducting into a frame is an association cost. The total cost is simply the sum of the contributing costs.

The options for various systems—the results, perhaps, of an initial selection process—are shown in table 7-2. For example, the structural system is composed of three subsystems: the framing, the reinforcing, and the slab. There are six, five, and five possible choices, respectively, in these subsystems.

The Generation Model

The generation model is simple: we investigate each decision option for each of our variables. The order in which we do so derives from the formulation of the problem for solution by dynamic programming.

The Optimization Model

We shall define the following terms:

1. *Stage variable*—the construction subsystem
2. *State variable*—the feasible alternatives for the subsystem
3. *Decisions*—the optimal choice of input state for each state at each stage.

The *objective function* is to minimize the sum of the costs associated with each choice for each subsystem and the costs associated with using al-

Table 7-2. Available elements after initial selection for floor–ceiling sandwich design.

Structural Systems

	Frame	*Reinforcing*	*Slab*
1.	concrete girders and beams	one-way slab	cast-in-place reinforced concrete
2.	concrete girders and joists	rib slab	precast reinforced concrete
3.	steel girders and beams	two-way slab	precast prestressed
4.	steel girders and joists	waffle slab	post-tensioned
5.	steel girders	cellular steel deck	concrete topping only
6.	concrete girders		

HVAC System

	HVAC System	*Ducting*	*Terminal Units*	*Return Air*
1.	independent	conventional low-velocity	mixing box	ducted
2.	central	single, high-velocity	mixing box with reheat	ceiling plenum
3.		double, high-velocity	mixing box with variable volume	
4.			reheat box	
5.			reheat box with variable volume	

Electrical System

1. through floor slab
2. below floor slab

Fire Protection System

1. sprinklers
2. no sprinklers

ternatives for linked subsystems (that is, for adjacent stages) in combination. This generates a nine-stage system. The interactions between the states in one stage and the states in another stage that need to be developed produce the feedforward loops. The solution methodology constrains these feedforward loops from intersecting. It is feasible to produce a good model of this problem within this restriction. One way is to rate the interactions between the subsystems, reducing the weak interactions to zero while increasing the strong interactions to unity in order to produce a binary interaction matrix that satisfies the above constraint. The resultant matrix may well be different for different designers and certainly will vary from one geographical region to the next.

Since minimum total cost is the criterion for solving this problem, the

	Frame	Reinforcing	Slab	HVAC System	Ducting	Terminal units	Return air	Electrical	Fire Protection
Frame	–	1	1	0	0	0	0	0	0
Reinforcing	0	–	0	0	0	0	0	0	0
Slab	0	1	–	0	0	0	0	1	0
HVAC system	0	0	0	–	0	0	0	0	0
Ducting	1	1	0	1	–	0	0	0	0
Terminal units	0	0	0	0	1	–	0	0	0
Return air	0	1	0	0	0	0	–	0	0
Electrical	0	1	0	0	0	0	0	–	0
Fire protection	0	0	0	0	0	0	0	0	–

Fig. 7-8. Interaction matrix for components of the floor–ceiling sandwich design problem.

interactions will relate the cost interactions. A typical resultant interaction matrix for this problem is shown in figure 7-8. The number of the forward interactions between one subsystem and another is the row sum from the matrix, while the number of backward interactions is the column sum from the matrix.

The ordinal function of the graph represented by this matrix (fig. 7-9)

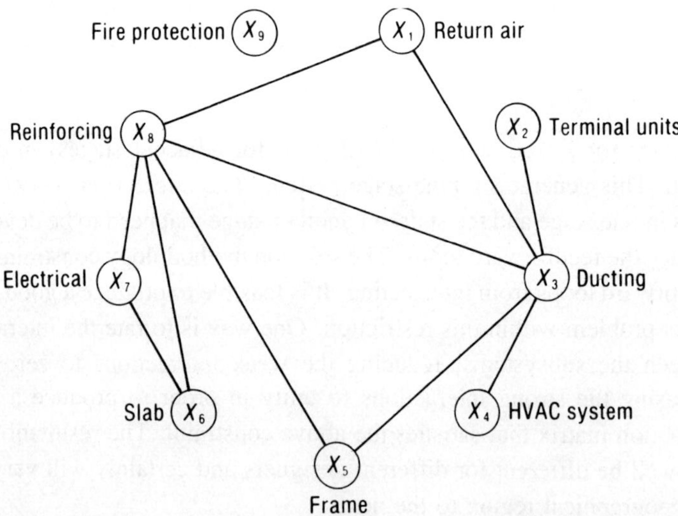

Fig. 7-9. Graph of a theoretical representation of relationships (arcs) between subsystems (nodes) in the floor–ceiling sandwich problem.

can be used to sequence these subsystems into stages. Here, the components are shown as nodes and the associations as paths between nodes. Using dynamic programming terminology, we shall refer to the component costs as *node costs* and to the association costs as *path costs*. Figure 7-10(a) shows the sequencing as a graph with six stages. Since each subsystem is to be treated as a stage, the graph can be "straightened out"—and the *Return Air* and *Fire* subsystems arbitrarily placed as the first and last stages—without altering its structure. Figure 7-10(b) shows this; the dotted connectivity lines are used to indicate that the path cost is zero.

The detailed model (fig. 7-11) now only requires numerical values for node and path costs. We shall label the decision variable at each stage j as X_j, and the ith value of each variable at stage j as x_j^i, for later reference. Again, the objective is to minimize the total cost of the floor–ceiling sandwich.

Careful study is required to produce the node and path costs, since they are in a form that is not customary. The node cost is the absolute cost of an item (states) in a stage. The path cost relates only to the cost of combining states, reflecting relative costs of different combinations. Thus, a path cost of zero would indicate that no supernumerary cost is associated with that combination. The path cost is used to prevent two states from being combined (because it is infeasible), by applying an infinite cost to that path. Shown in figure 7-12 are the node and path cost matrices associated with the problem as shown in figure 7-11.

Results

For the data given, the following optimal solution can be derived using feedforward nonserial dynamic programming:

Subsystem	*Optimal Element*
return air	ceiling plenum
terminal units	reheat box
ducting	conventional low-velocity
HVAC system	independent
frame	steel girders
reinforcing	one-way slab
slab	precast reinforced concrete
electrical	below floor slab
fire protection	no sprinklers

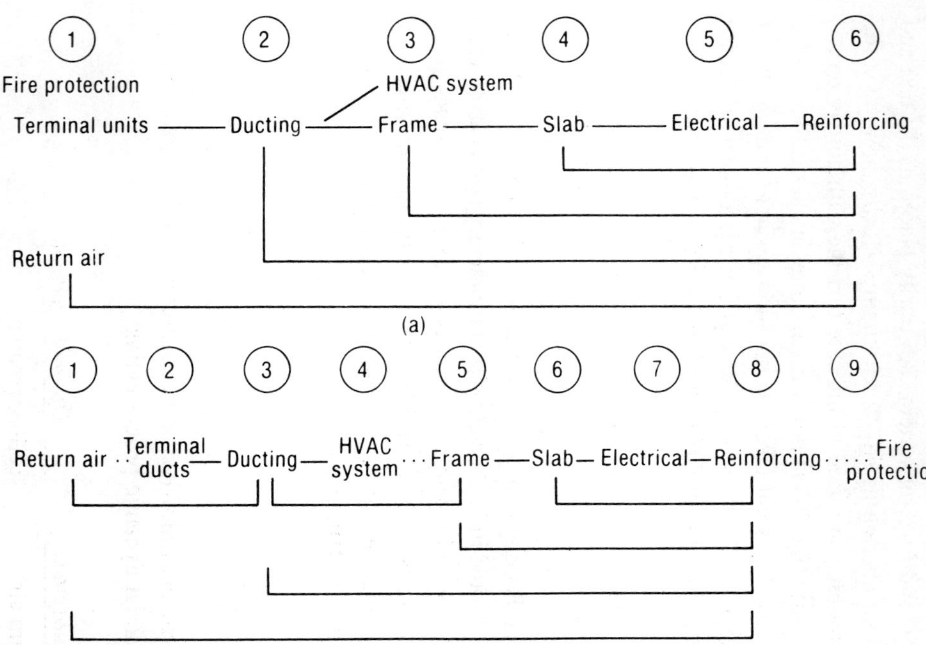

Fig. 7-10. (a) Graph of the sequencing of the dependent stages of the floor–ceiling sandwich problem.
(b) Graph of the "straightened" sequence of stages.
The heavy lines indicate nonzero path costs. The dotted lines indicate zero path costs (that is, independence).

This can be summarized for the four original systems in the following terms:

System	*Optimal Elements*
structural	steel girders with one-way precast reinforced concrete slab
HVAC	conventional low-velocity ducting with reheat box; an independent system with ceiling plenum for return air
electrical	carried below slab
fire protection	no sprinklers

Postoptimality Analysis

The optimal solution is interesting, but we would also like to know what other design options are open to us without major extra costs. Instead of just identifying the optimal solution, one pass of the optimization procedure was carried out to produce the four best policies (labeled 1 to 4, in table 7-3).

Solution number 1 (the optimal solution) is the one described in the preceding section; the numbers of the optimal states refer to the way in which the problem is formulated in figure 7-11. The costs are of relative rather than actual importance; they indicate the relative performance of different solutions, so solutions 2 and 3 (for example) are effectively equal within the accuracy of the models used.

The three suboptimal solutions generated (solutions 2 through 4) contain policies with different states from those in the optimal solution for one or more of variables X_1, X_3, X_6, X_7, and X_8. To provide alternatives for the other variables (X_2, X_4, X_5, and X_9), four further solutions were found by additional optimization passes; each time, one of the states x_2^4 (reheat box), x_4^1 (independent HVAC), x_5^5 (steel girders), and x_9^2 (no sprinklers)

Table 7-3. The four best policies.

Solution No.	*Cost of Solution†*	X_1	X_2	X_3	X_4	X_5	X_6	X_7	X_8	X_9
1	5,185	2	4	1	1	5	2	2	1	2
2	5,207	1	4	2	1	5	5	1	5	2
3	5,209	2	4	1	1	5	2	2	2	2
4	5,242	2	4	2	1	5	5	1	5	2

†The costs are expressed as relative numbers called cost units.

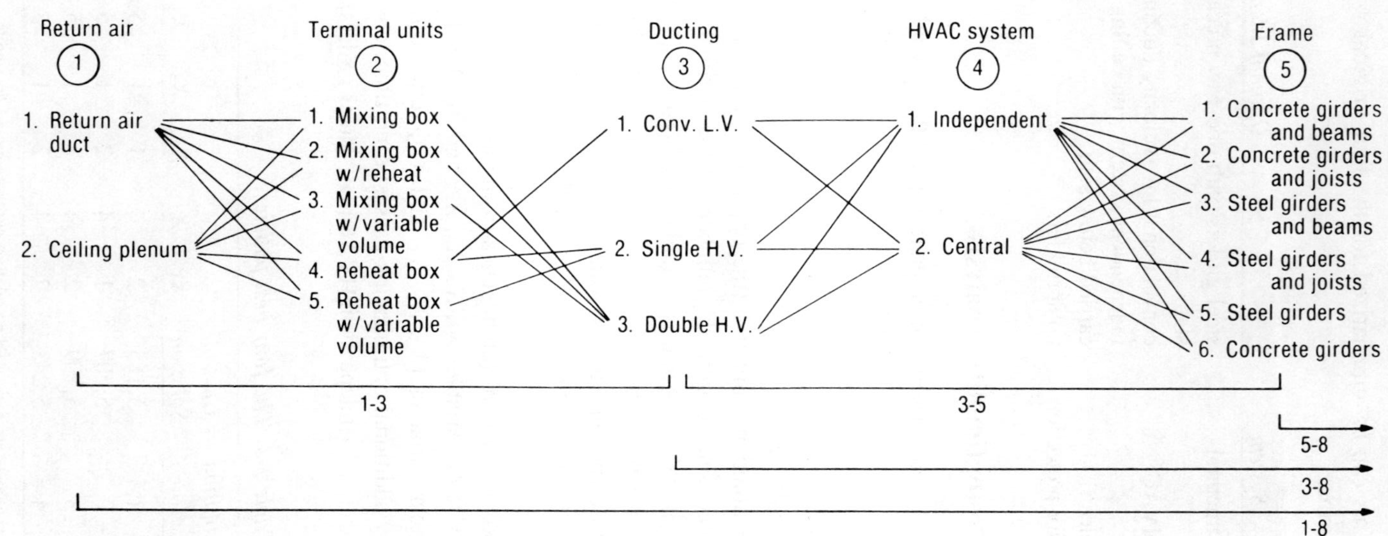

Return air
1
1. Return air duct
2. Ceiling plenum
Terminal units
2
1. Mixing box
2. Mixing box w/reheat
3. Mixing box w/variable volume
4. Reheat box
5. Reheat box w/variable volume
Ducting
3
1. Conv. L.V.
2. Single H.V.
3. Double H.V.
HVAC system
4
1. Independent
2. Central
Frame
5
1. Concrete girders and beams
2. Concrete girders and joists
3. Steel girders and beams
4. Steel girders and joists
5. Steel girders
6. Concrete girders
1-3
3-5
5-8
3-8
1-8

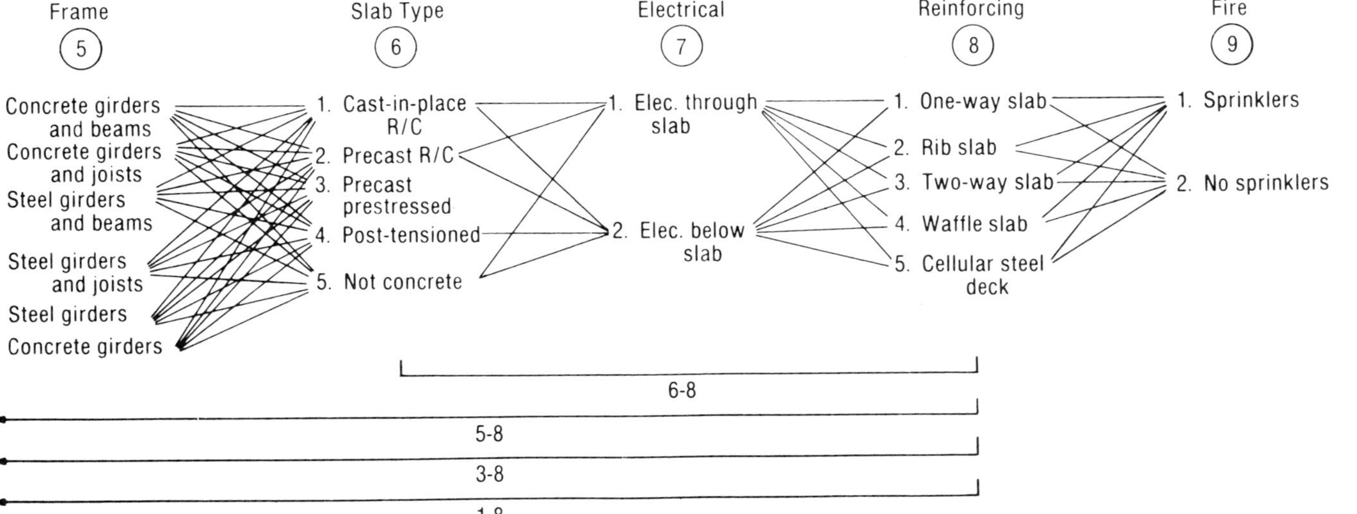

Fig. 7-11. Nodes and detailed paths for the floor–ceiling sandwich design problem, presented as a feedforward nonserial dynamic program with nine stages.

Node Costs

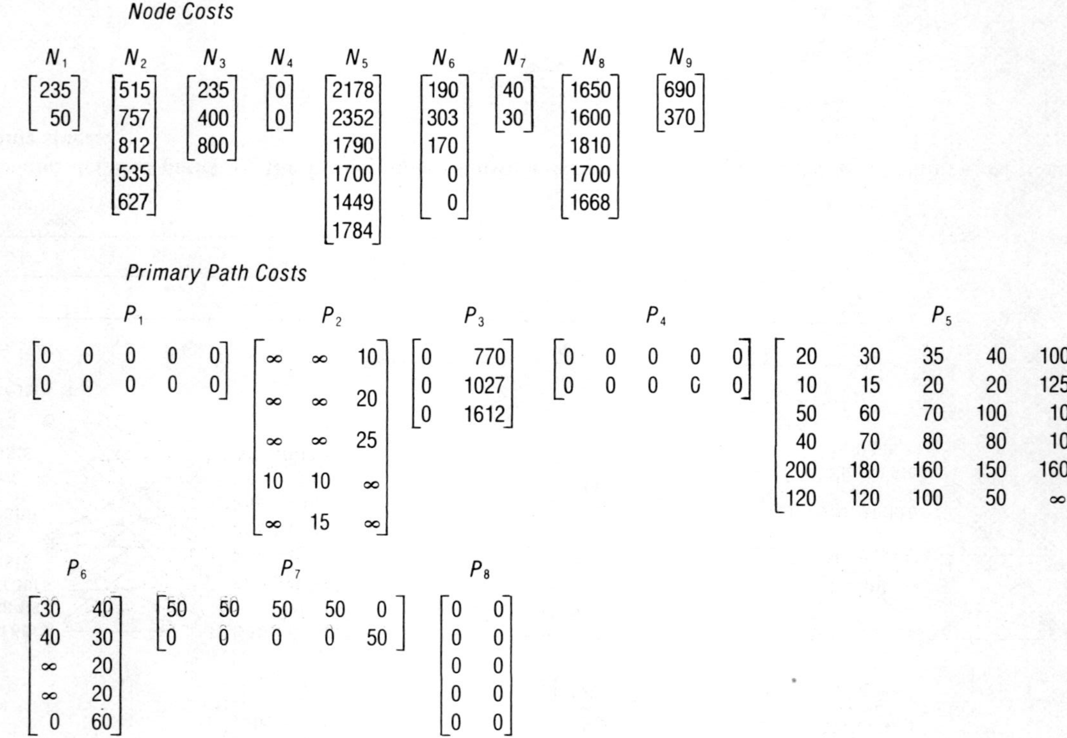

$$N_1 = \begin{bmatrix} 235 \\ 50 \end{bmatrix} \quad N_2 = \begin{bmatrix} 515 \\ 757 \\ 812 \\ 535 \\ 627 \end{bmatrix} \quad N_3 = \begin{bmatrix} 235 \\ 400 \\ 800 \end{bmatrix} \quad N_4 = \begin{bmatrix} 0 \\ 0 \end{bmatrix} \quad N_5 = \begin{bmatrix} 2178 \\ 2352 \\ 1790 \\ 1700 \\ 1449 \\ 1784 \end{bmatrix} \quad N_6 = \begin{bmatrix} 190 \\ 303 \\ 170 \\ 0 \\ 0 \end{bmatrix} \quad N_7 = \begin{bmatrix} 40 \\ 30 \end{bmatrix} \quad N_8 = \begin{bmatrix} 1650 \\ 1600 \\ 1810 \\ 1700 \\ 1668 \end{bmatrix} \quad N_9 = \begin{bmatrix} 690 \\ 370 \end{bmatrix}$$

Primary Path Costs

$$P_1 = \begin{bmatrix} 0 & 0 & 0 & 0 & 0 \\ 0 & 0 & 0 & 0 & 0 \end{bmatrix} \quad P_2 = \begin{bmatrix} \infty & \infty & 10 \\ \infty & \infty & 20 \\ \infty & \infty & 25 \\ 10 & 10 & \infty \\ \infty & 15 & \infty \end{bmatrix} \quad P_3 = \begin{bmatrix} 0 & 770 \\ 0 & 1027 \\ 0 & 1612 \end{bmatrix} \quad P_4 = \begin{bmatrix} 0 & 0 & 0 & 0 & 0 \\ 0 & 0 & 0 & 0 & 0 \end{bmatrix}$$

$$P_5 = \begin{bmatrix} 20 & 30 & 35 & 40 & 100 \\ 10 & 15 & 20 & 20 & 125 \\ 50 & 60 & 70 & 100 & 10 \\ 40 & 70 & 80 & 80 & 10 \\ 200 & 180 & 160 & 150 & 160 \\ 120 & 120 & 100 & 50 & \infty \end{bmatrix}$$

$$P_6 = \begin{bmatrix} 30 & 40 \\ 40 & 30 \\ \infty & 20 \\ \infty & 20 \\ 0 & 60 \end{bmatrix} \quad P_7 = \begin{bmatrix} 50 & 50 & 50 & 50 & 0 \\ 0 & 0 & 0 & 0 & 50 \end{bmatrix} \quad P_8 = \begin{bmatrix} 0 & 0 \\ 0 & 0 \\ 0 & 0 \\ 0 & 0 \\ 0 & 0 \end{bmatrix}$$

Secondary Path Costs

$$P_{s13} = \begin{bmatrix} 15 & 15 & 15 \\ 60 & 60 & 60 \end{bmatrix} \quad P_{s35} = \begin{bmatrix} 125 & 120 & 115 & 110 & 0 & 0 \\ 125 & 120 & 115 & 110 & 0 & 0 \\ 140 & 130 & 125 & 120 & 0 & 0 \end{bmatrix} \quad P_{s68} = \begin{bmatrix} 913 & 668 & 890 & 892 & \infty \\ 38 & 22 & 32 & 20 & \infty \\ 759 & 648 & 937 & 782 & \infty \\ 1313 & 1241 & 1394 & 1343 & \infty \\ \infty & \infty & \infty & \infty & 0 \end{bmatrix}$$

$$P_{s58} = \begin{bmatrix} 200 & 40 & 180 & 30 & 600 \\ 300 & 100 & 275 & 95 & 650 \\ 50 & 125 & 35 & 140 & 25 \\ 60 & 140 & 40 & 165 & 25 \\ 70 & 160 & 50 & 180 & 35 \\ 240 & 60 & 230 & 50 & \infty \end{bmatrix} \quad P_{s38} = \begin{bmatrix} 175 & 175 & 175 & 175 & \infty \\ 190 & 190 & 190 & 190 & 290 \\ 255 & 255 & 255 & 255 & 310 \end{bmatrix} \quad P_{s18} = \begin{bmatrix} 175 & 175 & 175 & 175 & 0 \\ 0 & 0 & 0 & 0 & 175 \end{bmatrix}$$

Fig. 7-12. Node and path costs for the floor–ceiling sandwich design problem depicted in figure 7-11. The node cost is the cost of an item (state) in a stage. The path cost is the cost of combining items (states) at different stages. For example, given a waffle slab with sprinklers, the slab and sprinklers are node costs, whereas the cost of fitting the sprinklers into a waffle slab is a path cost.

Table 7-4. Four constrained optimal policies.

Solution No.	*Cost of Solution*†	X_1	X_2	X_3	X_4	X_5	X_6	X_7	X_8	X_9
A	5,304	1	5	2	1	5	5	1	5	2
B	5,955	2	4	1	2	5	2	2	1	2
C	5,426	2	4	1	1	4	2	2	1	2
D	5,505	2	4	1	1	5	2	2	1	1

†The costs are expressed as relative numbers called cost units.

was constrained to be infeasible. These solutions are labeled A to D in table 7-4.

The permissible total change (node + arc costs) in the returns associated with each state in the optimal policy are shown in table 7-5. It is clear that the optimal policy is sensitive to changes in the costs associated with some of the states and fairly insensitive to changes in the costs for other states. For example, any increase greater than 1.1 percent in the costs associated with state x_1^8 (one-way slab) causes a different policy to become optimal. Column 3 in table 7-5 shows that the new optimal policy in such a case would be the original second-best policy. Further, table 7-3 shows that state x_8^5 (cellular steel deck) would replace state x_8^1 (the one-way slab), with changes in other state variables. On the other hand, only increases greater than 86.5 percent in the costs associated with state x_9^2 (no sprinklers) will cause a change in the optimal policy.

Table 7-6 shows the permissible changes in the returns associated with the relationship between states in the optimal policy (the arc costs only). This table indicates that the optimal solution is fairly stable in relation to changes in the relationship costs. The most critical relationship is (x_5^5, x_6^2), between the choice of steel girders for the frame subsystem and the choice of precast reinforced concrete for the slab subsystem, where a 12.2 percent increase in assumed cost causes a change in the optimal policy. Comparing tables 7-5 and 7-6, we can conclude that the critical costs in this case tend to be those associated with the states (the elements themselves) rather than those associated with the arcs (relationships between elements).

We can also obtain information about the stability of the optimal solution on the basis of changes in the returns associated with combination of states. For example, solution 2 will replace solution 1 as the optimal solution, given increases of 20.0 percent in the cost associated with x_1^2, or 4.6 percent in x_1^3, or 4.0 percent in x_6^2, or 36.7 percent in x_7^2, or 1.1

Table 7-5. Permissible total changes in cost of states in the optimal policy.

Stage	*Current State in Optimal Policy*	*Next-best Solution without Current State (see tables 7-3 and 7-4)*	*Cost of Next-best Solution over Optimal Solution*†	*Total Cost Associated with Current State (node + all arcs)*†	*Permissible Change (%)*
1	x_1^2	2	22	110	20.0
2	x_2^4	A	119	544	21.8
3	x_3^1	2	22	480	4.6
4	x_4^1	B	770	0	—
5	x_5^5	C	241	1,669	14.2
6	x_6^2	2	22	551	4.0
7	x_7^2	2	22	60	36.7
8	x_8^1	2	22	1,933	1.1
9	x_9^2	D	320	370	86.5

†The costs are expressed as relative numbers called cost units.

Table 7-6. Permissible changes in the relationship costs in the optimal policy.

Arcs from Stage	*Current Arc in Optimal Policy*	*Next-best Solution without Current Arc*	*Cost of Next-best Solution over Optimal Solution†*	*Total Cost Associated with Current Arc†*	*Permissible Change (%)*
1	(x_1^2, x_2^4)	2	22	0	—
	(x_1^2, x_3^1)	2	22	60	37.0
	(x_1^2, x_8^1)	2	22	0	—
2	(x_2^4, x_3^1)	2	22	10	220.0
3	(x_3^1, x_4^1)	2	22	0	—
	(x_3^1, x_5^5)	2	22	0	—
	(x_3^1, x_8^1)	2	22	175	12.6
4	(x_4^1, x_5^5)	C	241	0	—
5	(x_5^5, x_6^2)	2	22	180	12.2
	(x_5^5, x_8^1)	2	22	70	31.4
6	(x_6^2, x_7^2)	2	22	30	73.3
	(x_6^2, x_8^1)	2	22	38	57.9
7	(x_7^2, x_8^1)	2	22	0	—
8	(x_8^1, x_9^2)	2	22	0	—

†The costs are expressed as relative numbers called cost units.

percent in x_8^2, or any combination thereof. As another example, the analysis shows that, if state x_1^2 is not available, the optimal policy becomes solution 2, with a rise in total cost from 5,185 units to 5,207 units. If state x_2^4 then becomes unavailable, the optimal policy becomes solution A, with a total cost of 5,304 units. Looked at another way, this means that an increase of greater than 20.0 percent in the cost associated with x_1^2, followed by an increase of greater than 17.8 percent in the cost associated with x_2^4, causes a change in the optimal policy to solution A. Similar information is available about other variables that may be of interest.

Discussion

Two aspects of this example are of particular interest: the use of nonserial dynamic programming, which solved a problem that was not solvable by the standard serial form of dynamic programming; and the postoptimality analysis, which provided much more useful and complete information than was obtainable by the optimization alone.

PROBLEM: DESIGNING A HOTEL UNIT

You are designing a medium-size hotel that has rooms arranged on both sides of a central corridor (fig. 7-13). The planning decisions have been made, but many options for the building's structure and construction remain. The main areas where decisions are needed relate to the method of construction (prefabricated, in-situ, or a mixture), the standard of finish, and whether or not a balcony should be provided. There is also a fundamental decision to be made about structure. The choice here could be a series of cross walls providing the vertical load support and transverse bracing, with the floor and façade elements providing longitudinal bracing. Alternatively, the structure could consist of a frame with columns, beams, and nonstructural infill walls, or it could have a structural member every second bay and nonstructural cross walls every other bay carried by staggered steel trusses or wall beams. You want to obtain design information on the least-cost options.

The Description (Prediction) Model

We want to predict the cost of the building and therefore we need to describe the building in terms of the components that will contribute to that cost. As in the earlier floor–ceiling sandwich problem, we have to incorporate in the model both the direct cost of each component and the costs associated with using a component in combination with some other predicted component. The total cost is simply the sum of these contributing costs. In fact, in this model we take separate account of material, labor, and overhead costs so that some breakdown of the total can be made.

The building is described by twenty variables, each of which allows for several alternative choices (table 7-7). The major task involved in setting up the description model is to gather the cost information, calculated from current building price index lists. Since we are seeking a comparison of design options, relative costs are more important than absolute costs; it does not matter greatly if our cost data have become outdated, as long as the correct relativity is maintained.

The Generation Model

Once we have established the description model, the generation model is simple. We simply need to cycle in turn through each decision option for

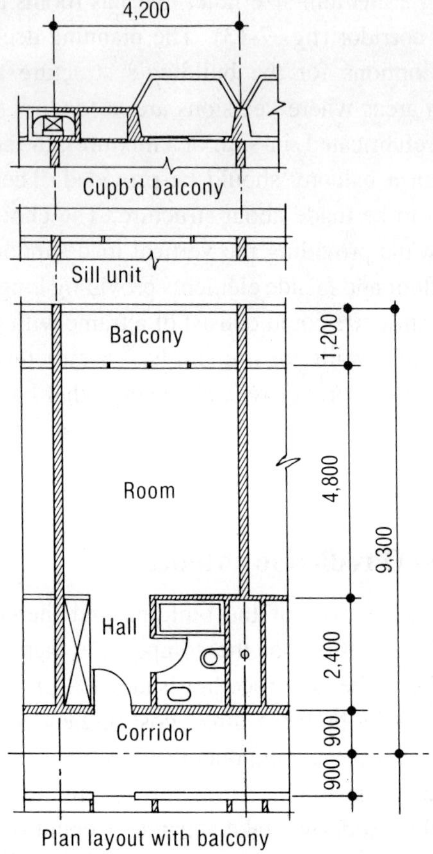

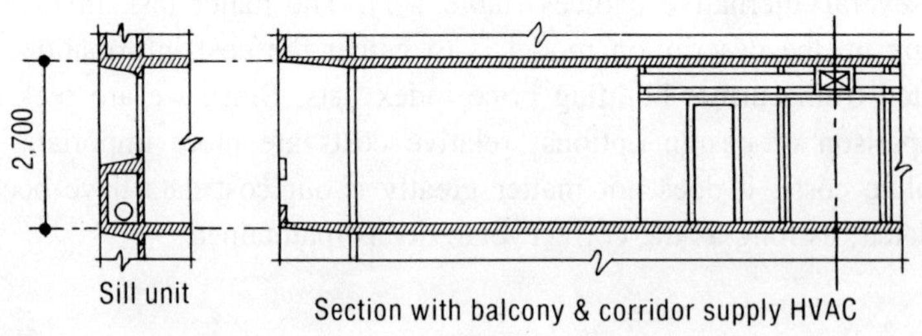

Fig. 7-13. Hotel room unit with façade options.

Table 7-7. Subsystems and alternatives for hotel unit.

1. Structural Cross Walls
1. In-situ RC
2. Precast concrete panels
3. Precast PC planks
4. In-situ concrete frame and concrete block infill
5. In-situ concrete frame and plasterboard infill
6. Tunnel construction
7. Steel STS and plasterboard infill
8. Precast PC wall beam as STS

2. Structural Cross Wall Finish
1. Paint
2. Render and paint
3. Wallpaper
4. Render and wallpaper

3. Structural Cross Wall Electrical Work
1. Prelaid in precast elements
2. On-site distribution

4. Nonstructural Cross Walls
1. None
2. Concrete blocks
3. $1^1/_2$ hours fire-rated plasterboard

5. Nonstructural Cross Wall Finish
1. None
2. Paint
3. Render and paint
4. Wallpaper
5. Render and wallpaper
6. Sprayed texture finish

6. Nonstructural Cross Wall Electrical Work
1. None
2. On-site distribution

7. Floor
1. None
2. In-situ RC
3. Metal deck and concrete topping
4. Precast concrete floor panels
5. Precast PC planks
6. Precast concrete permanent formwork and concrete topping
7. Patent beam and lightweight block infill and concrete topping

(*Continued*)

Table 7-7. Subsystems and alternatives for hotel unit (Continued).

8. Floor Electrical Work
1. Prelaid in precast elements
2. On-site distribution, in structure
3. On-site distribution, exposed

9. Room Ceiling Finish
1. Paint
2. Plaster and paint
3. Sprayed vermiculite
4. Plasterboard and paint
5. Patent suspended

10. Façade Element
1. Precast concrete full-width balcony unit
2. Precast concrete cupboard and half-width balcony unit
3. Precast concrete still unit
4. In-situ concrete full width balcony unit
5. In-situ concrete cupboard and half-width balcony unit
6. In-situ concrete sill unit

11. Glazed Element
1. Full-width window wall
2. Sliding doors only within precast element
3. Sliding doors only, on-site installation
4. Full-width window within precast element
5. Full-width window, on-site installation

12. HVAC
1. Perimeter-ducting HV
2. Perimeter-ducting horizontal distribution
3. Perimeter-ducting LV horizontal distribution
4. Corridor supply

13. Internal Partitions
1. Precast concrete wall panels
2. In-situ RC
3. Precast PC planks
4. Concrete block, 100 mm
5. Plasterboard wall construction

14. Internal Partition Finish
1. Paint
2. Render and paint
3. Wallpaper
4. Render and wallpaper
5. Sprayed texture finish

Table 7-7. Subsystems and alternatives for hotel unit (Continued).

15. Internal Partition Electrical Work
1. Prelaid in precast elements
2. On-site distribution

16. Corridor Partition
1. Precast concrete wall
2. In-situ RC
3. Precast PC planks
4. Concrete blocks 200 mm
5. $1^1/_2$ hour fire-rated plasterboard

17. Corridor Partition Finish
1. Paint
2. Render and paint
3. Wallpaper
4. Render and wallpaper
5. Sprayed texture finish

18. Ductwork
1. Prefabricated concrete duct and all plumbing
2. Prefabricated steel frame and all plumbing
3. Hole in floor and concrete block wall
4. Hole in floor and precast concrete panel
5. Hole in floor and precast plank
6. Hole in floor, asbestos cement

19. Plumbing
1. None
2. Conventional
3. Prefabricated "tree" and temporary frame, on-site erection

20. Hall and Corridor Ceiling Finish
1. Paint
2. Plaster and paint
3. Sprayed vermiculite
4. Plasterboard and paint
5. Suspended plasterboard and paint
6. Patent suspended

each of our variables. If we did this exhaustively, we would have around 4.9×10^{12} possible combinations of the decision, although many of these are infeasible. As in the other examples in this chapter, we embed the generation model within a dynamic programming optimization model so that we do not need to search the possibilities exhaustively.

The Optimization Model

The system is modeled as a stage–state optimization problem. As we did in the earlier floor–ceiling sandwich problem, we shall define the following terms:

1. *Stage variable*—the construction subsystem
2. *State variable*—the feasible alternatives for the subsystem
3. *Decisions*—the optimal choice of input state for each state at each stage.

The *objective function* is to minimize the total cost, which is the sum of the costs associated with each decision and of those associated with linked pairs of decisions.

Figure 7-14 shows the associations between the subsystems; that is, it shows pairs of stages where a cost is associated with the combination of decisions from the stages. This formulation is amenable to the heuristic nonserial dynamic programming algorithm described in chapter 6, where the stages are ordered to minimize nonseriality.

Results

A computer system SID (system for integrated design) was written for computer implementation. It uses the heuristic nonserial dynamic programming algorithm for the general class of problems that can be formatted in stage–state form with path and node costs. SID has three modules: a control and data input module through which the stages, states, and costs are described; an optimization module that carries out forward and backward optimization passes and orders a list of best solutions found; and a postoptimization module that carries out subsystem (costs associated with the choice of state at any stage) sensitivity analysis, connection (costs associated with the links between states at different stages) sensitivity analysis, and analyses involving the fixing of alternatives.

The optimal solution (fig. 7-15) has a total cost of \$13,511 for each unit, consisting of material costs of \$9,053, labor costs of \$3,628, and overhead costs of \$830. The design decisions leading to this lowest cost figure include precast concrete panels for cross walls and floors, rendered and printed wall finishes, and steel-framed prefabricated plumbing units. Taken alone, the information provided by this optimal solution is a cost yardstick by which to compare any other design or variation that might

	1	2	3	4	5	6	7	8	9	10	11	12	13	14	15	16	17	18	19	20
1. Structural cross walls	–	1	1	1			1			1			1			1		1		
2. Struct. cross walls finish		–																		
3. Struct. cross walls elect. work			–			1		1							1					
4. Non-struct. cross walls				–	1	1							1			1				
5. Non-struct. cross wall finish					–															
6. Non-struct. cross wall elect. work						–		1							1					
7. Floor							–	1	1	1			1			1		1		1
8. Floor electrical work								–	1						1					1
9. Room ceiling finish									–											
10. Façade element										–	1	1								
11. Glazed element											–	1								
12. HVAC												–								1
13. Internal partitions													–	1	1	1				
14. Internal partition finish														–						
15. Internal partition elect. work															–					
16. Corridor partition																–	1			
17. Corridor finish																	–			
18. Duct work																		–	1	
19. Plumbing																			–	
20. Hall & corridor ceiling finish																				–

Fig. 7-14. Binary association matrix showing associations between subsystems.

COMBINED FORWARD AND BACKWARD PASS

SOLUTION NO. 1				
	TOT. COSTS	IN $	=	13511.00
	MAT. COSTS	IN $	=	9053.00
	LAB. COSTS	IN $	=	3628.00
	OVER. COSTS	IN $	=	830.00

SUBSYSTEM	ALTERNATIVE
STRUCT. CROSS-WALLS	PRECAST CONC. PANELS
STRUCT. WALL FINISH	RENDER & PAINT
STRUCT. ELECTRICAL	PRELAID
NON-STRUCT. CR/WALLS	NONE
CROSS-WALL FINISH	NONE
CR/WALL ELECTRICAL	NONE
FLOOR	PRECAST CONC. PANELS
FLOOR ELECTRICAL	PRELAID
ROOM CEILING FINISH	PAINT ONLY
FACADE ELEMENT	P.C. CUPB/D & BALC
GLAZED ELEMENT	DOORS ONLY ON-SITE
HVAC	PERIMETER VERTICAL
INTERNAL PARTITIONS	PRECAST CONC. PANELS
INT. PART. FINISH	RENDER & PAINT
INT. PART. ELECT.	PRELAID
CORRIDOR PARTITION	GYPROK 1½ HRS
CORRIDOR FINISH	PAINT ONLY
DUCT	STEEL FRAME & PLUMB.
PLUMBING	NONE
HALL & CORRID. CEIL.	SPRAYED VERMICULITE

Fig. 7-15. Computer printout of the optimal results.

be considered as an indicative set of decisions leading to a low-cost design. The degree of confidence the designer has that this would indeed be the lowest cost design in practice depends on his or her confidence that the cost data in the model reflect the true cost relativities in practice. It must also be remembered that the optimization model here is heuristic and does not guarantee to produce the global optimum but a very good approximation of it. We can get much more information from the model, however, through postoptimality analysis.

Postoptimality Analysis

In the execution of the optimization model, the best forty decisions—rather than just the optimal decisions—were kept for each state at each stage. Further, both forward and backward passes through the stages were executed; because the optimization model is heuristic, the results of the two passes may differ. The first 200 performances were ordered, and the decisions for the first 5 performances on both forward and backward passes were examined.

Among these ten solutions, sixteen of the twenty subsystems display more than one alternative. The exceptions are the façade element (always precast concrete cupboard unit and balcony), the glazed element (always doors with on-site installation), the corridor partitions (always plasterboard), and the corridor partition finish (always paint). The stability of these decisions suggests that we could follow them with some confidence.

For the remaining sixteen subsystems, we can explore the sensitivity of our optimal solution to changes in the cost information that was used. Table 7-8 shows the costs associated with switching from the decision in the optimal solution to another decision for each of these subsystems. Column 2 shows the difference in total cost between the optimal solution and the cheapest solution displaying a different decision; column 3 shows the difference in costs directly attributable to the alternative decision (because of the interrelationship between decisions, these costs will not be the same); and column 4 shows the percentage by which the cost figures for the decision in the optimal solution for that subsystem could increase before another decision would be better. For example, if the costs of precast concrete panels for the structural cross wall system increased by 1.33 percent relative to other costs, some other decision might be better. On the other hand, the costs associated with the choice of no separate system for the plumbing subsystem (that is, of integrating the plumbing with the duct) can increase by 433.33 percent before another decision might be better. This is very useful information: it tells us which cost information needs to be accurate, where cost changes are and are not important in influencing our decisions, and adds more decisions (perhaps those with permissible changes of over 10 percent) to our list of what might be called stable decisions—decisions that can be adopted with confidence.

We want to go still further. One decision that was stable throughout our ten solutions was the façade element, which turned out to be a precast concrete cupboard and balcony. Using the method of postoptimality anal-

Table 7-8. Sensitivity analysis for subsystems drawn from the optimization results.

Subsystem	*Difference in Cost of New Solution over Optimal Solution in $*	*Total Cost Associated with Optimal Alternative in $*	*Permissible Change (%)*
1	40.00	3,018.00	1.33
2	5.00	330.00	1.52
3	60.00	455.00	13.19
4	247.00	0.00	—
5	247.00	0.00	—
6	247.00	0.00	—
7	85.00	2,615.00	3.25
8	247.00	280.00	88.21
9	10.00	330.00	3.03
12	247.00	2,950.00	8.37
13	25.00	775.00	3.23
14	25.00	240.00	10.42
15	25.00	410.00	6.10
18	50.00	1,180.00	4.24
19	130.00	30.00	433.33
20	22.00	100.00	22.00

ysis described in chapter 6 and resetting the cost of this option to infinity to ensure that it is not considered, we rerun the optimization; this time, we find a new "optimal" solution with a total cost of $13,916 and precast concrete sill units instead of the cupboard and balcony (fig. 7-16). (In fact, in this case the alternative was available within the originally generated solution set, and the optimization did not have to be rerun.) The cost of the change is $405, and it brings with it some other decision changes; the structural cross walls, for example, are now steel STS and gyprok (plasterboard) infill rather than the precast concrete panels of the original optimal solution. The most important information here is that the cost of the precast cupboard and balcony decisions can increase by up to 38.4 percent before the alternative design just described becomes economically preferable.

So far, our postoptimality analysis has investigated the effect of chang-

Fig. 7-16. (*facing page*) Computer printout of the results of postoptimality analysis.

RESULTS OF POSTOPTIMALITY ANALYSIS

SOLUTION FOR SUBSYSTEM 10 NOT FOUND IN ORDERED SET OF 200 SOLUTIONS
DO YOU WANT TO SEARCH NON-ORDERED SET OF 1200 SOLUTIONS?
(DEFAULTS TO NO.) - ELSE TYPE "YES" OR "Y"

? Y

SENSITIVITY ANALYSIS
SUBSYSTEM FACADE ELEMENT

SUBSYSTEM	ALTERNATIVE
STRUCT. CROSS-WALLS	STEEL S.T.S. & GYPROK
STRUCT. WALL FINISH	PAINT ONLY
STRUCT. ELECTRICAL	ON-SITE DISTRIBUTION
NON-STRUCT. CR/WALLS	GYPROK 1½ HRS
CROSS-WALL FINISH	PAINT ONLY
CR/WALL ELECTRICAL	ON-SITE DISTRIBUTION
FLOOR	PRECAST CONC. PANELS
FLOOR ELECTRICAL	ON-SITE EXPOSED
ROOM CEILING FINISH	BATTENS GYPROK PAINT
FACADE ELEMENT	P.C. SILL UNIT
GLAZED ELEMENT	WINDOW ONLY ON-SITE
HVAC	CORRIDOR SUPPLY
INTERNAL PARTITIONS	GYPROK
INT. PART. FINISH	PAINT ONLY
INT. PART. ELECT.	ON-SITE DISTRIBUTION
CORRIDOR PARTITION	GYPROK 1½ HRS
CORRIDOR FINISH	PAINT ONLY
DUCT	HOLE & ASB. CEMENT
PLUMBING	TREE & ON-SITE ERECT
HALL & CORRID. CEIL.	SUSPEND GYP & PAINT

TOT. COSTS OF NEW SOLUTION	IN $	=	13916.00
MAT. COSTS	IN $	=	9328.00
LAB. COSTS	IN $	=	3783.00
OVER. COSTS	IN $	=	805.00
DIFFERENCE BETWEEN OPTIMAL SOLUTION	IN $	=	405.00
TOT. COSTS SUBSYSTEM 10	IN $	=	1055.00
PERMISSIBLE CHANGE IN TOT. COSTS ASSOCIATED WITH P.C. CUPB/D & BALC		=	38.4%

ing decisions on the total cost of the design, and the extent to which the cost associated with a decision can change before another decision should take its place. But, we also have another kind of information we can explore. For each element (and for each association between pairs of elements used in combination), we have the separate labor, material, and overhead costs that contribute to the total costs. These are commensurable attributes of our cost criterion, commensurable meaning that they can be added together. What happens if labor costs rise faster than material costs, or vice versa, or if overhead costs (due, perhaps, to increasing interest rates) outstrip them both? Can we extract information from our model on how our decisions should change in response to these circumstances?

One way of dealing with this question is through the application of relativities or weights to the values of the three cost attributes. In finding the optimal solution, equal weighting (unity) was implicitly applied to each attribute; after all, we used cost information that we believed was correct in both absolute and relative terms. We could apply different weights, however—from the extreme of placing a zero weighting on two of the attributes and finding the least labor cost, least material cost, and least overhead cost solutions, to the opposite extreme of an equal weighting scheme, and any other scheme in between. We can change the implicit relativities between these attributes (to see how this influences the choice of optimal solution) by treating the attributes as noncommensurable criteria and using the method of postoptimality analysis by Pareto optimization that we described in chapter 6. (Much more on Pareto optimization can be found in chapters 8 and 9.)

Using a special database manipulation system, we identify fifty-nine Pareto optimal solutions from the already-generated solutions and display them as six graphs (figs. 7-17 through 7-22), where each graph combines two cost measures from the set of four in which we are interested (material cost, labor cost, overhead cost, and total cost). Note that we did not construct and have not executed a multicriteria Pareto optimization model; we have simply identified an approximation to the Pareto set by means of tests of domination on the database of performances we have already generated by single-criterion (total cost) optimization. With unit weighting, solution 1 on these graphs has been projected as the optimal solution; it is therefore at the extreme position on the total cost axis. We see, though, that it by no means offers the least labor cost, least material cost, or least overhead cost solution.

Consider figure 7-17, a graph of material costs against total costs. As

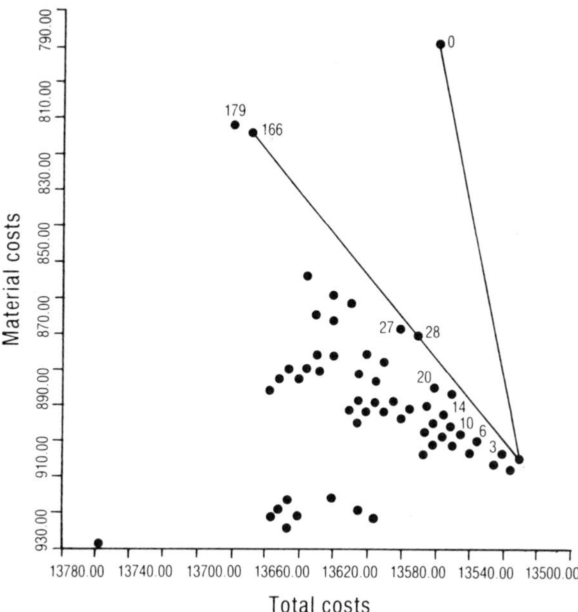

Fig. 7-17. Two-dimensional graphic display of Pareto optimal solutions: total and material costs.

material costs increase relative to other costs, the first solution to replace solution 1 as the optimal solution will be that for which the line segment joining the solution to solution 1 has the greatest slope. We can think of it as an isopreference line, where—if we use total cost alone as the criterion—the isopreference line is vertical; as we place increasing importance on material costs, this line slopes back towards the horizontal (the isopreference line in which material cost alone is used as the criterion). The point that makes this steepest line is solution 0; if we trace back to the decisions underlying it, we find that it uses tunnel-formed structural walls and floor and has relatively high labor and overhead costs. The negative slope from solution 0 to any other point indicates that any further proportional increase in material cost would cause no change in the preferred solution from solution 0.

We can get similar information for labor and overhead cost from figures 7-18 and 7-19, in each case assuming that the relation between the other two costs remains constant. We can quantify the results by looking at the slopes of these lines. Solution 1 ceases to be the optimal solution if material costs increase by 12 percent (when solution 0 takes over), or if labor costs

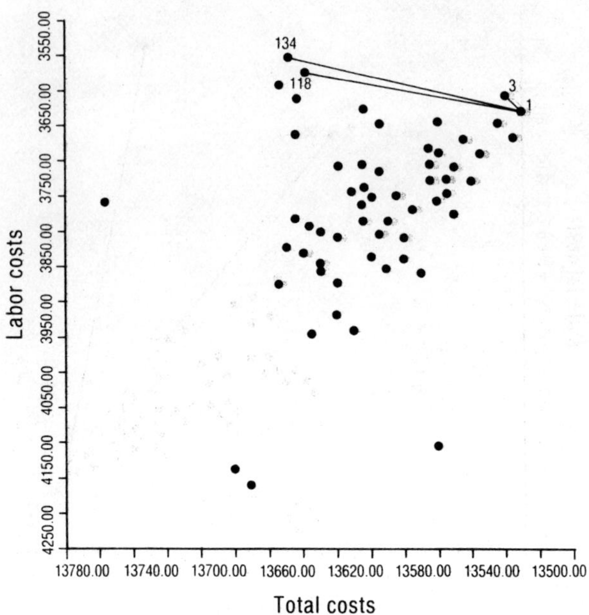

Fig. 7-18. Two-dimensional graphic display of Pareto optimal solutions: total and labor costs.

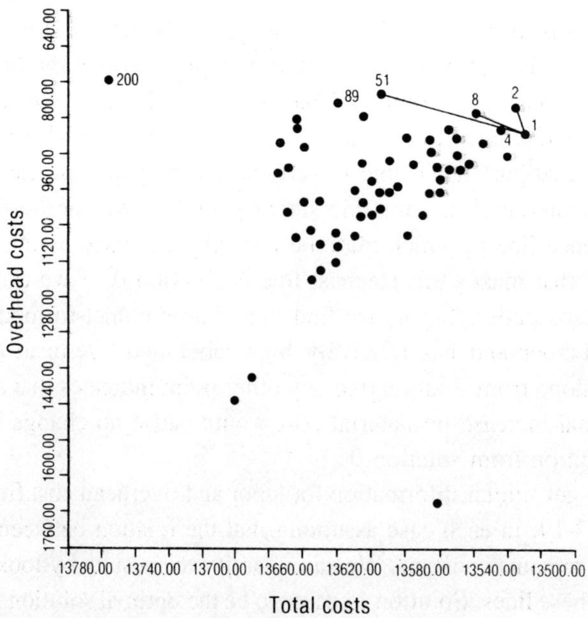

Fig. 7-19. Two-dimensional graphic display of Pareto optimal solutions: total and overhead costs.

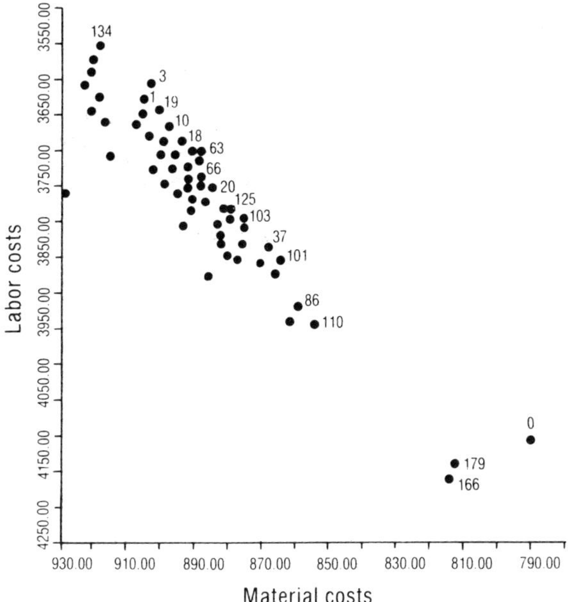

Fig. 7-20. Two-dimensional graphic display of Pareto optimal solutions: material and labor costs.

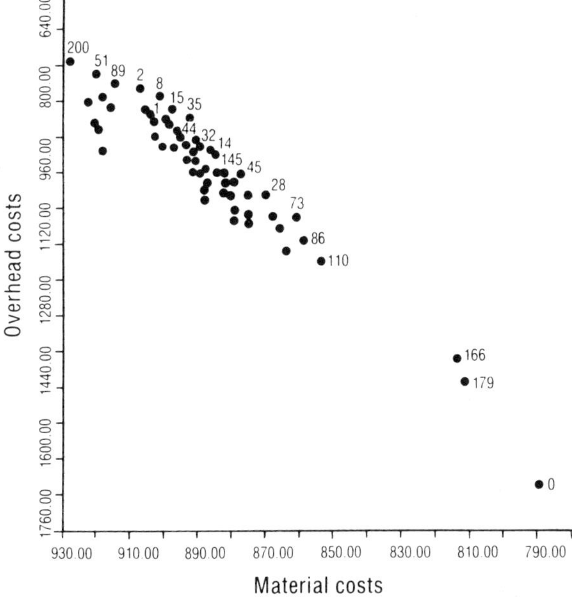

Fig. 7-21. Two-dimensional graphic display of Pareto optimal solutions: material and overhead costs.

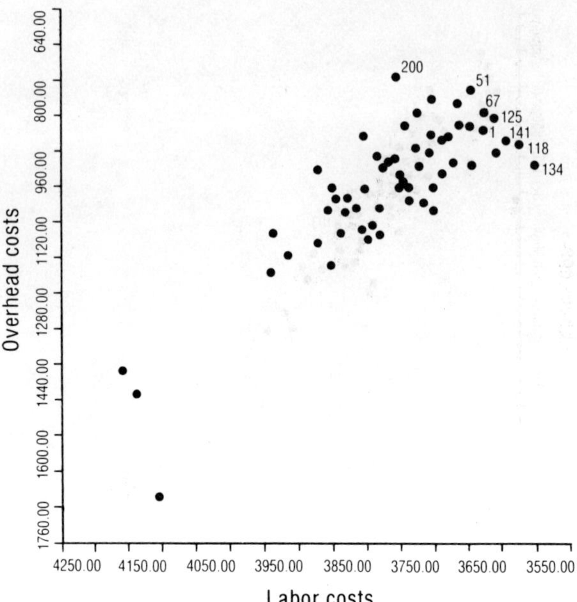

Fig. 7-22. Two-dimensional graphic display of Pareto optimal solutions: labor and overhead costs.

increase by 50 percent (when solution 3 takes over), or if overhead costs increase by 8 percent (when solution 2 takes over).

Figures 7-20, 7-21, and 7-22 illustrate some tradeoffs between the cost attributes of the Pareto set. As more is spent on materials, money can be saved on both labor and overhead (both graphs are, very roughly, linear); conversely, as more is spent on labor, overhead costs also tend to increase.

Discussion

Two points should be made about the formulation of this problem. The first is that, almost alone among the case studies quoted in this book, the optimization model here uses heuristics based on artificial intelligence techniques, and the optimal result is therefore not a guaranteed optimum but an approximation to it. The second is that the results depend on the cost data used, and in this case (with three component cost attributes) around 2,700 separate costs must be gathered and used. The former point should not worry us unduly: comparisons of the heuristic algorithm with guaranteed-optimum algorithms on the same problem show that good approximations are produced; and in our context of architecture and building, where many uncertainties and unforeseen events may exist or arise in the construction process, optimization to the last dollar is hardly meaningful anyway. We are looking for indicative information for designs, not for an exact prediction of minimum cost. On the second point, the number of costs to be gathered sounds daunting, but most of this information is routinely required for cost estimating and tendering anyway, and it is the use of this information at the design synthesis stage (rather than after the design has been finalized) that is unusual.

In the description of this example, we have concentrated on the post-optimality analysis—the information that can be extracted from the optimization model aside from the optimal solution and its performance. Designers in general are not used to having sensitivity and stability information of this kind available to them, and some thought and experience may be needed for designers to be able to exploit it well. Most design for low cost has been done on the basis of qualitative impressions rather than on the basis of quantitative data, and the idea of designing to take into account possible changes in the relative costs of labor, materials, and overhead is probably outside the past experience of most designers.

In the last part of this example, we carried out a postoptimality analysis using concepts of Pareto optimization, with the four commensurable cost attributes of labor, materials, overhead, and total costs expressed separately in an approximation of the Pareto set. This provides us with a good transition to the final part of this book, where we look at design problems that involve multiple noncommensurable objectives. In the example just presented, the approximation to the Pareto set was identified by exhaustive tests of domination among a corpus of near-optimal solutions generated by single-criterion optimization. In the next chapter, we shall describe some multiobjective optimization models that generate more accurate approximations to samples from the Pareto set.

FURTHER READING

The external lighting problem example is based on:

Gero, J. S., and Radford, A. D. 1977. A dynamic programming approach to the optimum lighting problem. *Engineering Optimization* 3(2):71–82.

The floor–ceiling system example is drawn from:

Gero, J. S.; Sheehan, P. J.; and Becker, J. 1978. Feedforward dynamic programming in building design. *Engineering Optimization* 3(4):183–92.

The example in section 7.4 is drawn from:

Rosenman, M. A., and Gero, J.S. 1980. SID—a system for integrated design. In *CAD80,* pp. 691–704. Guildford, England: IPC Press.

Rosenman, M. A. 1981. Computer-Aided Decision Making in the Design of Buildings. Ph.D. thesis, Department of Architectural Science, University of Sydney.

PART 4

MULTICRITERIA OPTIMIZATION IN DESIGN

Buildings and their component systems are rarely designed with a single aim in mind. Usually design problems have a number of quite distinct and disparate objectives, each of which is important to a greater or lesser degree. To encompass them all, the concepts of single-criterion optimization developed in parts 2 and 3 of this book must be extended to provide a framework for the multicriteria case. In this part, we examine two approaches to the solution of design problems that involve more than one objective, and we discuss some of the attendant difficulties of these approaches. Because Pareto (nonpreference) optimization methods make no assumptions about relative importance, they identify a field of equal-ranking solutions. It is left to the decision maker to choose from this field, based on knowledge of the tradeoffs required between performance in different objectives. Preference methods make use of explicit information on the relative importance of different criteria in order to identify a best overall solution.

In chapter 8, we present some techniques for the development and manipulation of design solutions based on both Pareto optimization and preference methods. We argue that the first approach is more realistic and useful for design because it allows subjective criteria to be taken into account. In chapter 9, we present two detailed case studies of design by Pareto optimization that show the power and utility of this approach. We conclude in chapter 10 with an examination of how multicriteria optimization and the derivation of knowledge about design are related to the formulation of design rules that can be used in expert systems.

CHAPTER 8

MULTICRITERIA OPTIMIZATION

In chapter 1, we discussed design as a decision-making process and in particular we noted the nature of design as a goal-directed activity in which the designer typically deals with several (often conflicting) objectives. We described decision and performance spaces and the nature of optimal and Pareto optimal performances and solutions. In the ensuing chapters, we concentrated on the use of optimization techniques in the production of design information in relation to just one of these objectives at a time. Now we want to return to those original ideas and look at techniques for examining multiobjective problems as wholes, rather than abstracting single-objective components from them and solving the components independently of each other.

The two general approaches we can take to building optimization models of multiobjective problems come under the headings of *nonpreference* and *preference methods*. With the nonpreference approach, we limit the model to the production of design information on nondominated (Pareto) performances and on the solutions that have those performances. A nondominated (Pareto optimal) solution is one for which no other solution exists that is capable of providing a better performance in one criterion and no worse performance in all other criteria. In other words if a solution is nondominated no alternative solution can dominate it. Given criteria that completely express the goals of a design problem, and a complete Pareto set of solutions for those criteria, the best solution must lie within the Pareto set. Which member of the set *is* best, though, depends on the designer's preferences as expressed in tradeoffs of performances in conflicting criteria. A designer's chosen solution from the Pareto set is often called a *best compromise solution,* to emphasize the fact that it is almost always a compromise between some decisions that would make for the best performance in one group of criteria and other decisions that would suit other criteria. Nonpreference optimization models, then, emphasize the need to present *information* about the multiple-objective problem, in a manner that allows the range of choice and the tradeoffs among objectives to be well understood by the designer charged with making this compromise decision.

In the preference approach, we place an expression of the designer's tradeoff preferences within the optimization model. Any available information or rationalization about the decision maker's preferences between objectives is used to narrow down the set of feasible solutions to be considered and, if possible, to identify directly a unique best solution. Rather than enumerating the whole field of nondominated solutions, the method searches for the subset or point that is of primary interest. Preference optimization models, then, emphasize the need to arrive at a *decision* on the chosen solution.

In this chapter, we describe both nonpreference and preference optimization models, and then we describe some interactive models in which the designer becomes engaged with the design model in the process of finding a best compromise solution. Finally, we compare nonpreference and preference approaches from the standpoint of their use in design.

NONPREFERENCE (PARETO) METHODS

Definition

The general Pareto optimization problem with N design variables, M constraints, and P objectives is

$$\max_{x} \, [Z_1(x), Z_2(x), \ . \ . \ . \ , Z_p(x)] \tag{8.1}$$

subject to

$$g_k(x) \leq G_k \qquad k = 1, 2, \ . \ . \ . \ , M \tag{8.2}$$

where x is an N-component vector consisting of design variables, and $g_k(x)$, $k = 1, 2, \ . \ . \ . \ , M$, represents M constraint functions, and $Z_1(x)$, $Z_2(x)$, . . . , $Z_P(x)$ are P objective functions.

A Pareto optimal solution $\mathbf{x}$ is a feasible solution to the problem, such that no other feasible solution x exists for which $Z_i(x) \geq Z_i(\mathbf{x})$ for some $i = 1, 2, \ . \ . \ . \ , P$ and $Z_j(x) \geq Z_j(\mathbf{x})$ for all $j \neq i$.

Consider the criteria space for a problem with two criteria (fig. 8-1). According to the definition of Pareto optimality, we can easily find that

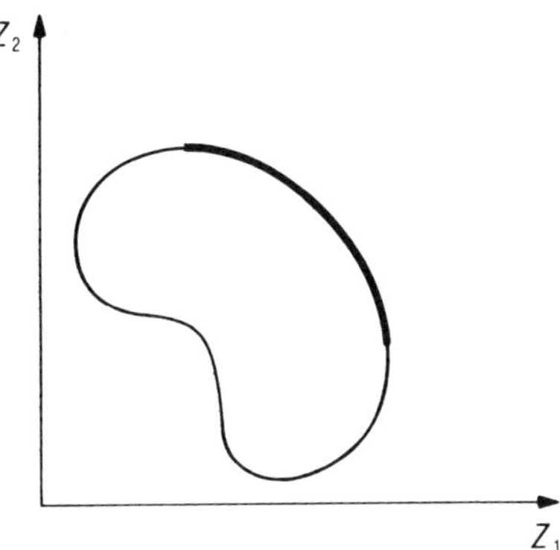

Fig. 8-1. Pareto optimal set for a problem with two objectives, Z_1 and Z_2.

the set of Pareto optimal performances lies along the northeastern boundary of the criteria space. In the general case of the P-criteria problem, the Pareto optimal set will form a surface in P-dimensional space. A graphical presentation of Pareto set for a two-criteria problem, as in figure 8-1, allows easy comparison of alternatives. A similar graphical presentation of higher dimensional problems is difficult; we discuss some approaches later in this chapter in the section on interactive methods.

Four approaches to generating Pareto sets can be identified. The first, the *constraint method,* is the most direct and intuitively appealing technique; but its usefulness suffers from the difficulty a designer encounters in formulating design problems so as to be able to use it. The second, the *weighting method,* is perhaps the oldest Pareto optimization technique; it is easy to apply but often gives a poor description of the Pareto set. The third, the *noninferior set estimation method,* is an extension from the weighting method; it allows better control over the results and is equally applicable. The fourth, *Pareto optimal dynamic programming,* gives good results (comparable to or better than the constraint method) but is expensive in terms of both computational effort and information storage; in addition, it requires that the design problem be expressed as a dynamic programming problem formulation.

The Constraint Method

One way of generating the Pareto set in figure 8-1 would be to fix values of Z_1 at intervals and find the optimal value of Z_2 for each value of Z_1. This is the reasoning behind the constraint method. It retains one objective as primary and treats the remaining $P - 1$ objectives as constraints, such that

$$\max_{x} Z_j(x) \tag{8.3}$$

subject to

$$x \in X \tag{8.4}$$

$$Z_i(x) \geq b_i \qquad i = 1, 2, \ldots, i - 1, j + 1, \ldots, P \tag{8.5}$$

where the jth objective was arbitrarily chosen for maximization, and b_i represents the lower bounds on the remaining $P - 1$ objectives (fig. 8-2). This formulation is a single-objective problem, so it can be solved by any applicable optimization technique. The Pareto optimal set is then generated by solving the above single-objective problem, with parametric variation of b_i.

The *constraint method algorithm* for a two-objective problem consists of four steps.

STEP 1. Solve two individual maximization problems to find the optimal solution for each objective alone.
STEP 2. Evaluate the performance of the other objective at each of these optimal solutions.
STEP 3. Convert the multiobjective form of the problem into its corresponding constrained problem,

$$\max_{x} Z_1(x)$$

subject to

$$x \in X$$

$$Z_2(x) \geq b_2$$

STEP 4. Solve the constrained problem for a number of values of b_2, where $b_2 = n_2 + [t/(r + 1)](m_2 - n_2), t = 1, 2, \ldots, r$; such that r = number of values of bound b_2 that will be used in the generation of Pareto solutions, m_2 = the maximum of Z_2, and n_2 = the minimum of Z_2 in the Pareto set.

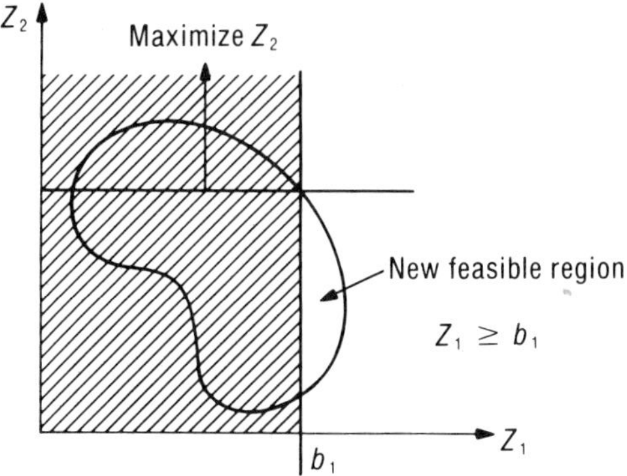

Fig. 8-2. Concept of constraint. A bound, b_1, is specified on Z_1, and Z_2 is maximized to find a Pareto solution.

For more than two objectives, all of the individual maximization problems are solved in step 1; step 2 remains the same, and additional constraints on the other objectives are imposed in step 3. For higher dimensions, the constraint method becomes increasingly less effective as a means of providing a good characterization of the Pareto hypersurface. Each constraint set does not guarantee the feasibility of the resulting solution; thus, for problems of three or more objectives, many iterations may not be useful. A major difficulty with the constraint method is that its formulation requires that the decision variables appear explicitly in the constraints. For many problems this cannot be assured.

The Weighting Method

Consider a line

$$Z_2 = -mZ_1 + R \tag{8.6}$$

superimposed on a solution space where the two criteria are Z_2 and Z_1. From elementary algebra (the equation is of the familiar form $y = mx + c$), we know that $-m$ is the gradient of the line (negative because of its direction), and R is a parameter specifying the point at which the line crosses the axis. When $R = 0$, the line passes through the origin. We can rewrite equation 8.6 as

$$R = mZ_1 + Z_2 \tag{8.7}$$

What happens if we optimize R—that is, push the line as far from the origin as possible, given the feasible values of $Z_1 + Z_2$? Clearly the feasible combination of values of Z_1 and Z_2 that maximizes R lies at a point on the boundary of the feasible region—namely, where $R = mZ_1 + Z_2$ is a tangent to the feasible region. We call this point A in figure 8-3.

But from our earlier definition, A is a Pareto optimal performance combination. Therefore, we have a method of identifying noninferior solutions to a two-criteria problem by optimizing the equation

$$R = mZ_1 + Z_2$$

where m is a factor applied to one of the attributes. The objective is usually written in the form $R = w_1Z_1 + w_2Z_2$, where the w variables are called weights (in our case, $w_2 = 1$). Note that we are interested only in the values of Z_1 and Z_2 resulting from the optimization; the return, R, has no meaning in the original multicriteria optimization problem, and the weight m is only an artifice to find a particular point. If we vary m and repeat the optimization, different points will be found. The resulting points are Pareto optimal, however, only if the gradient of the line is nonnegative—that is, only if the applied weight is nonnegative. Moreover, special conditions exist when one of the objectives is ignored. If the line is horizontal or vertical ($y = R$, or $x = R$), it passes through one Pareto optimal point, but it may also pass through other, inferior points.

Why the weighting method works is easy to understand with two criteria but more difficult with three or more criteria. In general terms, the method

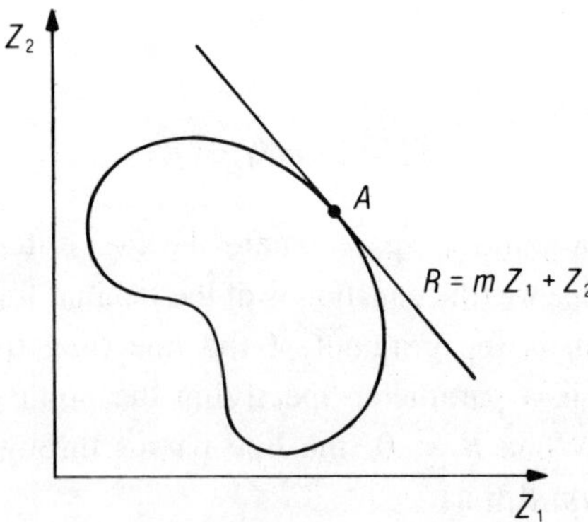

Fig. 8-3. Intersection of a line $R = mZ_1 + Z_2$ with the feasible region, where R is maximized for a given value of m.

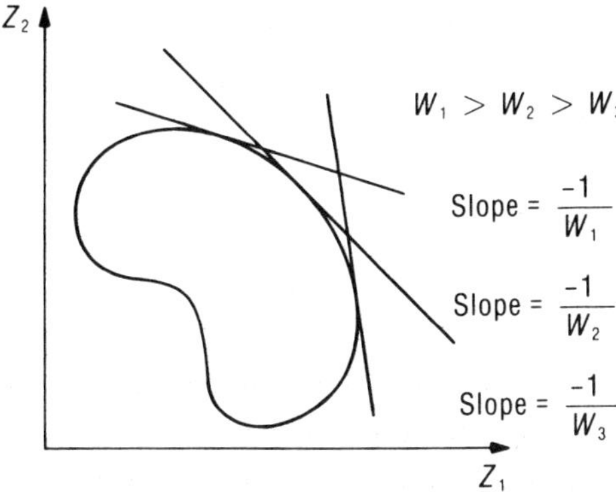

Fig. 8-4. Concept of weighting. The optimal solution to the weighted problem varies as the weight, W_1, varies.

involves solving for Pareto optimal solutions by converting the multicriteria problem to a scalar optimization problem in which the objective function becomes a weighted sum of the objective functions of the multiobjective model. That is,

$$\operatorname*{Max}_{x} \sum_{i=1}^{P} W_i Z_i(x) \tag{8.8}$$

subject to

$$x \in X \tag{8.9}$$
$$x \geq 0$$

where $W_i \geq 0$ for all i, and where it is strictly positive for at least one value of i.

The above problem is a single-criterion optimization problem that can be solved with traditional optimization methods. The optimal solution to the weighted problem is a Pareto optimal solution for the multicriteria problem, as long as all of the weights are nonnegative (fig. 8-4).

The *algorithm for the weighting method* is rather simple and straightforward. A number of different sets of weights are used, until an adequate representation of the Pareto set is obtained. Since the solutions that optimize each objective separately are the endpoints of the Pareto set, it is reasonable to begin by solving the weighted problem P times, with sets of weights as shown below.

Objective Number							
1	2	3	·	·	·	·	P
1	0	0	·	·	·	·	0
0	1	0	·	·	·	·	0
·	·	·	·	·	·	·	·
·	·	·	·	·	·	·	·
0	0	0	·	·	·	·	1

After each objective is optimized individually, a systematic variation of the weights may be imposed. For the special case in which one or more weights are set to zero, if alternative optima exist, some of them may be non-Pareto solutions. In this case, the Pareto optimality of the solutions must be checked. When all of the weights are strictly positive, however, alternative optima for the weighted problem are all Pareto optimal solutions.

One of the two major disadvantages of the weighting method is that it spans the Pareto solution space only under the condition that the criteria space is strictly convex. The method's other (equally important) disadvantage is that a unique set of weights does not guarantee to produce a unique Pareto solution: an infinite set of weights can be used to produce each Pareto optimal solution.

Noninferior Set Estimation Method

The weighting method produces a subset of the Pareto optimal set by manipulation of the weights, but distributing the weights in equal increments over the performance space does not guarantee an equal distribution of Pareto optimal values generated. A better approach is to adopt the Pareto points that are already known and to use weights to investigate the line segments between them. This extension to the weighting method is called the noninferior set estimation (or NISE) method.

As before, we shall begin with the bicriteria case. Suppose two noninferior points *A* and *B* have been found (fig. 8-5). The line segment between them is feasible and may or may not be noninferior. If the line segment is noninferior, moving in a direction outward from the line segment is infeasible. If the line segment is inferior, noninferior points lie in the outward direction. In the NISE method, Pareto points are found by choosing values for the weights so that the next Pareto point is the feasible point farthest out in a direction perpendicular to the line segment connecting two adjacent, previously found points. This method allows us to

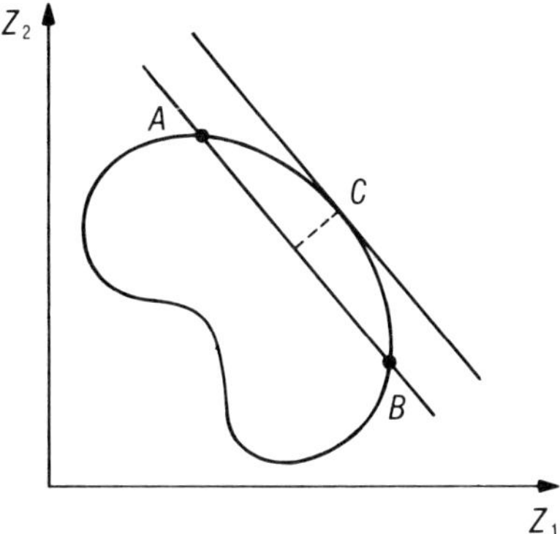

Fig. 8-5. Points on the line segment *AB*—where *A* and *B* are Pareto performances—may or may not be feasible and may be Pareto optimal or inferior, depending on the shape of the feasible region. If they are inferior, the feasible point *C* farthest out in a direction perpendicular to the line segment will be a Pareto point.

control the accuracy of the approximation of the noninferior set by prespecifying a maximum allowable error.

The weights used to generate point *A* in figure 8-6 can be used to compute the slope of a linear indifference curve corresponding to the weighted objective function. This linear indifference curve is shown as line *AC*. Line *BD* represents the linear indifference curve passing through *B* that corresponds to the weights used to generate point *B*.

The lines *AC* and *BD* represent an upper bound to the Pareto optimal set, since no other Pareto solutions can lie above these lines. Thus, if

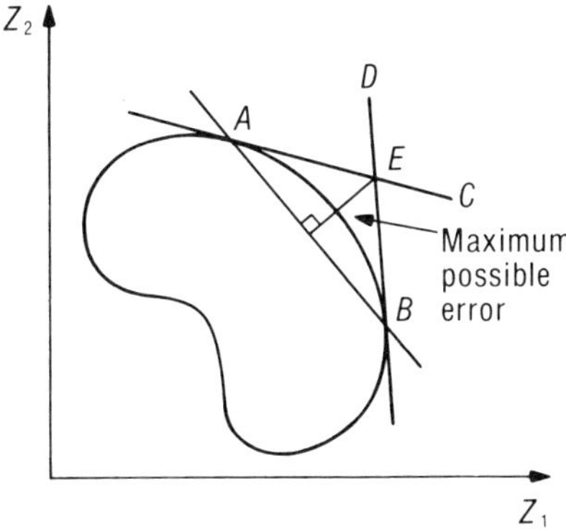

Fig. 8-6. Maximum possible error associated with a given line segment *AB* in the criteria space.

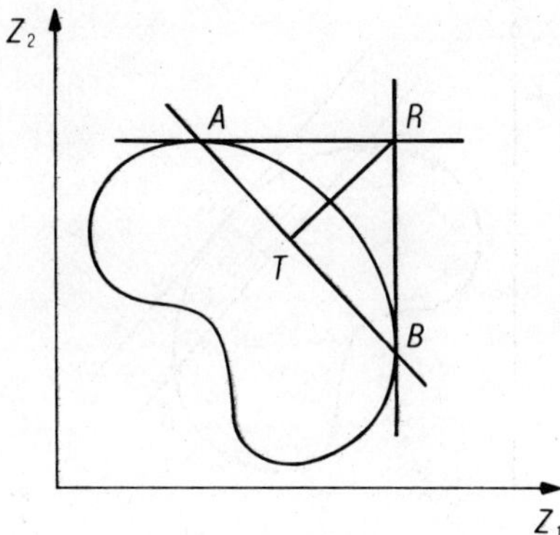

Fig. 8-7. Primary line segment and the maximum possible error associated with it. Points *B* and *A* represent the optimal solutions to Z_1 and Z_2, respectively.

there are Pareto solutions above the line *AB* they should lie within the triangle *AEB*. Therefore, if the line segment *AB* is taken as the approximation of the Pareto optimal set, the maximum possible error is represented by the perpendicular to *AB* drawn from *E*, as shown in figure 8-6. A value for the maximum allowable error must be selected prior to the start of the algorithm. Since the criteria space has axes that are measured in noncommensurable units, the distance in criteria space is not meaningful. Usually, the value of the maximum allowable error is designated as a percentage of the maximum possible error associated with the primary line (fig. 8-7).

In figure 8-7, *A* and *B* are the optimal solutions of the individual objectives, and *RT* is the maximum possible error for line *AB*. The maximum allowable error is set as a percentage of *RT* at the beginning of the algorithm. If the maximum possible error corresponding to an arbitrary line segment (say, *PQ*) exceeds the maximum allowable error, then the slope of the line segment *PQ* is used to compute the weights for use in the weighted problem; that is, the weights W_1 and W_2 are chosen to satisfy

$$-W_1/W_2 = \text{slope of } PQ \tag{8.11}$$

The new solution obtained by solving the weighted problem is then located in the criteria space. If the new solution lies above *PQ*, two new line segments are generated by joining the new solution to *P* and to *Q*, respectively. If the new solution lies on *PQ*, no other solutions lie above the line segment *PQ*.

The above procedure is repeated with each line segment until the maximum possible error in all parts of the Pareto optimal set is less than or equal to the maximum allowable error.

The *NISE algorithm* for the two-criteria problem consists of four steps. Let

S_i = Pareto optimal point having the ith highest value for Z_1 at a stage
MAE = maximum allowable error (preset)
MPE_{jk} = maximum possible error associated with the line segment S_jS_k
N = number of Pareto optimal points generated at a stage

STEP 1. Maximize the objectives individually. Let the image in the criteria space of the optimum for objective Z_1 be P_1, and for objective Z_2 be P_2; that is, $S_1 = P_1$, $S_2 = P_2$, $N = 2$. Compute MPE_{12} and set the value for MAE.
STEP 2. If $MPE_{i,i+1} \leqslant MAE$ for $i = 1, 2, \ldots, (N - 1)$, then stop; otherwise, proceed to step 3.
STEP 3. Find the value of i for the maximum of all $MPE_{i,i+1}$. Solve the weighted problem, using the line segment S_iS_{i+1}. If the new solution lies above the line segment S_iS_{i+1}, designate the new solution as P_{N+1}, and proceed to step 4. Otherwise, set $MPE_{i,i+1}$ to zero, and return to step 2.
STEP 4. Reorder the points P_t, $t = 1, 2, \ldots, (N + 1)$ such that

$$S'_t = S_t \qquad t = 1, 2, \ldots, i$$

$$S'_{t+1} = P_{N+1}$$

$$S'_{t+1} = S_t \qquad t = (i + 1), \ldots, N$$

The error terms are also relabeled:

$$MPE'_{t,t+1} = MPE_{t,t+1} \qquad t = 1, 2, \ldots, (i - 1)(i > 1)$$

$$MPE'_{t+1,t+2} = MPE_{t,t+1} \qquad t = (i + 1), \ldots, N\ (i < N - 2)$$

Compute $MPE_{i,i+1}$ and $MPE_{i+1,i+2}$. Set $N = N + 1$, and return to step 2.

Figure 8-8 shows a sequence of line segments that were generated by means of the NISE method.

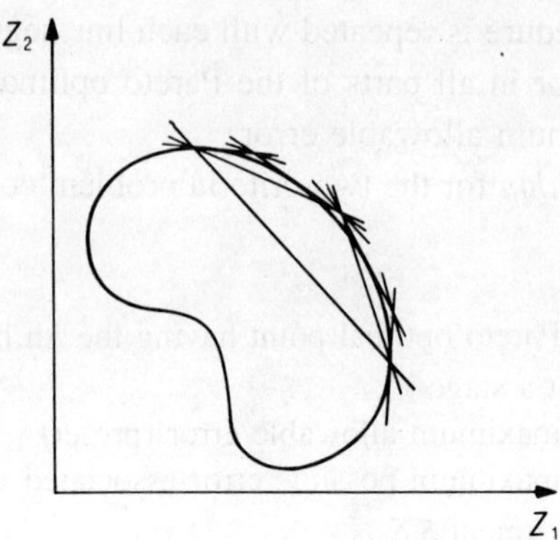

Fig. 8-8. Sequence of line segments generated by means of the NISE method.

Pareto Optimal Dynamic Programming

The method proposed for carrying out Pareto optimization using dynamic programming is similar in concept to conventional dynamic programming. Usually, at each stage n, for each state j of stage n, we carry out an optimization (make a decision, $D_j{}^*$) regarding a state i of stage $n - 1$, based on the optimal return, $F_j{}^*$, for state j. Similarly, for multicriteria problems, instead of carrying out a single-criterion optimization, we can carry out a Pareto optimization for state j of stage n and keep the set of Pareto optimal solutions, P_j, thus obtained and the corresponding set, DP_j, of states i of stage $n - 1$. By inspection, we can see that states i of stage $n - 1$ (which give part solutions that are dominated by part solutions contained in P_j) can never be part of a Pareto optimal policy.

From figure 8-9, we can see that—if the solution with a return of R_{11} dominates the solution with a return of R_{21}—then $(C_{11})_1$ dominates $(C_{21})_1$, and $(C_{11})_2$ dominates $(C_{21})_2$. In that case, any path through state 1 of stage n containing arc (1,1) must always dominate a path containing arc (2,1).

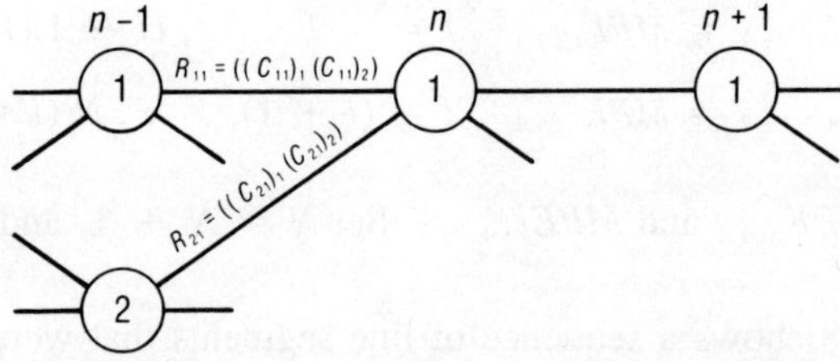

Fig. 8-9. Three-stage process of multiobjective dynamic programming problem.

Let us now compare the computations and storage required for three dynamic programming procedures: single criterion problems; multicriteria problems using the weighting method; and multicriteria problems using Pareto optimization. Tables 8-1 through 8-3 present a typical stage of the dynamic programming process for each of the three procedures.

Note that in the method proposed in table 8-3, no preferences or comparisons are made among the various criteria, nor is any other effort made to aggregate noncommensurate criteria. Each criterion is treated independently of the others. Theoretically, the whole Pareto set may be generated in one pass of the dynamic programming procedure. Practically, the use of this method will depend on the size of the problem and the amount of computer storage available. Since more than one Pareto solution is possible for each state j at every stage, the number of decision variables (states i for stage $n + 1$) may increase rapidly. As the number of criteria increases so does the likelihood of obtaining an increased number of Pareto solutions from a given set of solutions.

Discussion

Among these techniques, the weighting and constraint methods involve fairly straightforward computations. In the weighting method, the weighted problem is set up, and then several Pareto solutions are generated through changes in the objective function coefficients. The constraint method is used to generate Pareto solutions by changing the right-hand sides of the constraints on the objectives.

The NISE method requires more computations than are required for solving the weighted problem. At every step of the algorithm, error terms and new weights must be computed. The NISE method, however, generally calls for fewer solutions than do the weighting and constraint methods, because it exploits the shape of the Pareto set.

All the generating techniques treat the solution procedure as one in which the articulation of preferences is postponed until the range of choice is identified. When an approximation of the Pareto set is sufficient for decision-making purposes, any of these techniques can be implemented. Each technique, however, has its own weaknesses and its own advantages.

The weighting method can give poor coverage of the Pareto set by getting stuck at an extreme point or in a small range of the Pareto set while skipping over large portions of the Pareto set. On the other hand, if the weights themselves are considered important results, some degree

Table 8-1 Single criterion or conventional dynamic programming.

	Stage n − 1					
Stage n	$i = 1$	$i = 2$	. . .	$i = I$	F_j^*	D_j^*
$j = 1$	$R_{11} = C_{11}$	$R_{21} = C_{21}$	⋯	$R_{I1} = C_{I1}$	$F_1^* = R_{21}$	D_1^*
2	$R_{12} = C_{12}$	$R_{22} = C_{22}$	⋯	$R_{I2} = C_{I2}$	$F_2^* = R_{42}$	D_2^*
.	.	.		.	.	.
.	.	.		.	.	.
.	.	.		.	.	.
J	$R_{1J} = C_{1J}$	$R_{2J} = C_{2J}$	⋯	$R_{IJ} = C_{IJ}$	$F_J^* = R_{3J}$	D_J^*

(a) There is a single-valued return C_{ij} for each state j and state i.
(b) A single-criterion optimization is carried out for each state j.
(c) At each stage there are J values of the optimal return, F_j^*, and J values of the optimal decision, D_j—one value for each state j.

Table 8-2. Multicriteria dynamic programming using weighting methods.

	Stage $n-1$			
Stage n	$i = 1$	$i = I$	F_j^*	D_j^*
$j = 1$	$R_{11} = W_1(C_{11})_1 + \ldots + W_k(C_{11})_k \ldots$	$R_{11} = W_1(C_{I1})_1 + \ldots + W_K(C_{I1})_K$	F_1^*	D_1^*
2	$R_{12} = W_1(C_{12})_1 + \ldots + W_k(C_{12})_k \ldots$	$R_{I2} = W(C_{I2}) + \ldots + W_k(C_{I2})_k$	F_2^*	D_2^*
.	.	.	.	.
.	.	.	.	.
.	.	.	.	.
J	$R_{1J} = W_1(C_{1J})_1 + \ldots + W_k(C_{1J})_k \ldots$	$R_{IJ} = W_1(C_{IJ})_1 + \ldots + W_k(C_{IJ})_k$	F_J^*	D_J^*

(a) There is a single aggregated return $R_{ij} = \sum_{k=1}^{K} (C_{ij}))_k$ for each state j; and state i.

(b) A single-criterion optimization is carried out for each state j based on the aggregated return R_{ij}.

(c) At each stage there are J values of F_j^* and D_j^* one each for each state j.

Table 8-3. Multicriteria dynamic programming using Pareto optimization.

	Stage n − 1				
Stage n	*i = 1*		*i = I*	P_j	D_j
$j = 1$	$R_{11} = [(C_{11})_1, \ldots, (C_{11})_k]$	$\cdots$	$R_{I1} = [(C_{I1})_1, \ldots, (C_{I1})_k]$	$P_1 = (\ldots)$	$D_1 = (\ldots)$
2	$R_{11} = [(C_{11})_1, \ldots, (C_{11})_k]$	$\cdots$	$R_{I1} = [(C_{I1})_1, \ldots, (C_{I1})_k]$	$P_1 = (\ldots)$	$D_2 = (\ldots)$
.	.		.	.	.
.	.		.	.	.
.	.		.	.	.
J	$R_{1J} = [(C_{1j})_1, \ldots, (C_{1J})_k]$	$\cdots$	$R_{IJ} = [(C_{IJ})_1, \ldots, (C_{IK})_k]$	$P_J = (\ldots)$	$D_J = (\ldots)$

(a) For each state j and state i there is a multicriteria functional return.

(b) Pareto optimization is carried out for each state j.

(c) At each stage there are J sets of Pareto optimal solutions, P_j, and J corresponding sets of decisions, d_j, for each state j. Each set of Pareto solutions has mj members where $1 \leq mj \leq I$.

of control over their values is a significant attribute of the solution method. For instance, it may be worthwhile to communicate to decision makers that this solution implies that objective Z_1 has twice the weight of objective Z_2. In such situations, the weighting method is advantageous because the weights can be completely controlled. The major disadvantages of the weighting method are that it spans the Pareto solution space only under the condition that the Pareto set is strictly convex, and that it does not guarantee to produce any new solutions for any particular set of weights. Without an a priori knowledge of the applicable weights, the user can find this method to be very expensive computationally.

The NISE method is a powerful approach for generating a good approximation of the convex portion of the Pareto set in a manner that allows the accuracy of the approximation to be controlled. More important, every Pareto solution that this method identifies is chosen so as to reduce the error in the approximation as much as possible. The NISE method guarantees to identify the exact shape of the convex portions of the Pareto set. Like the weighting method, however, the NISE method is incapable of generating information on nonconvex portions of the Pareto set. The strength of the NISE method is most dramatic when the Pareto optimal set has sharp "elbows" in it.

The constraint method always generates the shape of the whole Pareto set; by contrast, the weighting and NISE methods span only the set's convex portion. Furthermore, the constraint method provides complete control of the spacing and coverage of the Pareto set. Its major weakness is the rather frequent occurrence of infeasible formulations for higher-dimensional problems. Furthermore, there may be difficulties in finding a formulation if the design variables do not appear explicitly in the objectives.

The relative merits of the constraint method, the weighting method, and the NISE method to solve a floor-dimensioning problem involving two objectives (maximizing area and minimizing cost) have been investigated. The problem was initially solved by using nonlinear programming. The results from the weighting method (fig. 8-10(a)) show that only five Pareto performances were actually generated from seventeen different sets of weights, with a large gap between two groups of performances. Controlling the weights through the NISE method increased the number of performances generated to seventeen different performances from the seventeen sets of weights (fig. 8-10(b)), but it did not extend the spread of the performances over the span of the Pareto set. It is unclear whether

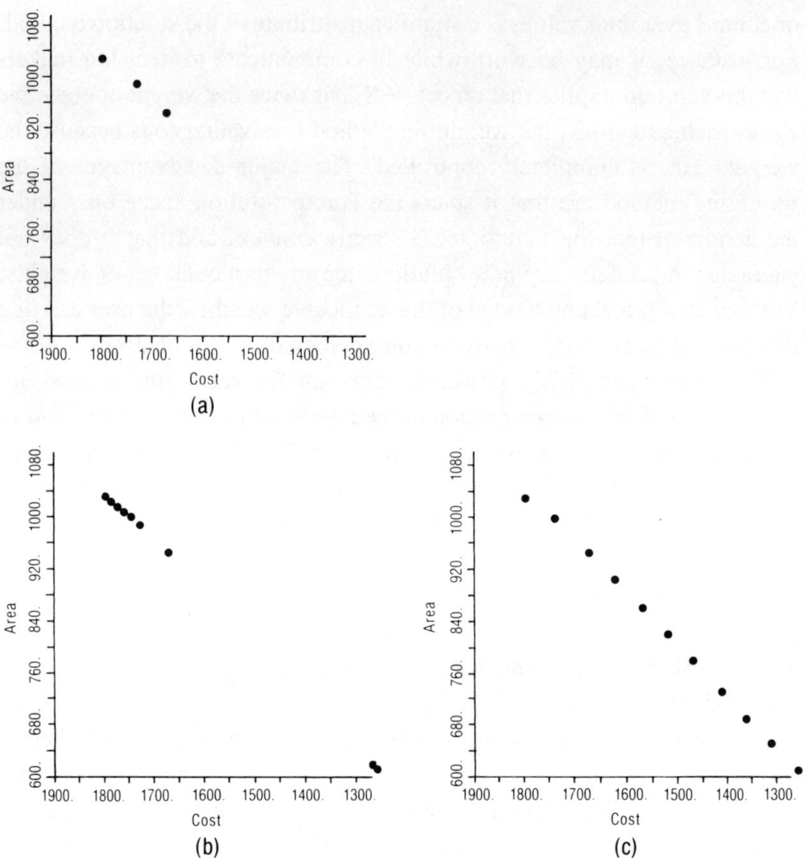

Fig. 8-10. Pareto optimal performances for criteria of maximum area and minimum cost for a floor-dimensioning problem, where the Pareto set is generated by (a) weights, (b) the NISE method, and (c) the constraint method.

the gap between the two groups is because of a concavity in the Pareto curve (weight-based methods will not generate performances in a concave sector) or because there simply are no performances in that region. The answer is provided by the constraint method; eleven iterations produced eleven evenly spaced performances, giving a very good indication of the shape of the Pareto set (fig. 8-10(c)). The problem with generalizing about the methods from this example is that, although weighting-based methods can always be used, constraint-based methods are only usable with particular problem types.

Pareto optimal dynamic programming is the most general method, provided the problem can be formulated as a dynamic program; however, it is expensive in terms of both computation and storage. The payoff is that it is capable of generating the entire Pareto set or any approximation of it that is desired.

PREFERENCE METHODS

We have seen that several different approaches are available to identify the Pareto set, all of which end in approximations to the same curve or surface—so that the information provided to the decision maker is the same, whatever the technique used for getting there. Several approaches to preference methods are also available, but these rely on different definitions of what is meant by *best* in a multicriteria context. The resulting solution presented to the decision maker is different for different techniques.

The Additive Composition Model

By far the simplest and most common of the rules that have been developed for integrating different criteria is the additive composition model. This reduces the multicriteria problem to a single-criterion problem by asserting that the performance of a multicriteria solution can be assumed to equal the sum of its weighted performances in the separate criteria. In mathematical form,

$$R = \sum_{i=1}^{P} W_i Z_i(X) \tag{8.12}$$

where R is the overall performance of the solution, and W_i is a weight attached to the performance $Z_i(X)$ in each of P criteria. The P-dimensional criteria space is thereby reduced to a single-criterion vector.

The use of weights is equivalent to the construction of linear indifference curves with the slope of the curve equal to the negative of the weights. The best solution is therefore the point at which the indifference curve is tangential to the feasible region; and the solution is given by

$$\underset{X}{\text{opt}}\ R = \sum_{i=1}^{P} W_i Z_i(X) \tag{8.13}$$

Indeed, this is exactly the formulation used in the weighting method for generating Pareto sets, except that there the weights and optimal returns were merely artifices used in the procedure. In the additive composition model, the weights are themselves meaningful because they state the preferences between objectives. In doing so, they imply some strong behavioral assumptions. The linearity of the indifference curve means that the marginal utility (which is a constant equal to the ratio of the weights) does not decrease with the level of an objective; the user's willingness to trade off one objective for another is independent of the level achieved.

The approach is attractive because of its simplicity and wide applicability, but the underlying assumptions must be borne in mind. For some purposes, the method can be rationalized by interpreting all the components in terms of a common measure of utility. In architecture, both energy and cost have been used as common factors. For example, energy has been used as a common factor to integrate lighting and thermal environmental components of building design in an optimization model. The qualitative aspects of natural or artificial lighting are ignored, and energy consumption serves as the measure of a lighting policy. The same approach has been adopted in producing a series of graphs to demonstrate the influence of daylighting and of surface-to-volume ratio in the energy performance of buildings. If the annual energy consumption in heating, cooling, and lighting is added for each solution (without weights, since the performance of each component is measured in the same units) a policy for minimum energy use can be identified.

In some ways, energy is a good measure of utility because it is neither time- nor market-dependent, but not all aspects of the environment have a bearing on energy consumption. Neither is it entirely valid to use an unweighted additive model in finding an optimum, since the real utility or value of the energy form used by, for example, lighting (electricity) may be greater than that used by heating or cooling (coal, oil, or gas). The other measure of utility commonly used—monetary cost—can take these differences into account and also allow for capital costs. The cost-in-use approach consists of setting the environmental performance required from the building at a constrained level and finding the minimum cost policy, measured as capital cost plus amortized running costs.

Decision by Exclusion

A development from the additive composition model has been the decision by exclusion rule. This operates on the *convex hull* formed by connecting extreme points in the criteria space that are assumed to dominate interior points. This is a much more restrictive assumption of dominance than in

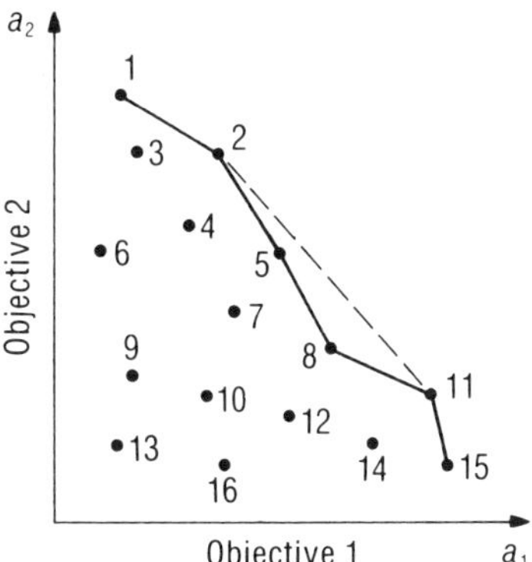

Fig. 8-11. The convex hull 1-2-11-15 for a two-criteria performance space may differ from the Pareto set 1-2-5-8-11-15.

Pareto optimality. As a result, the convex hull will contain fewer solutions than the Pareto set unless they are equal—that is, unless the Pareto set is itself a convex hull in the criteria space.

Thus, in figure 8-11, the Pareto set consists of solutions

1, 2, 5, 8, 11, 15

whereas the convex hull is formed of only solutions

1, 2, 11, 15

Earlier in this chapter, we saw that Pareto solutions forming part of the convex hull can be identified using the additive weighting method. This leads to the assumption of implicit additivity behind the decision by exclusion rule: it is assumed that the decision will be influenced by the contribution of all the attributes as if these were additive, although weights are never specified and addition of the component attributes is not explicitly performed. Thus, an alternative is said to be dominated by the others if the sum of its weighted attributes is less than the sum of at least one of the others alternatives for every possible set of nonnegative weights.

The convex hull 1–2–11–15, can be identified using the weighting system w_1, w_2, where w_1 and w_2 can take any values. A preference between criterion 1 and criterion 2 can be expressed as a constraint on these weights. Thus, the statement that objective 1 is more important than objective 2 could be expressed by the inequality

$$w_1 > w_2$$

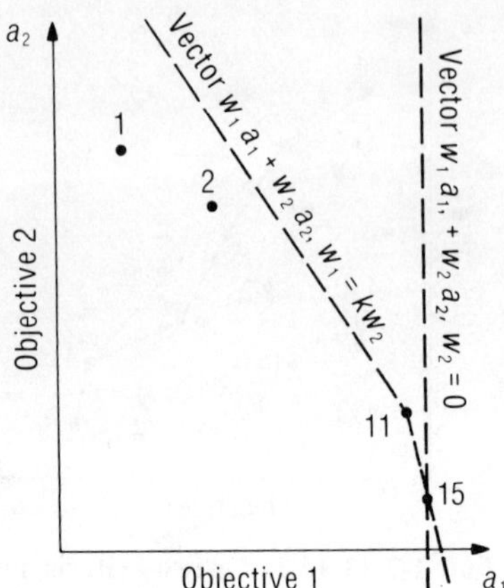

Fig. 8-12. Shape of the hull is modified by the limiting gradient of the vector $w_1a_1 + w_2a_2$. As preference for objective 1 increases, performances 1 and 2 (and then performance 11) are progressively eliminated.

If we identify the set of values on the convex hull by using weights subject to this constraint, we find the shape of the hull is modified by the limiting gradient of the vector $w_1a_1 + w_2a_2$ (fig. 8-12), where a_1 and a_2 are performances in objectives 1 and 2 respectively. As the preference for objective 1 increases—that is, where $w_1 \geq kw_2$, $k \geq 1$—the direction of this vector approaches a line parallel to the a_2 axis. For the case of $k = 2$—that is, where objective 1 is at least twice as important as objective 2—only alternatives 11 and 15 remain on the convex hull. In the limit, as k becomes infinitely large (only objective 1 matters) and the vector becomes parallel to the a_2 axis, only alternative 15 remains for consideration.

These concepts can be extended to the general case of n objectives and a criteria space in n-dimensional space. The design can then express either simple priorities (between any two objectives) or partially ordered sets of priorities. Simple priorities link one or more pairs of objectives:

$$w_1 \geq w_2$$

$$w_1 \geq w_4 \quad .$$

These priorities identify objective 1 as at least as important as objectives 2 and 4. Partially ordered sets provide a ranking of priorities among some or all of the objectives; for example,

$$w_1 \geq w_2 \geq w_3 \geq w_4$$

or (providing more information),

$$w_1 \geq 2w_2 \geq w_3 \geq 3w_4$$

These priorities identify objective 1 as at least twice as important as objective 2, which is at least as important as objective 3, which is at least three times as important as objective 4.

The following major assumptions underlie the decision by exclusion rule:

1. Performance objectives are independent of each other.
2. The designer can, at best, only rank the priorities among the performance objectives.
3. When the designer is appraising alternatives, an alternative's component performances contribute additively (although implicitly) to its overall worth.

The third assumption named above causes more alternatives to be eliminated as inferior to others than is the case where pure dominance (as in deriving the Pareto set) obtains. It allows priorities to be attached to the performance objectives and progressively refined so that a small set of "best" or "at least as good as" solutions is identified, from which the designer can make a final solution.

Geometric Descriptions

In figure 8-7, in relation to our discussion of the NISE method for generating Pareto optimal performances, we showed a primary line segment across the feasible performance space. One end of the line is marked by the performance that optimizes Z_1, and the other by the performance that optimizes Z_2; these two performances represent the solutions that optimize the single objectives of minimum weight and of minimum depth, respectively. The notion of an unobtainable ideal solution that would simultaneously optimize each objective individually is represented by point R in figure 8-13. Generally, it lies outside the feasible region (otherwise there would be no conflict among criteria). The best compromise solution is therefore defined as the point in the feasible region which is the minimum distance from the ideal solution.

Let Z_1^*, Z_2^* be the performances of the ideal solution, and let $Z_1(X)$,

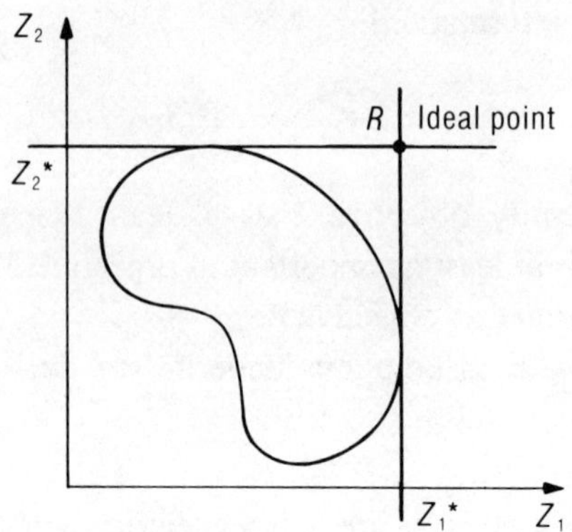

Fig. 8-13. Ideal point for a two-objective problem.

$Z_2(X)$ be the performances of a feasible solution. The best compromise solution is that which minimizes d,

$$\min d = \sqrt{([Z_1^* - Z_1(X)]^2 + [Z_2^* - Z_2(X)]^2)}$$

where Z_1^* and Z_2^* are constants. Clearly this equation can be used directly as an objective function, without plotting the Pareto set.

The distance minimized here is a distance in euclidean space; for convenience, we have chosen an example with two criteria and therefore a two-dimensional expression. If we generalize both the number of criteria and the space system, we find that the distance between two points with coordinates $(Z_1^*, Z_2^*, \ldots, Z_p^*)$ and $(Z_1(X), Z_2(X), \ldots, Z_p(X))$ is:

$$d_\alpha = \left(\sum_{i=1}^{P} | Z_i^* - Z_i(X)|^\alpha\right)^{1/\alpha} \tag{8.14}$$

This definition of distance corresponds to euclidean space when $\alpha = 2$. We are not restricted to euclidean space, however, and α can take any value from 1 to $+\infty$. The resulting different definitions of distance are known as *distance metrics* or *Minkowski distances*.

If we choose $\alpha = 1$, equation 8.14 becomes

$$d_1 = \sum_{i=1}^{P} |Z_i^* - Z_i(X)| \tag{8.15}$$

which states simply that the absolute differences on a component-by-component basis should be summed. If we choose values of $\alpha > 2$, we find that more weight is attributed to large component differences through raising them to an exponent. The effect of letting α increase to infinity is to place an infinite weight on the largest component difference, so that the others are ignored.

Returning to our example in figure 8-12, let us examine the effect of changing the distance metric. If we let $\alpha = 1$, equation 8.14 becomes

$$\min d = [Z_1{}^* - Z_1(X)] + [Z_2{}^* - Z_2(X)] \tag{8.16}$$

which, since $Z_1{}^*$ and $Z_2{}^*$ are constants, reduces to

$$\min d = -[Z_1(X) + Z_2(X)]$$

or

$$\max d = [Z_1(X) + Z_2(X)] \tag{8.17}$$

which, in turn, is simply maximizing the unweighted sum of the objectives.

Let α approach ∞. We have seen above that, when $\alpha = \infty$, only the largest deviation is significant; so equation 8.14 becomes

$$\min d = \max \{[Z_1{}^* - Z_1(X)], [Z_2{}^* - Z_2(X)]\} \tag{8.18}$$

Clearly the choice of distance metric will determine the best compromise solution that emerges. But it has been shown that, in general, these best-compromise solutions defined by different distance metrics form a subset of the Pareto set, ranging from the minimum distance solution found when $\alpha = 1$ to the minimum distance solution found when $\alpha = \infty$. All other best-compromise solutions found by $1 < \alpha < \infty$ will fall between these limits. Hence, we can map these different best-compromise solutions as a compromise set, and we can present them as a potentially useful subset of the Pareto set.

The major assumption underlying the minimum distance rule is that a good tradeoff between objectives is obtained when the solution is in some minimum geometrical relationship with an ideal solution that is itself deterministically selected. The subjective specification of preferences is avoided, but the validity of this fundamental assumption is itself a value judgment.

Goal Programming

The performance of the ideal solution used in the geometric description above was determined by the mechanistic application of a series of single-

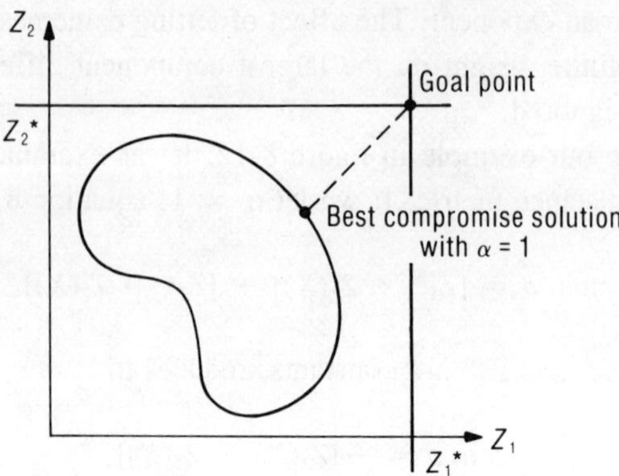

Fig. 8-14. Goal point and best compromise point for a two-objective problem where the distance metric α = 1.

criterion optimizations and the subsequent combining of the values achieved in the respective criteria. In goal programming, the ideal solution is specified directly by the decision maker, in terms of target values for each of the objectives (fig. 8-14). The best compromise solution is the solution in the feasible region that is located at the minimum distance from the ideal solution—usually (but not necessarily) determined by using the distance metric $\alpha = 1$.

For P criteria, the objective function for goal programming is to minimize

$$\sum_{i=1}^{P} (d_i^- + d_i^+) \tag{8.19}$$

subject to

$$Z_1^* - Z_i(X) = d_i^- - d_i^+), \; i = 1, \ldots, p$$
$$d_i^-, d_i^+ \geq 0, \qquad i = 1, \ldots, p$$

where d_i^-, d_i^+ are, respectively, the negative and positive deviations of the actual value of the performance in $Z_i(X)$ in the ith criterion from the goal performance Z_i^*. The formulation allows for modification of the basic idea to take care of some particular requirements. In particular, we can place weights on the deviations to express the relative importance of deviations from different goals, so that the objective function in equation 8.19 becomes to minimize

$$\sum_{i=1}^{P} w_i(d_i^- + d_i^+)$$

or even to minimize

$$\sum_{i=1}^{P} (w_i d_i^- + w_i^+ d_i^+) \tag{8.20}$$

Goal programming relies on the designer's being able to articulate a set of goals for the relevant objectives. Since these goals are specified without knowledge of the feasible region, it is always possible that the "ideal" solution thus specified lies within the region—that it is itself inferior to what might be obtained, given a better realization of the possibilities. If the ideal solution is attained in goal programming (a result that is indicated if the deviations are zero), the designer should suspect that the solution is inferior and that a better solution can be achieved if more demanding goals are specified.

Discussion

In this section we have described four approaches to multicriteria optimization in which the designer defines preferences among objectives beforehand and incorporates information about these preferences within the optimization model. In *geometric methods,* this expression is by default, since the preferences come from the optimal performances in each individual criterion—the combination of which is taken to be the designer's goal. In *goal programming,* the preferences are expressed as an ideal combination of performances. In the *additive composition model,* they are expressed as weights that identify the relative importance of the criteria. All of these methods are quite easy to implement. In the *decision by exclusion* approach, the preferences are expressed as an ordering of criteria that is less specific than the use of weights but still implicitly assumes the additivity of performances in different criteria. None of these methods has any real basis either in modeling how human designers make such tradeoff decisions or in extending an accepted theoretical argument as to how they ought to be made, and none can be regarded as a best approach.

INTERACTIVE METHODS

Rather than requiring all the preference information to be expressed in advance (as in the preference methods we have just described) or presenting the designer with a Pareto set and leaving him or her to choose from among this set unaided (as in the nonpreference methods we described earlier) we can combine the processing characteristics of the optimization model with the judgmental abilities of the human designer to produce a "best compromise" solution through interaction between the two. Of the interactive methods that have been developed for this purpose, we can identify two main classes: *interactive search* methods, which are concerned with searching for a best compromise solution without first identifying the whole Pareto set; and *interactive choice* methods, which are concerned with choosing a best compromise solution after first generating the Pareto set. Interactive methods could be classified as a subclass of preference methods, because they involve the explicit or implicit statement of preferences, but they work rather differently from the preference techniques we have described so far.

Interactive Search (The Surrogate Worth Tradeoff Method)

In an interactive search, the decision maker modifies his or her statement of preferences to take information provided by the analysis into account, and thereby to narrow the investigation down toward a preferred solution. A good example is the *surrogate worth tradeoff* method, in which the decision maker expresses tradeoff information at specific values to form a small subset of the Pareto set, rather than expressing it globally and equally for all values (as in the additive composition model). This is done by specifying the amount of one objective that the designer is prepared to forfeit in return for increasing another objective at the named points in the performance space; the tradeoff information can be different for each of these points. This information is then used by the model to construct a utility function that is compatible with the given tradeoff information. In turn, the utility function can be used to identify a best compromise solution. Thus, we have a neat and conceptually simple technique that generates just enough of the Pareto set to make the articulation of informed tradeoff preferences possible and then gets on with the problem of making decisions. The designer must, however, work with less information than would be available with the full Pareto set, and the justification for a choice is less clear. If feasible, a better approach is to generate the whole Pareto set, and then select a best compromise solution after assessing all of the options.

Interactive Choice (Inverse Goal Programming)

Pareto optimization eliminates clearly nonoptimal values, but with a large Pareto set—and particularly with three or more objectives, when the display of the Pareto set in meaningful ways to the decision maker becomes increasingly difficult—it may still leave a confusing range of tradeoff options open to the designer. *Inverse goal programming* is an approach to the structuring and exploration of the information contained in the Pareto set that helps a designer choose a best compromise solution.

The name comes from the relationship of the method to goal programming. We have seen previously that goal programming is a heuristic optimization method in which a search algorithm is used to identify the feasible solution whose set of performances is closest to a specified goal. It is a preference method, since the goal is some combination of values for all the criteria that are to be satisfied simultaneously, and since its specification implicitly quantifies preferences among the criteria. Thus, in goal programming, the goal is known even though the performance set and its boundaries are unknown. Indeed, the specified goal may lie inside or outside the boundaries of the performance set, and so may either be better or worse than any feasible performance combination.

The choice of the best compromise solution from among the options in the Pareto optimal set is conceptually the inverse of typical goal programming. Instead of knowing everything about the designer's goal and seeking information about feasible optimal performances and decisions in relation to that goal, we know everything about the feasible optimal performances and decisions and are seeking a goal. It can be tackled conceptually by inverting the goal programming approach so that the feasible optimal performances and decisions are progressively constrained until a best compromise solution is found—which is the goal. Inverse goal programming is a heuristic approach to choosing a best compromise solution from a Pareto optimal set by operating on a constraint set for criteria and for decision spaces.

Let

$$
\begin{aligned}
c_i \in C &= \text{the set of performance values for all feasible solutions} \\
c_i^P \in C &= \text{the subset of } c_i \text{ that lies in the Pareto optimal set} \\
d_j \in D &= \text{the set of decision values for all feasible solutions} \\
d_j^P \in D &= \text{the subset of } d_j \text{ that produces the Pareto optimal set}
\end{aligned}
$$

where C is the set of possible performances, and D is the set of possible decisions.

We can apply the following three classes of constraint operations to the performance and decision sets:

1. $c_i \geq l_i$, where l_i is a lower bound on performances. In this case, we would then check whether $\{d_j^P \mid c_i^P \geq l_i\} \in \emptyset$. If the set, $\{d_j^P \in \emptyset$, we would then release l_i. If the set $\{d_j^P\}$ is large, we would then apply further constraints.
2. $u_j \geq d_j > l_j$, where u_j is an upper bound and l_j is a lower bound on decisions; or $u_j \geq d_j$; or $d_j \geq l_j$. In this case, we would then check whether $\{d_j^P \mid u_i \geq d_j \geq l_j\} \in \emptyset$. If the set $\{d_j^P\} \in \emptyset$, we would then release u_j or l_j. If the set $\{d_j^P\}$ is large, we would then apply further constraints.
3. Some combination of the preceding two classes.

Desired levels of performance are set independently for each criterion, with no direct articulation of tradeoffs. Instead, the tradeoff decisions are made implicitly by the process of restricting the decision and performance spaces to an acceptable subset.

Discussion

The choice between interactive search and interactive choice methods is a tradeoff between the burden placed on the decision maker and the burden placed on the computer implementation of the optimization model. Articulation of the tradeoffs in numerical form in the surrogate worth tradeoff method is never going to be easy, although there is certainly more basis for doing so with this method than with the additive composition model. On the other hand, only a small subset of the Pareto set needs to be generated by the optimization model before it turns directly to finding the best compromise solution. Other interactive search techniques (for example, iterative techniques where attention moves from one Pareto solution to another in the direction the designer is interested in based on his or her information from early cycles of the procedure) operate in different ways, but the total number of solutions generated remains relatively small. In the interactive choice approach, the whole Pareto set (or at least a representative sample) must first be generated, involving more comprehensive coverage of the performance space and decision choices. On the other hand, the designer's process of asking "what if" questions to narrow down the Pareto set toward a preferred solution is an easier, more natural process to follow and makes the basis upon which a solution is chosen much more explicit.

COMPARISON OF APPROACHES

In this chapter, we have considered two alternative approaches to multicriteria optimization: nonpreference (Pareto) methods, and preference methods. The former is a bottom-up approach that provides a large information base for the designer to use in his or her decision making. The latter is a top-down approach that provides a much smaller information base by attempting to determine in advance the needs of the decision maker. We then discussed two interactive approaches in which the preferences are expressed not before but during execution of the optimization model.

We can compare the implications of choosing any of these approaches in terms of the amount of computation each requires in order to operate, the information each requires in order to work, and the information each provides. We have to accept the computational expensiveness of Pareto optimization—especially on large or complex problems and in situations involving large numbers of objectives (the number of solutions in the Pareto set increases exponentially with the number of objectives). In both the weighting method and the constraint method, each execution of the optimization procedure can generate (at most) only one Pareto value; and there may be no new value at all. Pareto optimal dynamic programming operates directly to determine the Pareto set within a single optimization procedure, but it is only effective if the problem is solvable by dynamic programming in the first place. On the other hand, the only information required for Pareto optimization is that necessary to operate the mathematical models behind the optimization—the same as for a series of single-criterion optimization models. In return for the computational burden, the decision maker receives a great deal of information to explore and use for understanding the implications of the decisions.

Preference methods involve much less computation because they generate only one solution or a small subset of the Pareto set. But this saving in computation is offset by the additional information that must be supplied in advance in specifying the tradeoff information between objectives. Obtaining this information can be time-consuming and expensive. We have looked, for example, at the use of cost–benefit analysis to introduce a common denominator into a multiobjective problem and have seen the difficulty of interpreting subjective values in terms of money. The information provided is a single result (the best compromise) or a small number of "equally good" solutions from which the decision maker can choose; such limited options do not provide the context information on the whole range of feasible solutions that is provided by the Pareto set. The major difference, then, is that nonpreference or Pareto methods place the major burden on computation and allow the designer to make decisions while fully aware of their tradeoff implications, whereas preference methods reduce computation but require the decision maker to articulate preferences in advance without knowledge of their tradeoff implications.

Another important difference between the two types of methods lies in the theoretical basis on which they stand. The theoretical basis of Pareto optimization is pure dominance, established by comparing like with like. The theoretical basis of preference methods requires some assumption about dominance or about the meaning of *best,* which varies from method to method. Thus, the additive composition model assumes that the utility of an alternative can be modeled by the sum of the weighted performances in each of its objectives, while the decision by exclusion rule assumes an implicit additivity model according to which only Pareto values forming part of a convex hull over the feasible region are of interest. Geometric descriptions and goal programming rely on a minimum distance assumption of *best:* that the best choice is the one closest to an ideal determined objectively by the application of a series of single-criterion optimizations or subjectively by the selection of goals. Is this a valid assumption? And even if it is, what basis is there for choosing any particular distance metric as the one for determining distance?

For these reasons, we believe that Pareto methods offer more to the designer than preference methods, despite the computational disadvantages. Still, it is useful to consider briefly how some of the concepts of preference methods can be used to draw additional information out of nonpreference methods.

In the section on nonpreference methods in this chapter, we saw the relationship between the Pareto set and indifference curves; and in the section on preference methods, we saw how disparate objectives can sometimes be interpreted in terms of a common denominator, if only some of their qualities are taken into account. This suggests the presentation of Pareto sets where one criterion is a hyperobjective embodying aspects of other objectives. A criteria space of daylighting, energy use, and sound levels, for example, may be supplemented by a hyperobjective of cost that embodies the financial consequences of the other objectives. This is different from stating categorically that the best solution is the least-cost solution, since it recognizes that certain qualities of daylighting cannot be measured by the cost of alternative artificial lighting, that certain implications of noise levels cannot be measured by cost benefit analysis, and that energy use may not be adequately interpreted by its cost alone. The tradeoff decision remains one involving all of the objectives, but in this instance we are mapping the available preference information onto a base of nonpreference information, to allow the designer to take both into account.

That leaves us with the interactive methods. We have suggested that they are preference methods—in that they involve the expression of preferences within the model—but they are preference methods well down the track toward nonpreference methods. It seems to us that the more complete the picture of the options in front of the designer becomes, the better. In the surrogate worth tradeoff method, some of this picture is apparent; in the inverse goal programming approach, all of it is apparent. Given that aim, the continuing support of the model right through the decision-making process to the selection of a particular "best compromise" design is entirely laudable.

FURTHER READING

Probably the best book on multicriteria optimization generally is:

Cohon, J.L. 1978. *Multiobjective Programming and Planning*. New York: Academic Press.

The classic text on preference methods is:

Keeney, R.L., and Raiffa, H. 1976. *Decisions with Multiple Objectives: Preferences and Value Tradeoffs*. New York: Wiley.

Excellent books that cover both preference and nonpreference methods are:

Chankong, V., and Haimes, Y.Y. 1983. *Multiobjective Decision Making*. New York: North-Holland.

Hwang, C.L., and Masud, A.S. 1979. *Multiple Objective Decision Making—Methods and Applications*. Berlin: Springer-Verlag.

The place of multicriteria optimization in design is examined in:

Gero, J.S., ed. 1985. *Design Optimization*. New York: Academic Press.

———. 1985. *Optimization in Computer-Aided Design*. Amsterdam: North-Holland.

A good book on goal programming is:

Ignizio, J. 1976. *Goal Programming and Extensions*. Lexington, MA: Heath.

Collections of papers on multicriteria decision making can be found in:

Nijkamp, P., and Spronk, J., eds. 1981. *Multicriteria Analysis in Practice*. London: Gower.

Starr, M.K., and Zeleny, M., eds. 1977. *Multiple-criteria Decision Making*. Amsterdam: North-Holland.

The constraint method and NISE algorithms are drawn from:

Balachandran, M., and Gero, J.S. 1984. A comparison of three methods for generating the Pareto optimal set. *Engineering Optimization* 7(4):319–36.

The method for Pareto optimal dynamic programming is described in:

Rosenman, M.A., and Gero, J.S. 1983. Pareto optimal serial dynamic programming. *Engineering Optimization* 6(4):177–83.

Decision by exclusion is described in:

Mattar, S.; Bitterlich, P.; Manning, P.; and Fazio, P. 1978. A decision model for the design of building enclosures. *Building and Environment* 13:201–16.

Inverse goal programming is further described in:

Radford, A.D., and Gero, J.S. 1985. Multicriteria optimization in architectural design. In *Design Optimization,* ed. J.S. Gero, pp. 229–58. New York: Academic Press.

Additional methodological developments can be found in:

Balachandran, M., and Gero, J.S. 1985. The noninferior set estimation method for three objectives. *Engineering Optimization* 9(2):77–88.

Beckingham, I. 1984. Pareto Optimal Critical Path Method. Master's thesis, Department of Architectural Science, University of Sydney.

Bell, A. 1986. Multicriteria Location Allocation. Master's thesis, Department of Architectural Science, University of Sydney.

Rosenman, M.A., and Gero, J.S. 1985. Reducing Pareto optimal sets. *Engineering Optimization* 8(3):189–206.

CHAPTER 9

PARETO OPTIMIZATION CASE STUDIES

This chapter presents two detailed case studies of the use of multicriteria Pareto optimization in the design of buildings. We have chosen these particular examples because they operate at different scales (first, whole buildings; then, a building element) while maintaining one of the same objectives (thermal comfort). The two most pertinent parts of these case studies are, first, the way in which they are formulated for solution, and second, the kind of information that has been extracted from the results. Both use dynamic programming optimization—one with Pareto optimal dynamic programming, and the other with the additive weighting method for identifying the Pareto set—and both use sophisticated models to predict performance, to generate solutions and partial solutions, and to evaluate these as part of the optimization process. We shall describe the two models in some detail.

This chapter demonstrates the application of some techniques already described to two complex problems. Since it introduces no new ideas or techniques, readers may wish to go straight on to chapter 10.

PROBLEM: DESIGNING BUILDINGS FOR THERMAL LOAD, DAYLIGHTING, COST, AND UTILITY

The first case study is concerned with the implications of designing for energy conservation and thermal performance in relation to three other important aspects of building performance: daylighting, capital cost, and planning efficiency. Its aim is to provide prescriptive quantitative information to assist the designer in selecting the form and construction of parallelopiped open-plan office buildings at early stages of the design process.

The design variables that affect the thermal performance of a building are shape, massing, orientation, window sizes, glass types, shading, surface finishes, material properties, and ventilation and infiltration. These same variables influence building performance in our other criteria of daylighting, capital cost, and planning efficiency. We want to develop a model that will allow us to explore the consequences of decisions relating to these variables at the conceptual stage of design, and hence will enable us to design a building that achieves a good balance between thermal performance and other objectives. In the following sections, we shall describe the models used for performance prediction (the descriptive models), for exploring variations of building form and construction (the generative models), and for seeking "best compromise" solutions (the optimization models). We shall then look at the computer program that implements the models and at some typical results.

The Description (Prediction) Models

The performance prediction models used here reflect the skeletal information available at early stages of design, while being responsive to the options usually available at such stages. For example, for thermal performance it is appropriate to calculate the building's thermal load rather than its energy use, since the latter calculation requires knowledge of the mechanical system's characteristics. In this section we shall describe models for predicting thermal loads, daylighting levels, capital cost, and utility for a building; in doing so, we shall go into rather more detail than we have done for our earlier examples, in order to illustrate the care and detail actually necessary. How we describe the building depends on the design variables for which we need values as a prerequisite to constructing the performance models.

The Thermal Model

Any technique for calculating the thermal load in a building must account for the heat transfer mechanisms of conduction, convection, and radiation. The resulting thermal environment is produced by the interaction of the enclosed space with the following things:

1. The outdoor climate—mainly air temperature and solar radiation
2. The thermo-physical properties of the enclosing structure
3. The energy sources or sinks resulting from internal heat inputs (such as occupancy, lights, and equipment), from ventilation, and from infiltration

Conduction heat transmission occurs from the warmer to the cooler surface of homogeneous elements. Many models are available for describing such heat flow. Here we use an analytic technique which accounts for transient heat flow and the dynamic effect of thermal inertia. Most readers of this book will not find it necessary to follow this model in detail, but we shall describe it since its form has a major effect on the building, generation, and optimization models.

The mean heat flow, Q_c, by conduction heat gain or loss through opaque elements is given by

$$Q_c = A_s U_s (T_o - T_i) \tag{9.1}$$

where

A_s = conduction heat gain/loss, in m^2 (ft^2)
U_s = heat transmission coefficient, in W/m^2K ($Btu/ft^2h°F$)
T_o = mean outside temperature, in °C (°F)
T_i = mean indoor temperature, in °C (°F)

The variation from the mean rate of heat flow, Q_c, at time $t + \phi$ is

$$Q_c = A_s U_s f(T_t - T_o) \tag{9.2}$$

where

f = decrement factor
T_t = outside temperature at time t, in °C (°F)
ϕ = time lag, in hours

Thus the actual rate of heat flow at time $t + \phi$ is

$$Q_{c_\phi} = Q_c + Q_c = A_s U_s [(T_o - T_i) + f(T_t - T_o)] \tag{9.3}$$

Convection heat transmission losses occur through the movement of air currents whenever an air space and a temperature difference are present. These occur in buildings through the following processes:

1. Air movement across air spaces within walls and between layers of glass
2. Air movement along building surfaces
3. Air infiltration through openings in buildings, including cracks around doors and windows, or as a result of forced ventilation

Even though air-film surface coefficients are known to vary over time, they are usually taken to be set values. Thus, air spaces in construction and air-film resistances on surfaces are usually combined with the heat transmission coefficient of the building element and expressed as an overall heat transmission coefficient, U_s; this combined value was used in equations 9.1, 9.2, and 9.3.

Air infiltration is calculated either by the crack method or by the air change method. In the crack method, buildings are assumed to be tightly built, such that leakage through walls, ceilings, and floors is negligible. The quantity of infiltering air is therefore taken as the length of any cracks around windows and doors (usually the perimeter length), multiplied by the expected wind velocity at the surface, multiplied by a coefficient that adjusts for crack width. The air change method assumes that a certain number of air changes occur per hour in a space. The quantity of air occupying the space in any hour is therefore equal to the number of air changes per hour, multiplied by the space volume; this computation provides a useful approximation in situations where the extent of crackage is difficult to estimate. Furthermore, with mechanical ventilating systems, a pressure is built up within a space that tends to offset the pressure on the outside that is due to the wind. In this situation the heat loss, Q_v, through ventilation is

$$Q_v = C_v(T_o - T_i) \tag{9.4}$$

where C_v = ventilation conductance. For low ventilation rates (≤ 2 air changes per hour),

$$C_v = 0.33\ Vn(\text{in } W°\text{C})$$

or

$$C_v = 0.018\ Vn(\text{in Btu/h°F}) \tag{9.5}$$

where V = volume of the enclosed space, in m^3 (ft^3), and n = number of air charges per hour. For higher ventilation rates,

$$C_v = [h_a\ \Sigma\text{A}(0.33Vn)]/(h_a\ \Sigma A + 0.33\ Vn)\ (\text{in W/°C})$$

or

$$C_v = [h_a\ \Sigma\text{A}\ (0.018Vn)]/(h_a\ \Sigma A + 0.018Vn)\ (\text{in Btu/h°F}) \tag{9.6}$$

where ΣA = sum of the area of all the surfaces, in m^2 (ft^2), and h_a = air/environmental conductance, in W/m^{2}K (Btu/ft^{2}h°F). A value of 4.8 W/m$^{2°}$K (27.3 Btu/ft^{2}h°F) is usually taken for h_a.

Radiant heat transfer arises from direct and diffuse irradiation from the sun. Arriving at a quantitative description of solar radiation is a difficult task. The most directly usable statistics come from meterological records; where these do not exist, statistical methods can be employed to compute the components of radiation, using multiplication factors to represent turbidity and using sunshine records to account for the influence of clouds.

When a surface is subjected to solar radiation, a rise in internal temperature is produced. A similar rise in internal temperature would occur in the absence of solar radiation, if the external temperature were increased. The increased external air temperature that would produce the same internal temperature rise as would solar radiation acting in conjunction with an unchanged external air temperature is termed the *sol-air temperature* and varies, of course, with the orientation and slope of the surface. It combines the heating effect of radiation intercepted by the building with the external air temperature to provide an effective temperature acting on opaque surfaces. Notionally, this is expressed as

$$T_{sa} = T_o + R_{so}aI_g - R_{so}eI_L \tag{9.7}$$

where

T_{sa} = sol-air temperature, in °C (°F)
T_o = external air temperature, in °C (°F)
R_{so} = external surface resistance, in m^{2}K/W (ft^{2}h°F/Btu)
a = absorptivity of surface
I_g = global radiation (direct + diffuse + reflected) on surface, in W/m^2 (Btu/ft^{2}h)
e = emissivity of surface
I_L = long-wave reradiation, in W/m^2 (Btu/ft^{2}h)

For our purposes, a value of 100 W/m^2 (315 Btu/ft^{2}h) for long-wave radiation from horizontal roofs to a clear sky can be assumed. In the case of vertical surfaces, eI_L can be taken as zero, since it can be assumed that the long-wave radiation the wall emits is approximately balanced by the radiation it receives from the ground.

The conduction heat flow equation (9.3) can now be rewritten as

$$Q_{c\phi} = A_sU_s[(T_{sa} - T_i) + f(T_{tsa} - T_{sa})] \tag{9.8}$$

where T_{sa} = mean sol-air temperature for a 24-hour period, in °C (°F), and T_{tsa} = sol-air temperature at time t, in °C (°F).

In order to calculate the total energy being transmitted through glass, we must consider the direct and diffuse irradiances separately. This is because, at any given time, the incident direct irradiance will strike the glass surface at a particular angle that has its own corresponding transmission coefficient. On the other hand, the diffuse irradiance will be striking the glass surface at all angles and consequently must be multiplied by a transmission coefficience different from that used for the direct irradiance. The equation for solar radiation heat gain through glass, Q_S, can be written as

$$Q_s = sI_g A_g \tag{9.9}$$

where

s = solar gain factor for the glass
I_g = solar radiation, in W/m^2 (Btu/ft^{2}h)
a_g = area of the glass, in m^2 (ft^2)

Internal heat gain arises from the occupancy of the space, the use of equipment in the space, and the use of artificial lighting to supplement natural illumination. The heat gain from occupancy is the product of the number of persons in the space and the nature of their activity. The allowed maximum number of persons to be accommodated in a space is usually specified in building regulations. For example, the building code in New South Wales, Australia, specifies that an area of 10 m^2 (108 ft^2) is required per person in office buildings. Thus,

$$N_p = \text{gross floor area}/A_p \tag{9.10}$$

where N_p = maximum number of persons that can be accommodated, and A_p = area required per person.

The heat gain per occupant can be found from tabulated values; these cite a figure of 100 W (29.3 Btuh) of sensible heat emission from human bodies engaged in office activities. The heat gain, q_o, from occupants is

$$q_o = N_p q_p H \tag{9.11}$$

where H = hours of occupation, and q_p = sensible heat emission per person.

The heat gain, q_e, from equipment is a function of the rating of the equipment being used. Thus,

$$q_e = RH \tag{9.12}$$

where R = rating of equipment, in W (Btu/h), and H = hours in use.

The need for artificial lighting arises when insufficient natural illumination is available. To calculate the heat gain from artificial lighting, we must assess the proportion of lighting in use at any given time. If we calculate a daylight factor distribution for a space, we can assume thereafter that artificial lighting will be required if the daylight factor over any specified area is less than a specified value. The heat gain, q_a, from artificial lighting is

$$q_a = (A/F)q_1 \tag{9.13}$$

where

A = area of lighting in use, in m^2 (ft^2)
F = floor area of the space, in m^2 (ft^2)
q_1 = heat output from the total lighting in use, in W (Btu/h).

The total internal heat gain, Q_I, is

$$Q_I = q_o + q_e + q_a \tag{9.14}$$

This gain is added to other loads when we are evaluating cooling loads only; any internal gains in the heating season are considered fortuitous.

Assuming that the inside air has negligible heat capacity, we can say that for *thermal balance*

$$Q_I + Q_s \pm Q_c \pm Q_v \pm Q_m = 0 \tag{9.15}$$

where Q_m = auxiliary heating or cooling load to maintain comfort conditions, in W (Btu/h).

The inside temperature, T_i, is assumed to be held at a constant value (at a fixed thermostat setting), that may be different in summer and winter and that may be subject to a setback temperature during periods of the day. The plus-or-minus signs in equation 9.15 indicate the potentially reversible direction of heat flow. We have the option of always treating the temperature difference as positive (by taking away the lower temperature from the higher), or of always subtracting the inside temperature from the outside temperature (in which case the difference will sometimes be negative, as for winter). In the former case, the thermal balance equation can be written (for winter) as

$$Q_m = Q_c + Q_v - Q_l - Q_s \tag{9.16}$$

and (for summer) as

$$Q_m = -(Q_c + Q_v + Q_l + Q_s) \tag{9.17}$$

If $Q_m > 0$ in equation 9.16, then heating is required. If $Q_m < 0$ in equation 9.17, then cooling is required.

In the latter case, the thermal balance equation for both winter and summer is

$$Q_m = -(Q_c + Q_v + Q_l + Q_s) \tag{9.18}$$

If $Q_m > 0$ then heating is required. If $Q_m < 0$ then cooling is required.

This model of the thermal system is now complete, insofar as it is capable of evaluating the thermal loads at the scheme design stage, and allows the designer to consider the effect of changes in the basic design variables that determine the shape, form, and construction of a building. It is sufficient for our purposes at early stages in the design process; for the design of heating and cooling systems, when the building design is finished or nearly finished, more complex models should be (and are) used. The thermal performance objective is to minimize the thermal load on the building.

The Daylight Model

Artificial lighting in a space increases the building's thermal load, so for the thermal model some kind of daylight prediction model is needed to establish whether and how much artificial lighting must be used. Quite apart from this purpose, though, good daylighting is a design goal in its own right. Windows are desirable both to provide visual contact with the exterior and to improve the quality of interior lighting.

The daylight illumination in an interior can be expressed either (in absolute terms) as an illumination value or (more usually) as a ratio of internal illumination to external illumination. This ratio, called the *daylight factor*, remains more or less constant during the day. The amount of daylight at any point in a room depends on the room layout and on the window locations relative to that point. On plan, the daylight distribution is usually shown by lines of equal illumination, which are termed *daylight contours*. When the shape of a window changes, the shape of the contours changes, too. A long, low window results in an ellipse parallel to the window, with poor penetration; a very high window gives a more or less circular contour with much greater penetration and area. Thus, a window geometry can be chosen to ensure the maximum degree of daylighting for a given percentage of window opening on a façade. Indeed, statutory requirements and codes of practice sometimes mandate that a given daylight factor be maintained over a certain area of a space, and they may specify the minimum penetration.

It is usual to identify the exposed area of glass on façades as a percentage of the wall surface. Obviously, a specified fraction can be configured in any of several ways, through combinations of width, height, and number of windows. It is possible, however, to determine—for any specified fraction of glass on a façade—the window geometry that permits the maximum daylight penetration contour area for a required level of illumination. The daylighting objective we shall use, then, is to maximize the area within the daylight factor contour for some specified illumination level (the precise level being chosen by the designer as appropriate to the building's use).

The Capital Cost Model

A building cost model should be sensitive to changes in design variables, should be appropriate to the information available at the design stage for which it is to be used, and should permit the original estimate to be checked continually as the design progresses. For this work, we need a cost model that reflects variations in plan shape, massing, window configurations, constructional properties, and surface finishes.

The method we have selected, the elemental estimating method, is one of the most commonly used cost estimating techniques. It uses a database of costs from the large amount of historic data available for different building types—in our case, open-plan offices. The method relates the rate of expense per square meter of the gross floor area of the building to each element of the building; thus, it requires that the building be split up into a number of elements that are individually priced and then added to provide the total. Approximate quantities are generated to build up the cost of the building in the form of an abbreviated bill of quantities, taking into account all design variables and all areas of significant cost.

As buildings grow taller, their cost per floor increases. This is partly covered by the use of approximate quantities (as for the net/gross floor area, structural cost, elevator costs, and fire protection costs, all of which are directly related to the number of stories), but it also needs to be reflected in unit costs for a number of structural and service elements. For example, the cost of pouring concrete is higher on the tenth floor than at ground level. The increase in cost with increase in height is discontinuous, as statutory requirements and plant size changes produce thresholds of changes in rates. From an analysis of cost information, it was found necessary to make available four sets of cost data, associated with single-, two- to five-, six- to twelve-, and greater than twelve-story heights.

The cost criterion, then, is to minimize the total capital cost. As a by-product of the cost analysis, a fully enumerated cost plan for a building can be produced with the model.

The Usable Area Model

To express the utility of a particular building configuration, we need something akin to its net rentable area; but a figure for rentable area (as it is normally defined) cannot be calculated at the early stages of building design because no information on internal space partitioning is available. Instead, we calculate a net usable area, taking the area inside the external walls, less the area occupied by services, such as elevators and staircases, less the following allowances for circulation and toilet facilities:

> Circulation: ground floor, 10% of net area; upper floors, 5% of net area
> Toilet facilities: 5% of net area

In the calculations for this model, net area is gross floor area, less the area occupied by external walls. For a single-story building,

$$\text{net usable area} = 0.85\ (\text{net area}) \tag{9.19}$$

For a two- or three-story building,

$$\begin{aligned}\text{net usable area} = {} & 0.85\ (\text{net area}) + 0.9\ [\text{net area}(\text{stories} - 1)] \\ & - \text{area of staircases}\end{aligned} \tag{9.20}$$

For a building of four stories or more, regression studies have shown that

$$\text{net usable area} = -355A_1 + 9325A_2 - 7552A_3 + 100.8A_4 + 0.9365A_5 + 6{,}644 \quad (9.21)$$

where

A_1 = number of floors
A_2 = number of elevator zones
A_3 = number of elevators
A_4 = elevator arrangement
A_5 = total gross area

The net usable area calculated is expressed as a percentage of the gross floor area.

The Building Model

The kind of description of the building (and of the environment in which it is located) that we need to construct in order to carry out the study follows from the models we have chosen for describing the building's behavior in terms of heat, light, cost, and usable area. For each of these separate behavioral models, we need values for certain endogenous and exogenous variables. If we want to use all four behavioral models together, we need values for every endogenous or exogenous variable that arises in any of the models. Figure 9-1 brings this information together by simple aggregation. It establishes the scope of the complete problem, the data required for its operation, and their relevance to each of the performance criteria. The number of design variables is large, with just two independent design variables (orientation and light transmittance). Clearly, the design variables for the thermal and capital cost subsystems possess a high degree of connectivity. Far fewer variables affect the daylight and usable area criteria, and these are independent of each other.

The exogenous variables are variables over which the designer has no control. As a result, they form a fixed set of input data required for a particular problem. The endogenous variables are the design variables for which the designer seeks optimal decisions as part of the solution process. All design decisions relating to shape and massing affect usable area, capital cost, and thermal criteria simultaneously. Wall, roof, and floor construction variables affect thermal load and capital cost, while window construction variables also affect the daylight criterion. The two independent design variables are orientation, which only affects the thermal load criterion, and light transmittance, which only affects the daylight criterion.

The Generation Model

If our model were only concerned with description—that is, with the simulation and prediction of how a building will behave in a given environment—all we would need are the models we have already set up. A given building could then be evaluated by providing values for all the variables in figure 9-1, running the model, and looking at the values of the performance variables. But we want to look at a whole field of possible solutions, so we need a generative as well as a descriptive model.

Let us consider what we need to generate. We want to be able to investigate different window geometries; therefore, we need a model that can generate a range of feasible widths and spacings. We want to investigate different wall and roof constructions as they affect thermal behavior; therefore, we need a model that can generate a range of feasible insulation types and thicknesses. Similarly, we need a model that can generate a range of feasible glass types, window shading factors, building orientations, aspect ratios, floor areas, and number of floors. In general, we need to generate all feasible values of the endogenous variables (within constraints) so that we can find the best combination of these feasible values. Sometimes the feasible values will be discrete (as in number of floors), and sometimes they will be discretized values at intervals within a continuous range (as in floor area). The generation model we shall use is quite simple: it enumerates exhaustively all the possible values of a design variable, given a description of as much of the rest of the design as is necessary to ascertain the effect of the variable. The model, shown diagrammatically in figure 9-2 is a state/stage model; the description of the building is generated stage by stage, and the state of the design as it is output from one stage becomes the input state to the next stage. The window, wall, and roof subsystems are generated separately and combined at later stages.

What has decided the ordering of these stages in the generative model? If each endogenous variable were to have three possible values (a very conservative estimate), the number of feasible design solutions created by arranging these different variable values in every possible combination is about 1.4×10^9. Clearly, exhaustive enumeration will not work; instead, we must use Pareto optimal dynamic programming. The ordering of the

Utility	Capital Cost	Daylight	Thermal	Subsystem				
Net Usable area	Cost/sq m of gross floor area	Daylight contour area	Thermal load	Criterion	Primary Variable	Characteristic	Element	
•	•		•		Gross floor area	Capacity	Building	EXOGENOUS VARIABLES
			•		Minimum area/floor			
		•	•		Height/floor			
		•			Lintel depth	Windows		
		•			Sill height			
		•			Dirt allowance			
		•			Frame allowance			
•			•		Area/person	Occupancy	Use	
			•		Heat emmission/person			
			•		Ventilation rate			
		•			Daylight factor			
			•		Heat gain	Equipment		
			•		Thermostat settings	Control, temperature		
			•		Mean annual temperature	Temp. averages	Climate	
			•		Mean daily temperature			
			•		Annual amplitude			
			•		Daily amplitude			
			•		Hottest month of the year			
			•		Peak daily temperature time			
		•			Sky luminance distribution			
			•		Latitude	Radiation		
			•		Altitude			
			•		Mean value of solar constant			
			•		Turbidity factor			
			•		Relative sunshine distribution			
	•				Cost/element	Elements	Costs	
•	•		•		Aspect ratio	Shape	Building	ENDOGENOUS VARIABLES
•	•		•		Number of floors	Massing		
•	•		•		Floor area			
	•		•		Material thermal properties	Construction - ext. walls		
•	•		•		Material thickness			
			•		Solar absorptivity			
	•		•		Shading			
	•		•		Material thermal properties	- roof		
	•		•		Material thickness			
			•		Solar absorptivity			
	•		•		Material thermal properties	- floor		
	•		•		Material thickness			
	•	•	•		Size - width	- windows		
	•	•	•		- height			
		•	•		- spacing			
	•	•	•		Glass type			
	•	•	•		Shading			
		•			Light transmittance			
			•		Relationship to North	Orientation		

Fig. 9-1. Relationship between performance models and exogenous and endogenous variables.

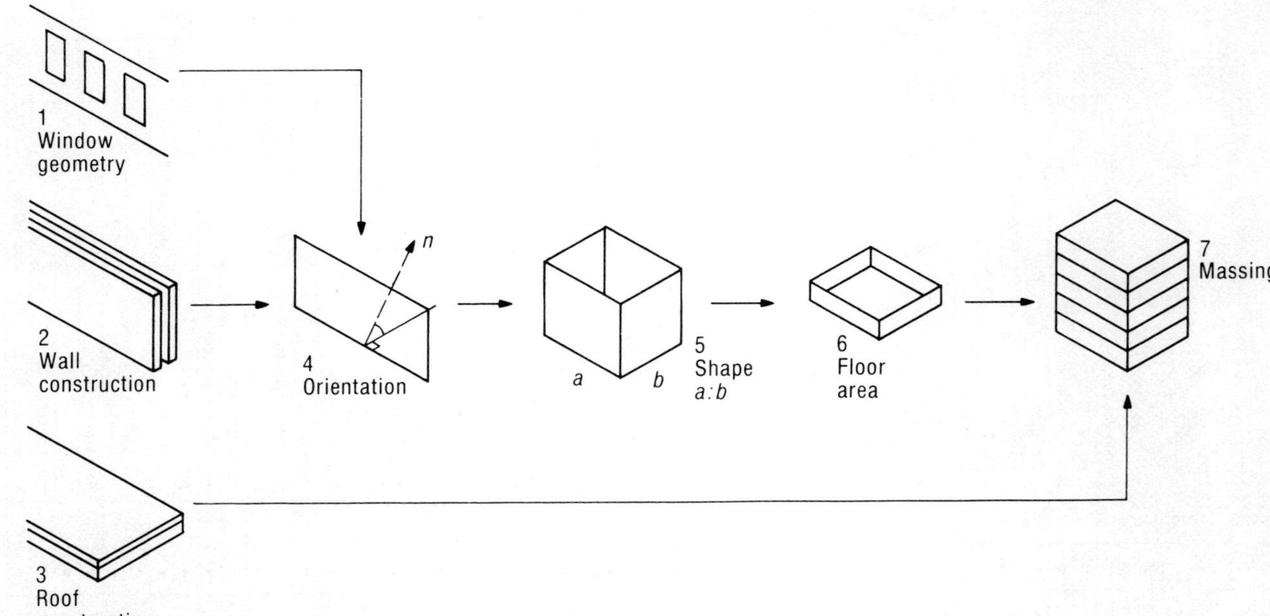

Fig. 9-2. State/stage generation model. The output states from stages 1 to 7 are transformed at the next stage by the addition of further design variables.

stages, therefore stems from the need to incorporate this generative model within an optimization model.

The Optimization Model

To use dynamic programming optimization, we need to develop a problem formulation that will satisfy the dynamic programming conditions of separability and monotonicity. Since the thermal model is the most complex of our prediction models and involves the most endogenous variables, we shall begin by looking back at it.

The equation for conduction heat transfer through an opaque surface (equation 9.8) is

$$Q_{c_\phi} = A_s U_s[(T_{sa} - T_i) + f(T_{tsa} - T_{sa})]$$

The sol-air temperature terms inside the brackets are a function of the total solar radiation on the surface, which in turn is dependent on the surface orientation.

The surface thermal transmittance, U_s, and decrement factor, f, are a function of its construction, while the area of the surface A_s, can be expressed in terms of the gross floor area, the aspect ratio (ratio of the length of the northmost wall to the length of the eastmost wall), and the number of stories in the building. For example, for a parallelopiped building,

$$\text{area of north and south walls} = n \times h \times b \tag{9.22}$$

where

n = number of stories
h = height per story
b = building length

$$\text{area of east and west walls} = n \times h \times w \tag{9.23}$$

where w = building width

$$\text{floor area } (F) = n \times b \times w \tag{9.24}$$

$$\text{aspect ratio } (R) = b/w \tag{9.25}$$

By substitution

$$F = n \times R \times w^2 \tag{9.26}$$

from which

$$\text{building length } (b) = \sqrt{(F \times R/n)} \qquad (9.27)$$

$$\text{building width } (w) = \sqrt{(F/n \times R} \qquad (9.28)$$

Thus, for a building comprising only opaque surfaces, a stage ordering might be developed through the following decision sequence:

orientation → wall construction → shape → massing

When glass surfaces are added, the ordering is complicated by the fact that the area of the windows are usually expressed as a percentage of the wall surface. The solar gain through glass (equation 9.9) is

$$Q_s = sI_gA_g$$

and

$$A_g = pA_w \qquad (9.29)$$

where p = percentage of glass on the surface, and A_w = wall surface area.

It is also evident from equation 9.9 that the solar gain through glass is dependent on solar radiation (orientation) and on the transmission property of the glass.

Besides resulting from the transmission heat flow through the construction surfaces, additional heat gain is generated from the occupants' bodies and from the use of artificial lighting in the building. The gain from artificial lighting can be minimized through the use of large windows that permit as much natural light as possible, but this approach disproportionately increases the heat gain in summer (with a consequent increase in the cooling load).

Considering the relationship between the criteria and the endogenous variables in figure 9-1, we can see that the daylight criterion is only dependent on window construction. We can certainly make a decision on the best window geometry (in terms of width, height, and spacing)—that is, on the geometry that permits the maximum daylight penetration for specified window fractions and daylight factor. Independently of this, we can evaluate the effect of thermal transmittance and inertia through the wall and roof construction on the thermal and cost criteria.

This suggests separate branches converging toward a stage where the effect of the wall/window combination has to be considered. At this stage, the effect of solar radiation can be evaluated through both the glass and the opaque parts of the building enclosure. Because we have only considered a unit length of surface up to this stage, the effect of the shape, floor areas, and massing of any building remains to be resolved, as indicated by equations 9.27 and 9.28. A decomposition of the problem in this form enables us to evaluate components of the performances in the four criteria as they apply at each stage. Expressed in dynamic programming terminology, the problem has been formulated as a seven-stage forward nonserial dynamic programming problem with converging branches (fig. 9-3).

Stage 1 – Window Geometry

It is usual to express the exposed area of glass on the façades of a building as a percentage of the total wall surface area, but a specified fraction can be configured in many ways through combinations of width, height, and number of windows. When the shape of the window changes, the contour of daylight (for a specified daylight factor) entering a space also changes. In this stage, we determine the best window geometry (width, height, and spacing) for any specified fraction of glass on a façade by choosing the geometry that permits the maximum daylight penetration contour area for a given daylight factor.

Consider an infinite length of wall. For any given spacing between windows, a specified fraction of window size can be obtained, as follows.

$$\text{window area } (A_g) = w_1 \times w_h \qquad (9.30)$$

where w_1 = window length, and w_h = window height.

$$\text{wall area } (A_w) \text{ between spacing} = w_s \times h \qquad (9.31)$$

where w_s = spacing between windows, and h = floor-to-ceiling height of wall. For any specified fraction, p of window size on a façade,

$$p = A_g/A_w = (w_1 \times w_h)/(w_s \times h) \qquad (9.32)$$

$$w_h = (p \times w_s \times h)/w_1 \qquad (9.33)$$

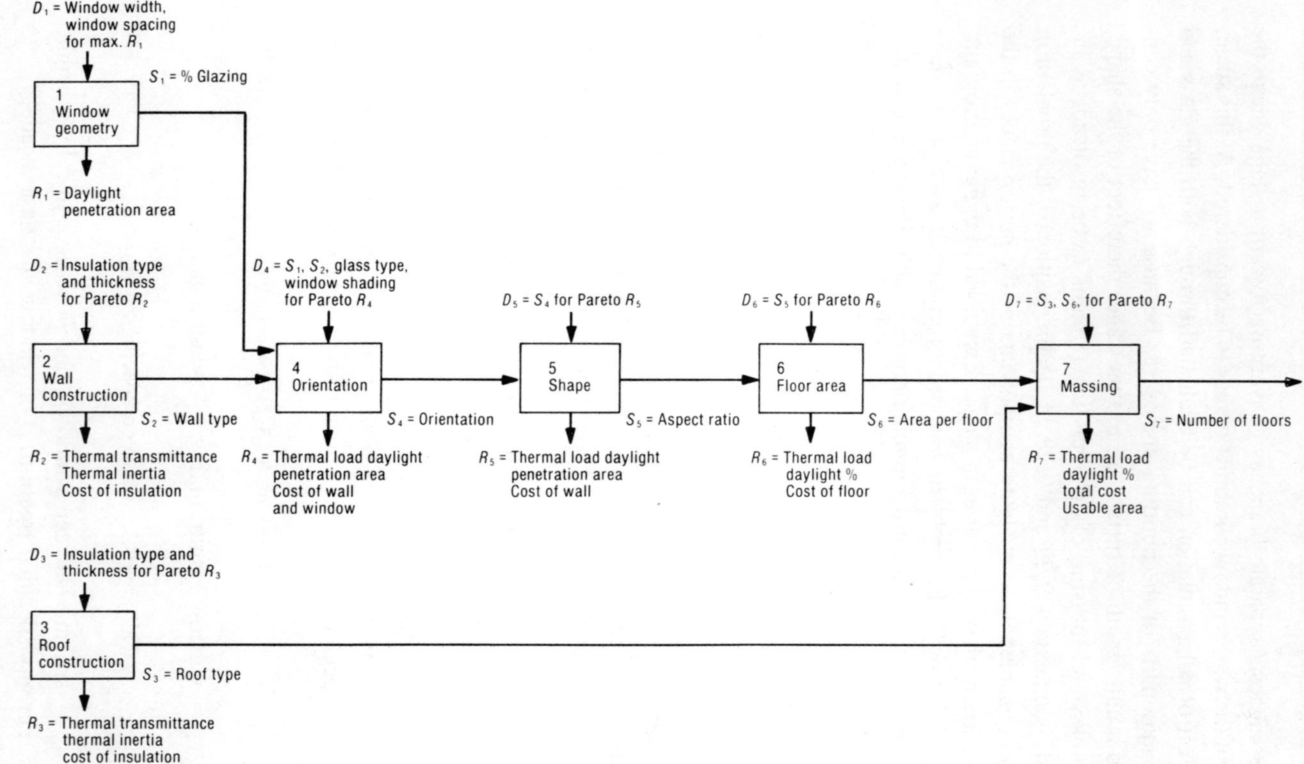

Fig. 9-3. Optimization model. The parallelopipedal building design problem is formulated as a seven-stage nonserial dynamic programming problem with converging branches.

Thus, for any specified window fraction, a range of window sizes can be generated by combining various window spacings and lengths (fig. 9-4); and for each shape, the daylight contour area can be calculated for a specified daylight factor. A decision can be made on the best window geometry for a specified fraction of window size by choosing the geometry that yields the maximum daylight contour area.

Stage 2 – Wall Construction

The thermal performance of a wall is influenced by its thermal transmittance and inertia. The first parameter indicates how fast heat is conducted through the wall, while the second describes how fast the wall heats up or cools down. When climatic conditions vary diurnally, an objective of thermal control is to prevent heat loss when cold conditions prevail and to prevent heat gain when hot conditions prevail. Usually, however, wall construction has to meet several objectives (for example, structural, fire protection, and sound control objectives)—apart from thermal considerations. Although due consideration is often given to the thermal properties of the construction materials, thermal performance rarely dominates other wall construction objectives. Once the broad lines for the design of the wall construction have been conceived, better thermal performance is most easily achieved with insulation. The addition of insulation reduces the wall's thermal transmittance (U-value), which in turn reduces all forms of conduction heat transfer through the building envelope.

The thermal properties of insulation depend on its thickness, and hence on its cost. Higher capital cost attributable to improved wall insulation should be judged in relation to possible savings in energy consumption. Apart from the wall's resistance to the flow of heat, economy of energy use is also influenced by the capacity of the wall construction to absorb heat. Walls with low thermal transmittance but high inertia can perform as well as those with high thermal transmittance and low thermal inertia. This gives rise to the concept of *thermally equivalent* walls. Thus, a balance between U-value, thermal inertia, and cost of insulation is needed.

In this stage, the effect of various insulation types and thicknesses are evaluated. If we assume that the wall construction (apart from insulation) is fixed, and we consider various insulation types and thicknesses, we can compute the U-value and thermal inertia of the composite wall, as well as the cost of insulation. The Pareto set of solutions for these three criteria is carried forward to the next stage.

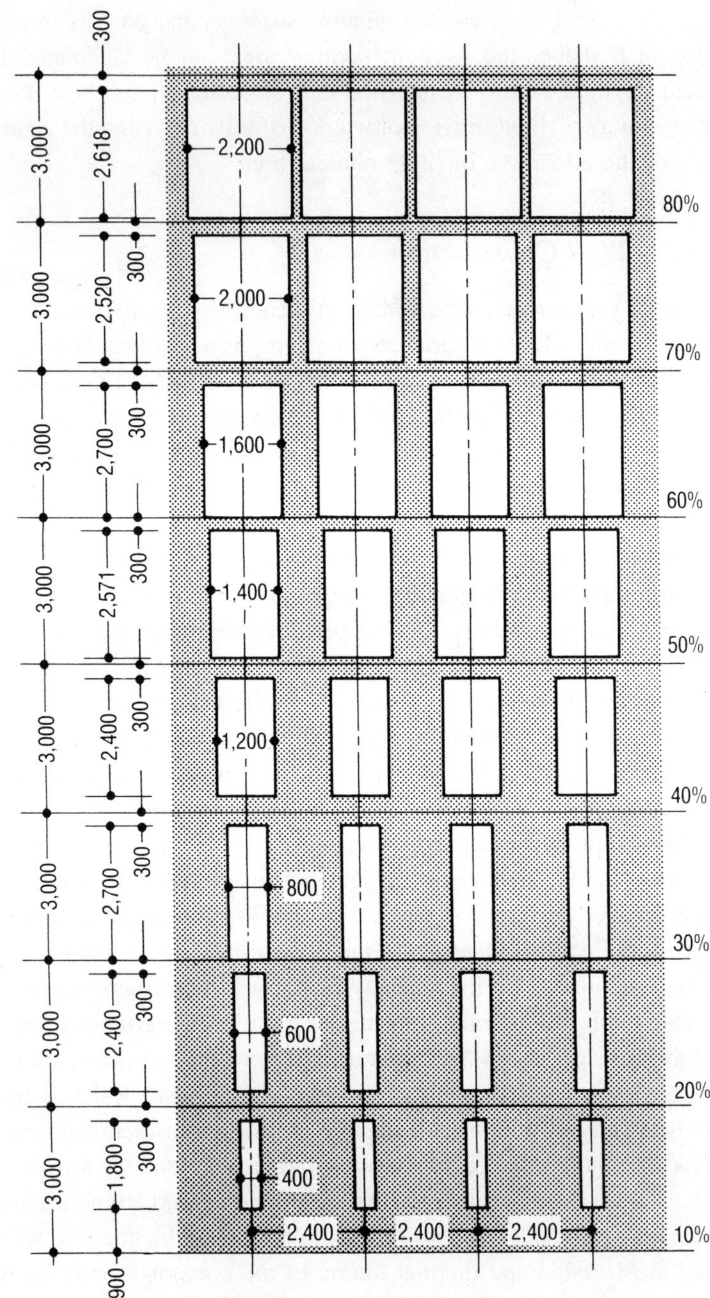

Fig. 9-4. Window geometry for specified glass percentages.

Stage 3 – Roof Construction

Like the wall construction's thermal load the roof construction's thermal load is affected by the roof's thermal transmittance and its thermal inertia, which in turn can be related to the type and thickness of insulation used. Unlike the situation with walls, though, the incident radiation on a flat roof is not orientation-dependent. At this stage, roof insulation types and thicknesses are considered, carrying forward the Pareto set of roof *U*-value, thermal inertia, and cost of insulation. This branch need only join the main optimization sequence at stage 7, when the decision relating to roof insulation type and thicknesses can be made.

Stage 4 – Orientation (Opaque/Glass Surfaces)

The input state to this stage consists of the best window geometry for each of the specified window fractions from stage 1 and the Pareto set of wall insulation types and thicknesses from stage 2. In this stage, the effects of orientation, glass types, and window shading, and the cost of glass and of shading are considered. The amount of solar radiation striking the façade of a building is dependent on time and on the orientation of the surface. The property of glass that enables it to transmit high-temperature radiation while trapping low-temperature radiation means that virtually all of the incident radiation heat will pass directly through the glazing and contribute to warming the interior. Given this heat gain, it is possible to reduce the amount of auxiliary winter heating; but conversely, the gain can cause summer overheating and a consequent increase in the cooling plant requirements. A design objective, therefore, is to maximize the solar radiation gain through glass in winter while minimizing it in summer. The heat flow from radiation through glazing is always directed into the building.

The effect of solar radiation on opaque surfaces is usually combined with that of the outside air temperature by using the sol-air temperature concept. At any given time, (depending on orientation), each façade receives a different amount of temperature gain from solar radiation. Likewise, the time of occurrence of the peak irradiance is different, resulting in different sol-air temperature profiles for each façade.

The rate of heat flow through an opaque element varies directly with the difference in temperature between the element's outside and inside surfaces. Since the sol-air temperature profiles are different on each façade, so will be the temperature differences, and hence the heat flows; and these are dependent on the relative position of the opaque surfaces.

In winter, the expected conduction heat flow through opaque surfaces is from the inside to the outside surfaces, with the reverse flow taking place in summer. But regardless of its direction, the heat flow should be minimized—since in winter it is desirable to retain heat within the building, and in summer heat should be kept out. Because the building under consideration is a parallelopipedal shell, the heat flow through the four façades can be calculated for any orientation. Using a unit length of wall, we can calculate the combined net effective solar and conduction thermal load over summer and winter through the wall/window combination.

Here, again, we calculate the modified daylight contour area arising through the use of different glass types and different shading for each window fraction, as well as calculating the cost of each insulation type and thickness and the cost of each glass/shading combination. The Pareto set of wall constructions is generated for the three criteria of thermal load, daylight contour area, and cost of wall for each value of orientation; and this Pareto set is carried forward to stage 5.

The Pareto set could be very large at this stage, and hence could increase significantly the computational burden at later stages. In such a case, clustering of similar-valued solutions is used to reduce the Pareto set.

Stage 5 – Shape

The heat flow rates calculated in stage 4 relate to a unit length of wall. This heat flow rate is different for each façade and should therefore be related to the shape of the building. The shape of the building is considered here through its aspect ratio—that is, through the ratio of the length of the northmost facing wall to the length of the eastmost facing wall.

The thermal load, cost of walls, and daylight penetration area can be calculated for each aspect ratio, and the associated Pareto set can be obtained. Then a decision can be made as to the best orientation for the solutions in the Pareto set. These decisions are carried forward to the next stage.

Stage 6 – Floor Area

Two exogenous variables considered as fixed for this problem are the gross floor area and the minimum area per floor of the building. Within these fixed values, a range of floor areas can be considered by initially massing the entire gross floor area of the building on a single floor and then reducing the area per floor in some increment until the minimum area per floor is reached. The range of floor areas considered can be related to the possible ways of massing the building.

The input to this stage is the Pareto set of thermal load, cost, and daylight penetration area for each value of aspect ratio. For each floor area, the appropriate contribution of heat gain due to space utilization and artificial lighting required can be included, and the adjusted Pareto set of thermal load, cost, and daylight penetration area can be obtained.

Stage 7 – Massing

Here, a field set of buildings with different gross floor areas can be evaluated; or alternatively, only the story combinations that allow a specific gross floor area for a building to be configured may be considered. Additional inputs to this stage are the Pareto set of thermal parameters and the cost for roof construction from stage 3.

Given the massing of the building, its usable area and its capital cost can be calculated. The Pareto set of thermal load, daylight availability, usable area, and capital cost can then be produced, which is the design information we originally sought.

Implementation of the Models

The suite of computer programs that implements the models consists essentially of eight computer programs operating independently—one for each of the seven stages of the formulation, plus a program to trace back and present the decisions pertaining to a building specification. It also includes a set of routines grouped into a library consisting of all routines required by two or more of the programs (for example, those required for Pareto optimization, cluster analysis, and solar radiation). The input required at any stage is minimal, self-explanatory, and specific to that required for the operation of the stage. Communication between programs occurs through binary data files that carry forward the stage returns and all input data required at a later stage.

The system structure is essentially sequential, and program execution is meant to follow the stage ordering of the problem formulation. Since the programs for each stage are independent, it is possible to rerun a program for any stage, using a different set of input data. In the case of stages 1, 2, and 3, no previous stage input data file is required, while for the remaining stages a data file output from a run of the previous stage is required. The restriction, of course, is that it is not possible to reorder the stages.

Example: Design for a Building in Perth, Australia

To illustrate the implementation and the kinds of information produced, we shall use the design of a 2,000-m^2 (21,520-ft^2) office building in Perth, Australia. The Pareto solutions are shown graphically in figure 9-5, where thermal load is plotted against capital cost, usable area, and daylight, respectively. The seemingly odd solutions in the set is solution 1, which qualifies for the Pareto set because it provides the highest daylight contour area. The range of performance values is broadest for the thermal load, where values range between 19.51 W/m^2 (6.18 $Btuh/ft^2$) and 85.05 W/m^2 (26.96 $Btuh/ft^2$)—a difference of 77 percent in performance. The next broadest range of values is daylight, with 23 percent, while for both capital cost and usable area, the spread in the range is 14 percent.

The rationale for picking a solution for development of a design from this set depends on the user's requirements. For example, we might view usable area as providing the return on the investment (capital cost), the thermal load as indicating running costs, and daylight as providing a qualitative assessment of the interior environment of the building. From this viewpoint, we might disregard solution 1 as being too expensive and as providing the lowest return. We might also disregard solution 2 for providing too little daylight. The remaining solutions all envision two-story constructions. The difference in usable area for these solutions suggests that the solutions are grouped by aspect ratio: solutions 3, 4, 5, and 6 with an aspect ratio of 1.0; solutions 7, 8, and 9 with an aspect ratio of 1.5; and solution 10 with an aspect ratio of 2.0. The most attractive solutions would appear to be 7 and 9, which—though not providing the best performance in any individual criteria—seemingly provide a balance of performance in all.

By tracing back (this is carried out by a separate program in the computer implementation), we can find the design decisions that lead to any one of these Pareto optimal performances; as an example, figure 9-6 shows the complete set of decisions that underlie solution 7.

It is interesting that no constraints were applied here; the common wall

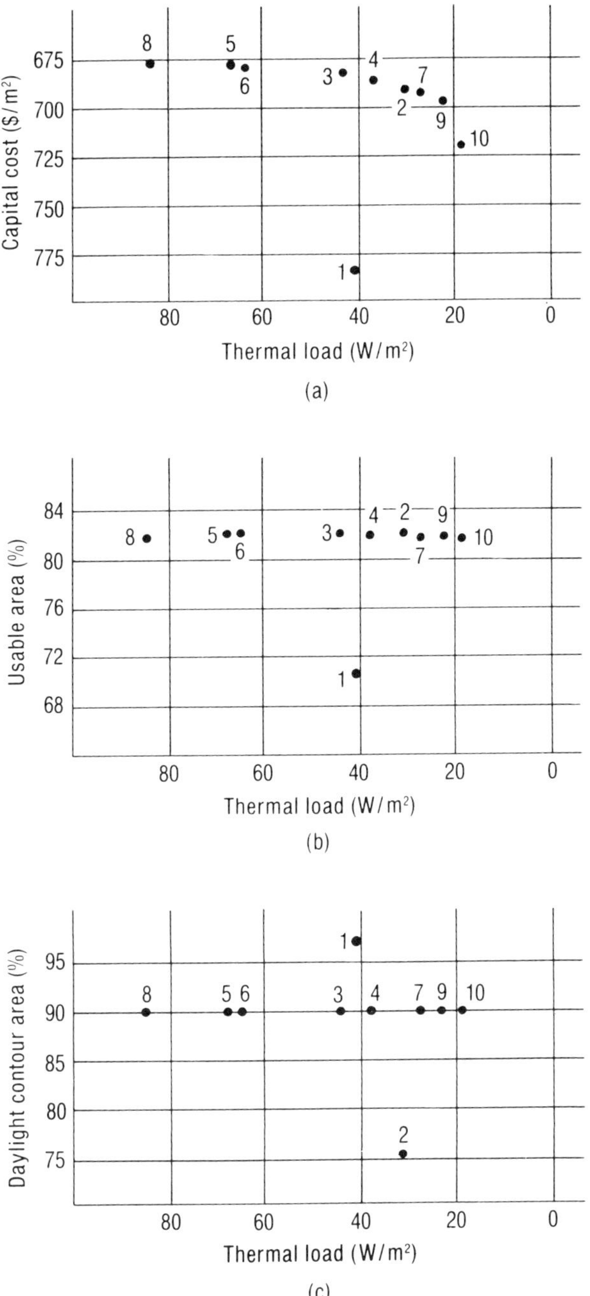

Fig. 9-5. Ten representative Pareto performances (abstracted by cluster analysis) for the criteria of minimum thermal load, minimum capital cost, maximum usable area, and maximum daylight contour area. The graphs show the projection of the set onto three faces of a four dimensional criteria space.

BUILDING SPECIFICATION

Gross floor area	2000.00 m^2
Area per floor	1000.00 m^2
Number of stories	2.00
Aspect ratio	1.50
Building length	38.73 m
Building width	25.82 m
Orientation	0.0 deg

	WALL				ROOF
	N	E	S	W	
Insulation type (polyurethane)	21.	21.	21.	21. (glass wool)	4.
Insulation thickness (mm)	100.	50.	100.	50.	50.

GLASS

	N	E	S	W
Type (plain)	1.	1.	1.	1.
Size (%)	70.	10.	10.	10.
Shading summer (%)	0.	100.	100.	100.
Shading winter (%)	0.	0.	0.	0.
Width (mm)	2000.	400.	400.	400.
Height (mm)	2520.	1800.	1800.	1800.
Spacing (mm)	2400.	2400.	2400.	2400.

BUILDING PERFORMANCE

Thermal load	28.33	W/m^2
Daylight availability	90.00	% GFA
Capital cost	692.85	$\$/m^2$
Usable area	82.13	% GFA

ELEMENTAL COSTS ($)

(Without rounding the figure up or down)

Preliminaries	91672.78
Substructure	34274.90
Superstructure	
columns	10971.44
upper floors	191045.49
staircases	6787.33
roof	91341.63
building envelope	406608.65
internal construction	52488.69
Finishes	
wall finishes	15746.61
floor finishes	72398.19
ceiling finishes	75113.12
Fittings	6221.72
Services	
hydraulic services	25339.37
fire protection	22986.43
mechanical services	12107.73
electrical services	12107.73
elevators	0.00
Site works	32863.83
External services	12107.73

STRUCTURE

Number of columns	35
Spacing along width (m)	6.45
Spacing along depth (m)	6.45
Column size (mm)	325.00 square
Spandrel beam depth (mm)	550.00
Spandrel beam width (mm)	275.00
Width of column footing (mm)	950.00
Depth of column footing (mm)	400.00

SERVICES

Number of elevators	0
Number of staircases	2
Area of staircase (sq m)	19.52
Total number of risers	68.00
Total number of landings	10.00

Special provisions	36323.18
TOTAL CAPITAL COST	1386485.60

Fig. 9-6. Design decisions for solution 7 in figure 9-5. The structure, services, and elemental costs are generated only for costing purposes within the cost model.

insulation and glass type over the four façades have been generated by the program. Since we rejected solutions 1 and 2 as being unsuitable, figure 9-7 shows a shortened list of the design decisions for solutions 3 through 10. The solutions fall into three groups (for the three aspect ratios input), within which the following subgroups are evident:

Group No.	*Subgroup Label*	*Aspect Ratio*	*Solution No.*
1	(a)	1.0	3 and 4
	(b)	1.0	5 and 6
2	(c)	1.5	7 and 9
	(d)	1.5	8
3	(e)	2.0	10

Design → performance relationships can be inferred from the results. For the various combinations of design variables, the performances in the four criteria are available. The differences in performance for the solutions in subgroup (a) are attributable to wall insulation thickness. In solution 4, thicker wall insulation is recommended, which has improved the thermal performance but increased the capital cost. The same comments apply to subgroups (b) and (c), where the increase in wall insulation thickness has improved the thermal performance but simultaneously increased the capital cost: in subgroup (b), with solution 6 over solution 5; and in subgroup (c), with solution 9 over solution 7.

Between subgroups (a) and (b), the differences in thermal performance and capital cost are more pronounced. The increase in thermal load in subgroup (b) is attributable to orientation, to an increase in glass percentages on the south and west façades, and to the absence of shading on the west. The decrease in capital cost is due to the relative cheapness of glass (versus opaque wall), as well as to the reduction in cost for the lack of shading on the west façade. The same comments apply to subgroups (c) and (d). Here, although the solutions have the same orientation, solution 8 in subgroup (d) has more glass on the east, south, and west façades, and it has no shading on any façade. As a result, it has the worst thermal performance but qualifies for the Pareto set because it represents the lowest capital cost solution.

Solution 10 in subgroup (e) stands alone. As might be expected for the climate of Perth, Australia—given an orientation due north and the glass

SOLN NO.	ASPECT RATIO	ORIEN-TATION DEG.	GLASS %				SUMMER SHADING				WALL INSULATION THICKNESS				THERMAL LOAD	DAYLIGHT AVAIL.	CAPITAL COST	USABLE AREA
			N	E	S	W	N	E	S	W	N	E	S	W	W/M^2	%	$	%
3.	1.0	10	60	10	40	10	0	100	0	100	100	50	75	50	44.5	90	683.4	82.2
4.	1.0	10	60	10	40	10	0	100	0	100	100	100	75	100	38.3	90	686.4	82.2
5.	1.0	20	60	10	80	40	0	100	0	0	100	50	75	100	68.4	90	677.9	82.2
6.	1.0	20	60	10	80	40	0	100	0	0	100	100	75	100	65.2	90	679.6	82.2
7.	1.5	0	70	10	10	10	0	100	100	100	100	50	100	50	28.4	90	692.9	82.13
8.	1.5	0	70	30	80	30	0	0	0	0	100	75	75	75	85.1	90	677.7	82.13
9.	1.5	0	70	10	10	10	0	100	100	100	100	100	100	100	23.3	90	695.6	82.13
10.	2.0	0	50	10	10	10	50	100	100	100	100	100	100	100	19.5	90	720.8	81.99

For all ten Pareto solutions, glass type is plain, winter shading is 0%, wall insulator type is polyurethane, roof insulator type is glass wood, and roof insulator thickness is 50mm.

Fig. 9-7. Design decisions for solutions 3 through 10 in figure 9-5. Solution 1 has been excluded on cost grounds, and solution 2 has been excluded because it provides too little daylight.

percentages, summer shading, and wall insulating thickness recommended—it is the best thermal solution. It is also the most expensive, for the reasons outlined above.

Performance → *performance* relationships can also be inferred. In comparing the performances of the solutions within the subgroups for each aspect ratio grouping, we may interpret an improvement in capital cost as meaning an increase in the thermal load. The performance tradeoff choice thus involves improving thermal performance at the expense of increasing capital cost.

For *design* → *design* relationships we need to look at daylight availability and usable area. Daylight availability maintains the same percentage for all solutions, while usable area remains the same within each aspect ratio grouping. If the intent was to design for usable area, all of the solutions within each aspect ratio grouping are possibilities. Design freedom exists as to decisions on orientation, glass percentages on the south and west façades, shading on the west façade, and insulation thicknesses on the east, south, and west façades. Within subgroups (a), (b), and (c), choice is allowed only as to insulation thickness on the east and west façades. If the intent was to design for daylight availability, all of the solutions (3 through 10) are options to be considered. Design freedom in this case may relate to all of the design variables, or to a restricted set within the aspect ratio groupings, or to an even more restricted set within the subgroups.

Discussion

Of particular interest in the formulation of the preceding model is the presence of *invariant imbedding*. For example, because the combination of floor areas and number of floors (stages 6 and 7) can generate buildings possessing very different total floor areas, one operation of the optimization model can generate the Pareto optimal sets for a wide range of building size problems at once, embedding within these solutions the solution for any specifically nominated total floor area. We have looked at a problem for a 2,000-m^2 (21,520-ft^2) office building; but in the implementation procedure, that specific problem was embedded within a wider one that generated solutions for buildings of 1,000 m^2 (10,750 ft^2), 2,000 m^2 (21,520 ft^2), 3,000 m^2 (32,290 ft^2), and so on, up to 10,000 m^2 (107,600 ft^2). Further, the cumulative results prior to each stage could stand alone, to provide the basis for an analysis of the performances of the design variables included up to that stage. From stage 4, for example, we get a Pareto set of performances and their associated decisions in terms of wall insulation types and thicknesses, window sizes, glass types, and shading—all of which could be applied to the design of an office floor for minimum thermal load, minimum wall cost, and maximum daylight contour area at different orientations (fig. 9-8).

Among the uses of the model are the following five:

1. It provides a design tool for the architect in dealing with a specific project.
2. It generates generalized information and advice on building form in a specific climate, which can be presented in either graphical or tabular form.
3. It enables the relationship between climate and building form to be explored.
4. It facilitates studies between different building constructions (that is, heavy and lightweight structures) and thermal performance.
5. It offers a powerful educational tool for understanding the relationships between design decisions and the criteria considered. It can also be applied to a number of parametric research studies, including studies of the threshold relationship between aspect ratio and floor area, and the associated sets of decisions for differing orientations and patterns of external shading for sites at different latitudes.

In this section, we have discussed the conceptual formulation and the practical development of a model intended to aid the designer at the scheme-design stage of building design. The model we considered provides prescriptive quantitative information for the design of the building form and enclosure, gauging thermal performance in relation to the daylighting and usable area available, as well as in relation to its capital cost. As a model, it can be practically applied after simple substitution of the actual design options in any particular situation.

PROBLEM: DESIGNING WINDOW WALLS FOR PASSIVE SOLAR ENERGY

This problem, like the last, is concerned with the design of buildings for good thermal performance. This time, though, we consider a later stage in the design process. The building's massing, orientation, and layout have been decided, and the site and the buildings around it are known. What we seek now is information about the implications for comfort

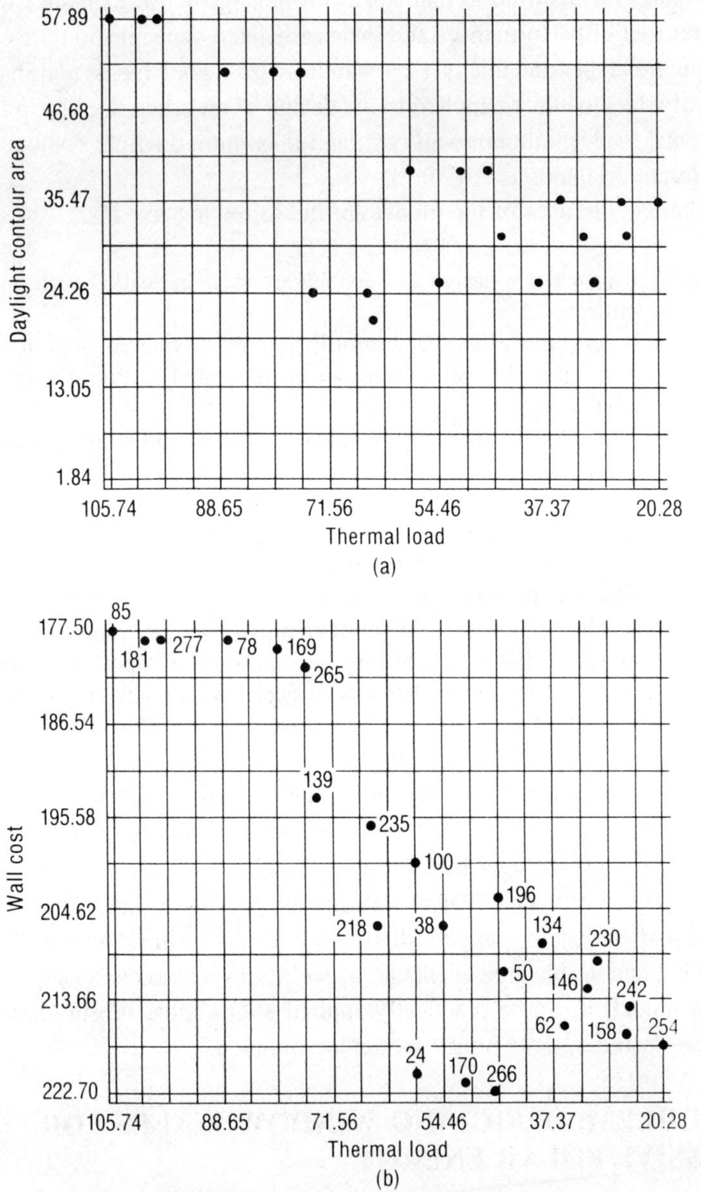

Fig. 9-8. Pareto set of (a) thermal load and daylight contour area, and (b) thermal load and wall cost, for a floor of an open-plan office building with orientation due north.

conditions in the building's rooms of design decisions about the window walls.

Buildings are increasingly often being designed to make use of passive solar energy; to this end, their orientation, windows, and sunshading are organized to facilitate solar heat gain in winter and consequently to reduce both the capital costs and the running costs of space heating. The effect of solar heat gain, though, can be detrimental as well as beneficial: sun penetration that makes a room comfortably warm in winter can make it unbearably hot in summer and artificial cooling is more expensive than artificial heating. On unobstructed sites, the necessary design principles are well understood, and the solar effects are fairly predictable. In urban, obstructed situations, however, it is not always easy to foresee either the qualitative or the quantitative thermal effects of window and sunshade design. Using criteria of predicted minimum winter and peak summer internal temperatures during occupied hours (in the assumed absence of artificial heating or cooling), we could carry out two optimizations to find the best window designs for winter and summer conditions, and then we could compare the resulting forms. But the real interest lies between these extremes, in finding an acceptable compromise between design exclusively for the winter and design exclusively for the summer. This middle ground can be traced through multicriteria Pareto optimization.

The Description (Prediction) Models

We need a thermal model that is sensitive to the effects of window size, shape, and position and to any sunshades over the windows. Since internal temperature must be related to a specific point or space in order to be meaningful, a model of the building/environment system must be based at a level of individual rooms or areas. Earlier simulation models have followed this same rationale. If it is to be practicable as a basis for optimization, some form of structure must be imposed on the system so that the system is ordered into manageable parts without having the integrity of the interactions between parts compromised. We shall describe first the performance prediction model, and then the building model within which it is implemented.

The Thermal Model

The thermal analysis is based on the admittance procedure developed in Great Britain by the Building Research Establishment. It is best suited to predicting "worst case" conditions, for which reference days can be chosen to represent extreme points in the range of climatic conditions encountered. The actual heat exchanges in a room (by convection between air and surfaces, and by radiation between surfaces) are replaced by exchanges between a single "environmental point" and the surfaces.

The calculation sequence that follows uses the concept of *environmental temperature* to deal with both radiant and convective energy interchanges at the surfaces of the enclosed space. Environmental temperature is a weighted mean between mean radiant temperature and air temperature. Although its use as a direct index of comfort has been questioned because of temperature variations within a room, it provides a better index of thermal comfort than does air temperature alone. At low air speeds its value is not very different from that given on either the equivalent temperature scale or the resultant temperature scale (the two most common indices of comfort that are independent of humidity).

The value of environmental temperature is given approximately by the formula

$$T_{ei} = 0.33T_a + 0.67T_r \tag{9.34}$$

where

T_{ei} = environmental temperature
T_a = air temperature
T_r = mean radiant temperature

There are two ways of expressing the results. The environmental temperature that results when heating and cooling systems are absent is easy to compare with a desired value, and its value will indicate the comparative performance of different building solutions. The alternative approach is to calculate the heating or cooling load imposed on the building in order to keep the internal environmental temperature within a desired comfort range. A return expressed in terms of load, however, is less immediately meaningful to an architect than one expressed in terms of temperature, and it is less easily compared with experience in other situations. It has no physical meaning unless the plant capacity for heating and cooling is a system variable and cost or energy optimization is involved. Initially, the peak and minimum environmental temperatures that would result in the absence of artificial systems appear to offer the most appropriate index of thermal performance. It can be argued that an optimum design with respect to temperature will in any case be optimum with respect to load minimization, since the two parameters are interrelated.

The Building Model

The exogenous and endogenous variables we must use to describe the building in order to use the thermal model are listed in figure 9-9. The exogenous variables describe the nature of the room (fixed by requirements other than thermal performance) and the external environment. The endogenous variables encompass a range of material characteristics, sizes, and positions.

The effect of any element of the room enclosure on the internal environment depends primarily on two pieces of information: the construction or material of the element, and the location of the element. The conceptual basis of the building model involves systematizing the locations variable by superimposing a notional grid over the plane of the enclosing surface (fig. 9-10). The external wall is thereby divided into numerous subplanes or cells, while internal walls, floor, and ceiling (which may be required to be all of one construction) are divided coarsely and perhaps as whole planes.

Windows, solid areas and open areas are made up of numbers of these subplanes, and sunshades are positioned on the grid so formed. The effect of any particular location on the internal environment can then be predicted, given the properties of the construction form that occupies it, the external environment impinging on the external surface, and certain physical characteristics of the room as a whole. The resulting internal environment in the room is determined by combining the contributing effects of all the locations over the notional grid and adding any effects that cannot be attributed to a particular location.

The basic geometric description of both building and site is founded on a hierarchy of three-dimensional coordinate systems (fig. 9-11). The topography of the site and any buildings or walls on the site are described as planes in a global coordinate system based on any convenient origin. The outline of the building to be investigated is described according to the same system, and—as far as external obstructions are concerned—no differentiation is made between the buildings within which the investigated room is set and any other building. The effect of reentry corners are therefore covered automatically. But the building under study also has

CRITERION	Peak or minimum internal environmental temperature		
	element	*variable*	*characteristic*
EXOGENOUS VARIABLES	ROOM	Height	
		Length	
		Width	
		Orientation	
	CLIMATE	Air temperature	
		Sun path	Solar altitude
			Solar azimuth
	EXT. OBSTN.	Position	
		Size	
	USE	Occupancy	Heat flow rate
		Equipment	Heat flow rate
ENDOGENOUS VARIABLES	EXT. WALLS	Ext. surface	Surface resistance
			Solar absorptivity
		Construction	Thermal transmittance
			Decrement factor
			Time lag
			Admittance
(either)	ROOF	Ext. surface	Surface resistance
			Solar absorptivity
			Long-wave radiation loss
		Construction	Thermal transmittance
			Decrement factor
			Time lag
			Admittance
(or)	CEILING	Construction	Admittance
	INT. WALLS	Construction	Admittance
	FLOOR	Construction	Admittance
	WINDOW	Position	
		Length	
		Height	
		Glass/blind	Solar gain factor
			Alternating solar gain factor
			Thermal transmittance
			Admittance
		Wall depth	
	HORIZONTAL SUN SHADE	Position	
		Projection	
		Angle	
	VERTICAL SUN SHADE	Position	
		Projection	
		Angle	
DEPENDENT VARIABLES		Number of air changes/hour	
		Heat flow rate from artificial lighting	

Fig. 9-9. Relationship between the performance model and exogenous and endogenous variables. In this case, the same model is used for two different performance measures, for summer and winter conditions.

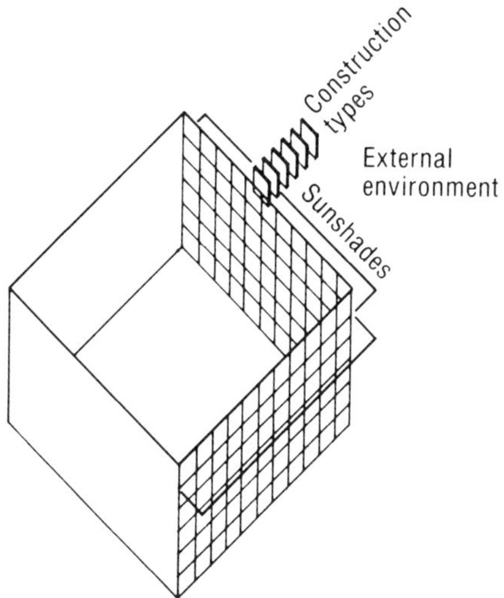

Fig. 9-10. Rectangular room with notional grid over enclosing surfaces.

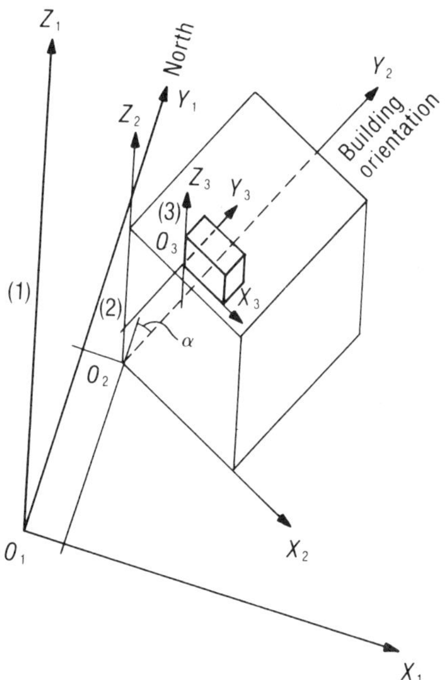

Fig. 9-11. Geometric description of built form using coordinate systems for (1) the site, (2) the building, and (3) the room. The origin of (3) is defined on (2), and the origin of (2) is defined on (1).

associated with it a secondary coordinate system having an origin at one corner of the building. This is for convenience in manipulating the position of the room to be investigated. Rotation and transformation algorithms are used to transform the origin of this geometric description system to a reference point on the external wall surface, as required to establish shaded or nonshaded conditions at any location.

The endogenous and exogenous variables in the model can be linked through the system model to the criteria they control, by using a network analog. In figure 9-12, the system model is divided into the parts concerned with the external environment system (encompassing the basic climate on the site and its modification up to the wall line) and the parts concerned with the internal environment system. Thus, the output of the external environment system is independent of the variables that describe the room enclosure. There is no conceptual differentiation between opaque and glazed areas of wall, although the mathematical equations that express the links may vary. External conditions at a particular site are partly extracted from a database of historical weather records and partly simulated by mathematical model. The actual effect of the conditions underlying this time-variant climate information is modified by external obstructions and shading devices before the conditions impinge on the external surface of any wall element of a building. The effect of these obstructions can be characterized by two dependent variables: isolated condition and obstruction factor.

In order to calculate direct solar radiation on the wall surface, we need to know whether or not each location occupied by the element is shaded at each hour of a reference day. The isolated condition of each location is established in the model by testing each obstructing plane against solar position for each time interval and for each location on an external wall.

In order to calculate the diffuse solar radiation incident at any location, we need to know the proportion of the sky that is obstructed by sunshades or external obstructions. This proportion can be represented as an obstruction factor established by a numerical integration over the half-hemisphere of space seen by each location on an external wall.

Reflected radiation from obstructions is more difficult to predict, although methods do exist for the relatively simple case of a continuous obstruction parallel to the wall surface.

In the model, the present value of ground-reflected radiation is calculated and used directly, without any modification for obstructions. In practice, the reflected component of radiation is small in comparison to the direct component.

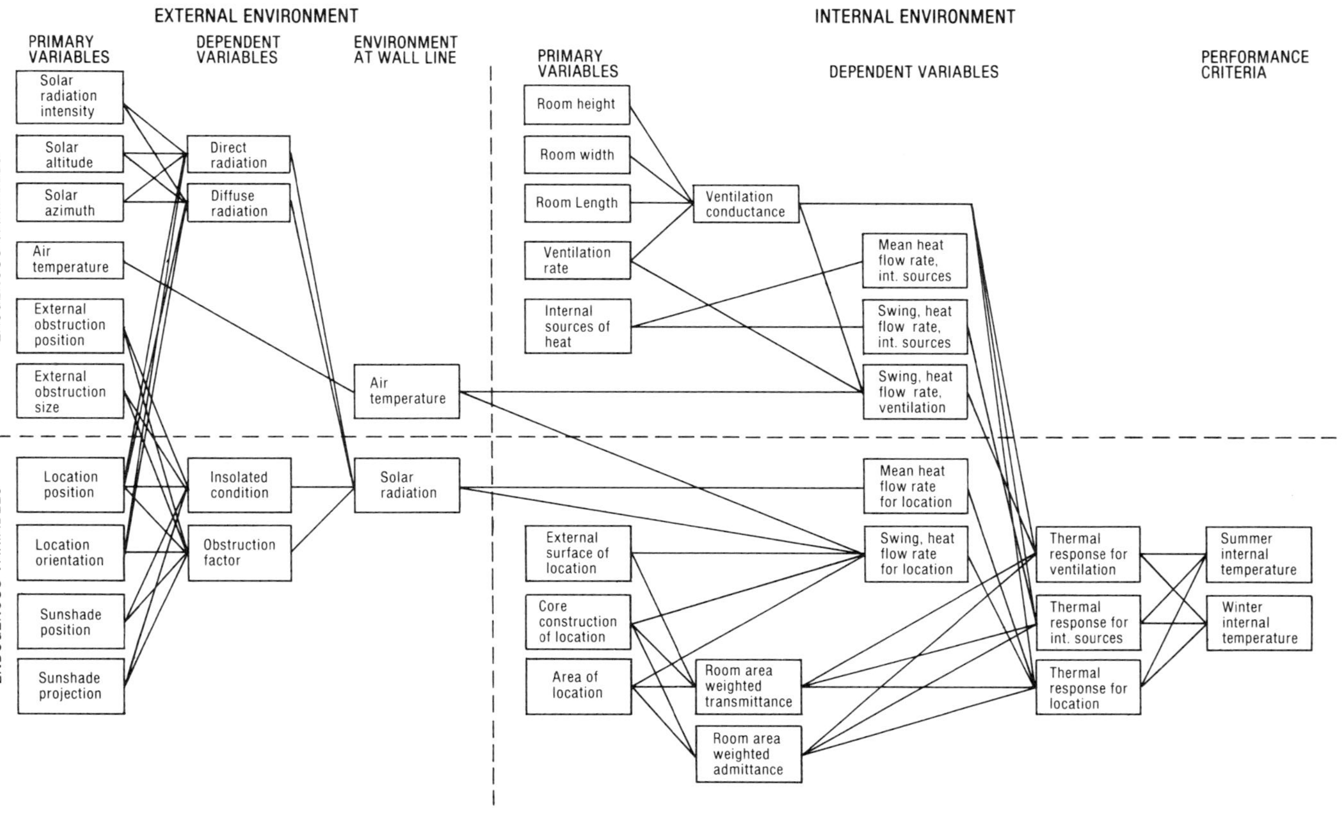

Fig. 9-12. System model, with links between component variables.

The effect this quantifiable external environment has on the interior of the room depends on the material that occupies the location and on certain physical characteristics of the room as a whole. Solar radiation and conduction, the sources of heat flow through external surfaces, are expressed as a mean heat flow rate for the reference day; swings from that mean are recorded at hourly intervals. A component of internal environmental temperature ascribable to a particular location at a particular time can then be calculated from the mean and swing values of heat flow rate through that location, as well as from values for ventilation conductance and area weighted transmittances and admittances. The resulting internal environmental temperature in the room is an integration of the effects of each location over the notional grid, together with the effects of heat flow from ventilating air and of internal heating sources (such as artificial lighting, human occupancy, and mechanical equipment).

The Generation Model

Within this building model structure, the design process can be represented as the selection (for each part of the room enclosure) of a construction form that maximizes the total benefit of the enclosure on the internal environment. Clearly, it would be impossible in practice for every location to be occupied by a different type of building construction—even if that situation resulted in good environmental performance. Therefore, we must recognize practical restrictions on the sizes and shapes of building elements and on the way materials can be fitted together to produce a feasible solution. Equally important, architects often have specific ideas of their own about the form the envelope design can take without violating aesthetic or other nonquantifiable demands. These requirements are modeled as a set of design rules, expressed as three classes of constraint:

1. *Topology*—restrictions on the number and spatial relationship of windows and other elements
2. *Geometry*—restrictions on the position, shape, and minimum and maximum size of an element
3. *Materials*—restrictions on acceptable forms of construction, the number of different materials, and the points at which they meet.

The ability to handle these constraints must be built into the generative procedure. In fact, they were taken as the starting point for the formulation itself. If a required topology for the wall can be specified, optimal sizes and materials can be determined through application of an optimal dimensioning algorithm adapted from work on floor plans.

The Optimization Model

The Pareto optimal set is generated by a method very similar to the noninferior set estimation (NISE) method. A pseudo-objective function is formed by aggregating the weighted performances in each criterion.

Assume a given topology K windows in an external wall. We can then define J vertical divisions in the wall, where $J = 2K + 1$ (fig. 9-13). Let

W = room width
H = room height
g = glass type
c = wall construction type
s = sunshade projection
l_{min}, l_{max} = minimum and maximum window lengths
h_{min}, h_{max} = minimum and maximum window heights
s_{min}, s_{max} = minimum and maximum sunshade projections
$x_1, \ldots, x_J$ = horizontal dimensions defining the window edges
$y_1, \ldots, y_3$ = vertical dimensions defining sill and lintel heights

Our aim is to determine the values of $x_1, \ldots, x_J$, $y_1, \ldots, y_3$, c, g, and s, in order to maximize the combined return from both window and opaque areas of the wall, subject to the following five constraints:

$$x_1 + x_2 + \cdots + x_J = W$$
$$y_1 + y_2 + y_3 = H$$
$$l_{min} < x_j < l_{max},\ j = 2, 4, \ldots, J - 1 \text{ or } x_j = 0$$
$$h_{min} < y_2 < h_{max} \text{ or } y = 0$$
$$s_{min} < s < s_{max} \text{ or } s = 0$$

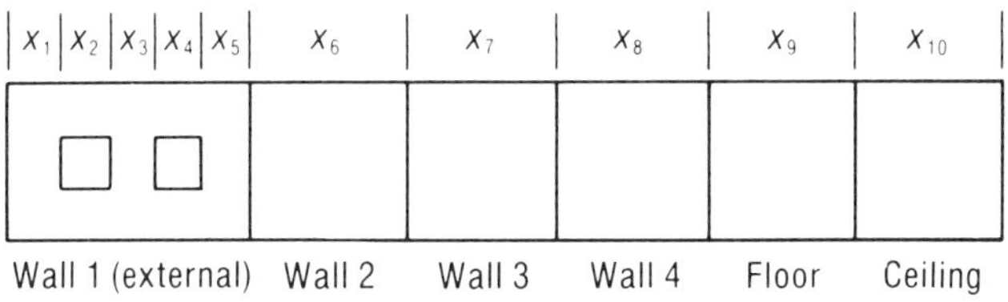

x_1 x_2 x_3 x_4 x_5 x_6 x_7 x_8 x_9 x_{10}

Wall 1 (external) Wall 2 Wall 3 Wall 4 Floor Ceiling

Fig. 9-13. Room surfaces expressed as contagious rectilinear areas.

This can be solved as a dynamic programming optimization problem, with the stage and state variables and the objective defined in the following terms:

Stage Variable
The vertical zone of wall j, $j = 1, J$
State Variables
The length of the jth zone, x
Vertical dimensions y_1, y_2, and y_3
Glass type, c
Wall construction type, g
Sunshade projection, s
Objective
To maximize the total return from all wall areas; that is,

$$\max \sum_{j=1}^{J} \sum_{i=1}^{3} f(g,c,s)_{i,j}$$

where $f(g,c,s)_{i,j}$ is the return associated with the wall area given by the pair (x_i, y_j) for stage j.

The component of the internal environment temperature at time t due to a location is given (using the admittance procedure) by

$$T_{ei(t)} = Q/(\Sigma AU + C_v) + Q_{(t)}/(\Sigma AY + C_v) \tag{9.35}$$

where

$T_{ei(t)}$ = addition to environmental temperature at time h, in °C (°F)
Q = mean rate of heat flow through the location, in W (Btu/h)
$Q_{(t)}$ = swing in rate of heat flow through the location at time h, in W (Btu/h)
ΣAU = sum of the area-weighted thermal transmittances of the enclosing surfaces
ΣAY = sum of the area weighted admittances of the enclosing surfaces
C_v = ventilation conductance for the room

In terms of the dynamic programming problem formulation, the mean heat flow rate, Q, and the swing in heat flow rate, $Q_{(t)}$, are additive and are functions only of the stage and state variables. The ventilation conductance, C_v, can be assumed to be constant for the room and to be independent of the enclosing surfaces (and therefore independent of the stage decisions). A difficulty is caused by the area-weighted sums of thermal transmittance, ΣAU, and admittances, ΣAY, which are functions of decisions at every stage. These sums can be expressed in dynamic programming as involving the transfer of information between a stage and every other stage—that is, as including both feedforward and feedback loops.

Considering thermal transmittance first, and taking one stage in isolation, we require information on the average thermal transmittance from previous stages (the feedforward) and the average transmittance from future stages (the feedback) in order to calculate a stage return. For the feedforward part, to ensure that the present decision will be correct in relation to all future stages, we must make that decision for every feasible value of the average transmittance represented by the decisions at future stages. Further, we must base our calculation of the returns from all stages in a decision path on the same (and correct) assumption of overall average thermal transmittance.

One solution to this problem is to use two additional state variables—one representing quantized values of an assumed overall average transmittance, and the other representing quantized values of the average transmittance of construction forms in the locations considered up to that stage. The assumed feedback value could be found (if required) from the assumed overall value and the actual feedforward value. The first of these state variables must keep a constant value for all stages of a decision path, and its values can therefore be examined sequentially—simply by multiplying the amount of computation by the number of values considered—without requiring significant additional storage. Each quantized value of the second state variable acts as a constraint on feasible values of the decision variables, which must comply with its requirements. As the stages progress, its value can be pruned as it becomes impossible for any decisions made at future stages to bring the average to the value assumed by the value of the first state variable.

This procedure of optimizing for quantized values of feedforward or feedback information can be applied when the information concerned is groupable into classes for all of the stages before or after the stage being considered. Thus, the same reasoning can be applied to thermal admittance, and—given this procedure—any number of locations can be taken as stages in a dynamic programming optimization. The smaller the intervals are between the quantized values for these state variables, the greater the accuracy of the result is.

Implementation of the Models

The total model is implemented as a suite of computer programs. The system structure is essentially sequential. The design situation is specified first; then the specific problem is defined, in terms of the environmental components of interest; then the design rules are nominated; and finally a set of Pareto optimal solutions is generated. During execution, it is possible to return to an earlier stage or to reenter at any stage after interrupting a session, but it is not possible to reorder the stages. Since the execution of any program uses the output of earlier ones, a redefinition of a room (for example) requires reexecution of the environmental component programs before the design rules and optimization stages of the redefined room are entered. Two principal databases are created: a sequential file containing the problem description, which is read, modified, and rewritten by each component program; and a random access file containing performance information in the nominated environmental components, which is read by the optimization program. Additional sequential data files contain default values and keep records of the instruction set for the program session so that, if needed, the same values can be recovered in the next session.

Example: Design for a Building in Hobart, Australia

The case study we shall present here involves a corner room of area 4.5 m × 6 m (14 ft 9 inches × 19 ft 9 inches) and of floor/ceiling height 2.7 m (8 ft 10 inches) in an office building situated in Hobart, Australia. The shorter external wall faces 60 degrees west of north; the longer one faces 30 degrees east of north. The office building is situated at an urban street corner. The position of the room under investigation and the positions of buildings on the opposite sides of the streets are shown in figure 9-14. In this case, sill height and wall and glass construction types are assumed to be fixed, and applicable design rules place restrictions on the window topology and geometry.

The Pareto set of performances (fig. 9-15) follows the classic convex shape. The extreme points of the graph (solutions 1 and 10) demonstrate the best that can be achieved in either criterion—that is, the optimal

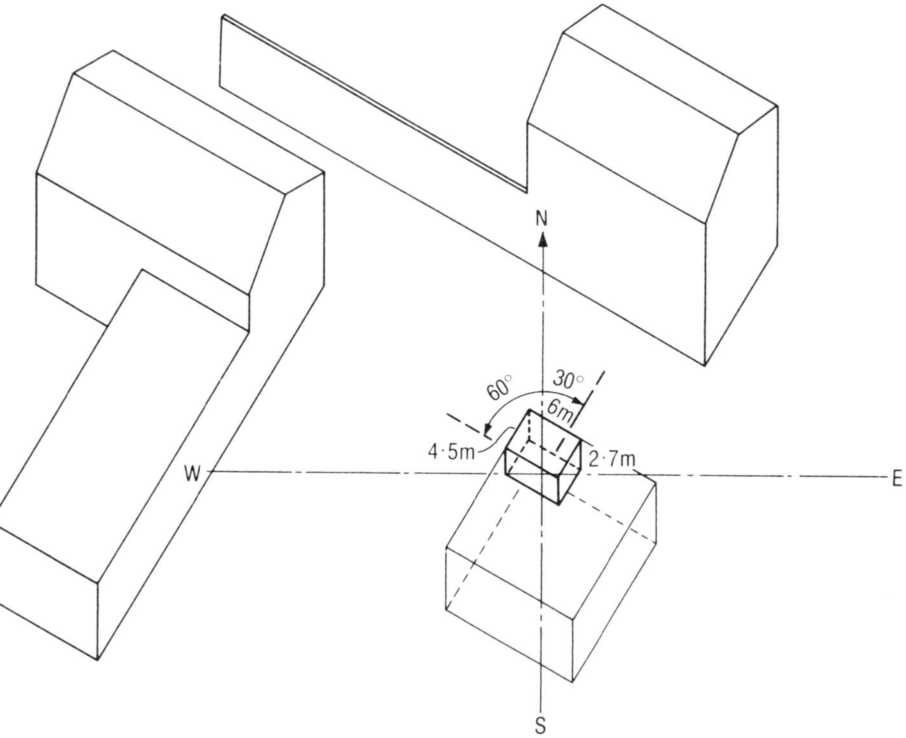

Fig. 9-14. Design situation for the example: a small office with two external walls in Hobart, Australia, latitude 42°53′S, longitude 147°20′E.

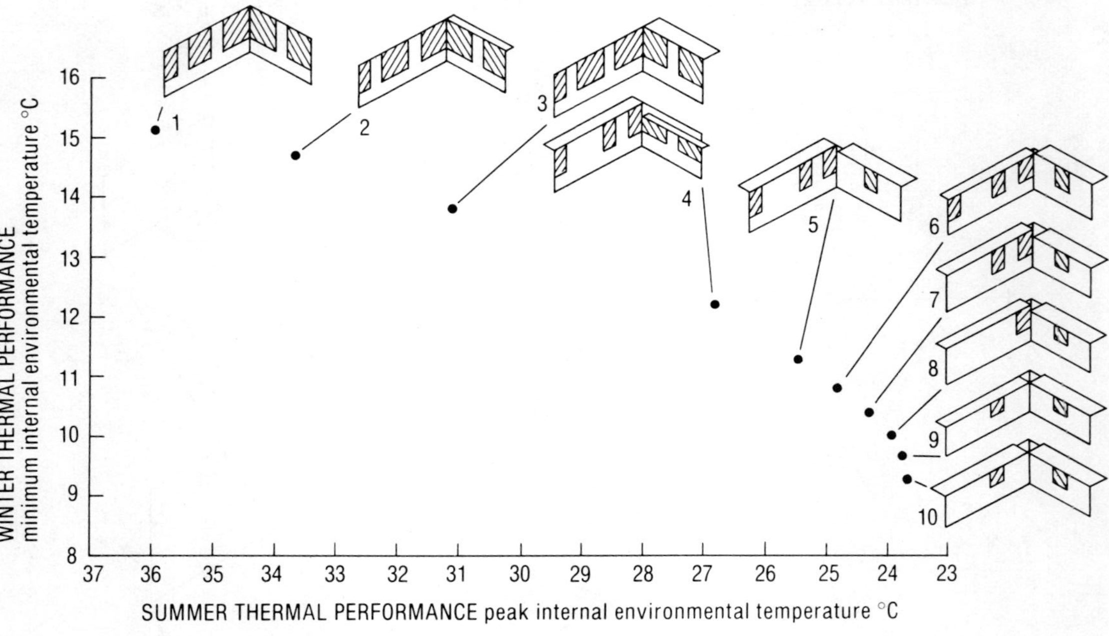

Fig. 9-15. Pareto set of performances, and associated solutions.

solutions to the two separate single-criterion optimization problems. The extremes define the range within which the designer can work. Thus, the best winter conditions are achieved by a window design with much glass and no sunshades, but this design brings with it a high peak summer temperature.

Looking at the numerical values, we find that reducing this peak summer temperature to 34°C (93°F), while keeping the winter minimum temperature as high as possible requires placing a small sunshade over one wall (solution 2). No other solution within the given constraints offers the same level of summer performance and a better winter performance. A major improvement in peak summer temperature to 27°C (80°F) with least worsening of winter temperature can be achieved by placing sunshades on both walls and adopting a different window arrangement (solution 4). A performance combination outside the area bounded by this curve (a minimum winter temperature of 13°C (55°F) and a peak summer temperature of 26°C (79°F) for example) cannot be achieved without recourse to artificial services, whatever the design decisions.

The qualitative information provided by the diagram is as important as the quantitative information; sources of such information include the shape of the graph (showing a steady reduction in the rate of improvement in winter thermal conditions as further reductions in peak summer conditions are allowed), the trends in shading and window area, and the differences in behavior of the two walls as emphasis shifts from one criterion to the other. The solutions go through several distinct formal stages in the course of their progress along the tradeoff curve. The design of the northwest (shorter) wall changes at each plotted point for solutions 1 to 5, holds this form (solution 5's) for solution 6, and then remains constant for solutions 7 to 10. The design of the northeast (longer) wall is unchanged for solutions 1 through 3, holds a different form for solutions 4 and 5, and is then different for each solution 5 to 10. Only between solutions 3 and 4 (which are relatively far apart in summer performance, although not in winter performance) and between solutions 6 and 7 do the designs of both walls change together.

Since the Pareto set is small, the choice of a preferred solution is straightforward. A best compromise solution will come from the middle group—perhaps from among solutions 4, 5, and 6—where summer peak temperatures are acceptable as worst conditions and where minimum winter temperatures at least offer a reasonable starting point for space heating.

Discussion

The model provides an approach to sizing windows in obstructed situations by explicitly quantifying the effects of different window sizes and sunshade projections on summer and winter thermal performance. As a result, the designer can trade off the beneficial effects of solar heat gain in winter against its detrimental effects in summer. The aim has been to generate enough points to make clear the trend in both performance values and design solutions—not to identify the whole set of Pareto optimal solutions. The tradeoff decision is left to the designer; but by identifying the Pareto set, the designer obtains prescriptive quantitative information to base that decision on.

An important point that has not been discussed thus far is the influence of the assumed external conditions on the shape of the tradeoff diagrams and on the relative performance of different forms of solution. For example, the shape of the Pareto set in figure 9-15 would be different if the assumed winter conditions consisted entirely of overcast skies with little solar radiation. The assumption that the climate included some sunshine was made to investigate the potential contribution of design for passive solar energy. In further use of the model, the effects of different assumptions of external climates should be investigated. Indeed, one useful application of the model is to generate tradeoff curves for performance at the same time of year, given two different assumptions of external conditions.

The system could also be used to investigate the variation of window design for passive solar energy over different geographical locations and derive generalized information through using notional descriptions of the physical environment around the building as degrees or types of obstruction rather than using the model with a description of a single, real, site.

THE CONSTRUCTION OF PARETO OPTIMIZATION MODELS

In this chapter, we have described the models used in two Pareto optimization case studies, and we have done so at a more detailed level than was adopted for most of the examples in this book. Our intention here was to illustrate the components of a Pareto optimization model for solving a nontrivial building problem—to show how the components fit together and how they relate to the notions of descriptive, generative, and optimizing models that we discussed in chapter 2.

To construct a Pareto optimization model, we must first identify the general design goals that we wish to explore. Then we must interpret these goals as single-valued criteria—a difficult task, which we discussed at the beginning of this book. Our next task is to put together the performance prediction models for each of these criteria, using methods that are appropriate to the information available at the stage of the design process for which the model is intended. The endogenous and exogenous variables for which values are needed in these prediction models tell us what needs to be described and what level of detail is necessary for the building model. By this point, we have already done the equivalent of constructing a whole series of simulation models. We need, next, a generative model—a means to explore potential design solutions within any bounding set of design constraints. Then we need an optimization model, chosen from available optimization techniques (exhaustive enumeration, classical calculus, linear programming, nonlinear programming, dynamic programming, and so on). We also need to select a model for identifying the Pareto optimal set of performances, from the models available (exhaustive testing, the weighting method, the constraint method, Pareto optimal dynamic programming, and so on). Finally, we might need a model such as inverse goal programming (chapter 8) to help us structure and interpret the results.

This model construction process is made more difficult by the interrelationship between the components. The generative model is so closely linked to the optimization model that most books do not identify it as a separate component. The models for identifying Pareto optimal sets are linked to the optimization models: using Pareto optimal dynamic programming means using dynamic programming optimization. Conversely, using the constraint method means using an optimization technique that allows constraints to be imposed on values of the objective functions (this is generally not possible with dynamic programming because of the decomposition of the problem into linked subproblems). Even the form of the performance prediction models influences the choice of optimization model and (indeed) whether an optimization formulation is possible.

If all this seems difficult, that is because it often is. The effort is worthwhile only if the problems addressed are of sufficient significance to be worthy of exploration. But once constructed, the models can be used for many different buildings in many different locations—either directly or with minor modifications to suit different building types, climates, and so on. In the two examples presented in this chapter, we have concentrated on the models rather than on their applications, and both could be (and to some extent have been) used to explore a wide range of design situations. It all begins to seem worthwhile if we think of the purpose of models as being to add to human knowledge, rather than just as being to solve a particular problem. The idea of optimization as knowledge is the subject of chapter 10.

FURTHER READING

The thermal load, daylighting, cost, and utility problem is drawn from:

D'Cruz, N. 1984. Multicriteria Performance Model for Building Design. Ph.D. thesis, Department of Architectural Science, University of Sydney.

The window walls problem is drawn from:

Radford, A. D. 1979. A Design Model for the Physical Environment in Buildings. Ph.D. thesis, Department of Architectural Science, University of Sydney.

Further, large-scale applications can be found in:

Rosenman, M. A. 1981. Computer-Aided Decision Making in the Design of Buildings. Ph.D. thesis, Department of Architectural Science, University of Sydney.

Murphy, N. S. H. 1984. Design of Multifunctional Opaque Building Enclosures. Ph.D. thesis, Department of Architectural Science, University of Sydney.

Additional descriptions related to these applications can be found in:

D'Cruz, N.; Radford, A. D.; and Gero, J. S. 1983. A Pareto optimization formulation for building performance and design. *Engineering Optimization* 7(1):17–33.

Gero, J. S.; Radford, A. D.; and D'Cruz, N. 1983. Energy in context—a multicriteria model for building design. *Building and Environment* 18(3):99–107.

Gero, J. S.; Radford, A. D.; and Murthy, N.S.H. 1982. What if? Exploring the consequences of design and performance decisions in computer-aided design. In *CAD 82*, ed. A. Pipes, pp. 633–46. Guildford, England: Butterworths.

Murthy, N. S. H.; Radford, A. D.; and Gero, J. S. 1985. Computer-aided decision making for multiobjective problems. *COMPINT 85*, pp. 212–16. Washington, D.C., IEEE.

Radford, A. D., and Gero, J. S. 1980. Tradeoff diagrams for the integrated design of the physical environment. *Building and Environment* 15(1):3–15.

Radford, A. D.; Gero, J. S.; Rosenman, M. A.; and Balachandran, M. 1985. Pareto optimization as a computer-aided design tool. In *Optimization in Computer-Aided Design*, ed. J. S. Gero, pp. 47–69. Amsterdam: North-Holland.

CHAPTER 10

OPTIMIZATION AND KNOWLEDGE

In all of the design examples we have quoted in this book, we have assumed that the designer is only interested in a solution to the particular problem presented and is not seeking to discover rules or principles to apply in any general sense. Yet the information generated by optimization often is generally applicable; for example, we developed general information about the relationship between window sizes and types of external environment and about building design for climate in the two case studies of chapter 9. In this chapter we look at the kinds of knowledge that can be learned from the results of multicriteria optimization and at how such knowledge might be represented and used in computer-aided design systems.

LEARNING FROM OPTIMIZATION

A Pareto set contains some knowledge about design and performance relationships that might otherwise be built up through years of practical experience. We can learn from both the form of the Pareto set of performances and the relationship between the Pareto set of performances and the corresponding solutions.

Learning from the Relationship between Pareto Performances in Different Criteria

Figure 10-1 shows five projections of a Pareto set onto the space defined by two criteria; it does not matter here whether these are the only criteria of interest in a design problem or whether they are just two criteria from a larger applicable set. We can classify the patterns exhibited by those projections according to the following five characteristics:

(a) *No conflict exists between two criteria.* We learn that optimizing performance in one criterion also tends to optimize performance in the other criterion. Further, we can see from figure 10-1(a) that the spans of Pareto set in each of its criteria is very small. From this we learn that, irrespective of the decisions taken, the performances in these criteria will be similar; that is, regardless of which decision is implemented, the result will be essentially the same.

(b) *The Pareto set for two criteria is heavily convex.* We learn that a balance exists between the two criteria at a point where performance in both is near optimal, but we observe that improving performance in either criterion beyond this point causes a major loss in performance in the other criterion.

(c) *Pareto performance in one criterion is a function of Pareto performance in the other criterion.* We sometimes find that the Pareto set in the criteria space defines a straight line or hyperbolic curve that has a fairly simple mathematical description. We learn that a rule allows us to predict a Pareto performance in one criterion, given a Pareto performance in the other criterion.

(d) *The Pareto set for two criteria is heavily concave.* We learn that conflict exists between the criteria, and we observe that attempts at compromise between them are likely to result in bad performance in both.

(e) *The Pareto set is partly convex, partly concave.* We learn that the relationship between the criteria varies over the span of Pareto set, and we find that no simple rules can be applied in this situation.

Learning from the Relationship between Pareto Performances and Solution Forms

In addition to learning from the relationships between criteria, we can learn from the relationships between Pareto performances and decision

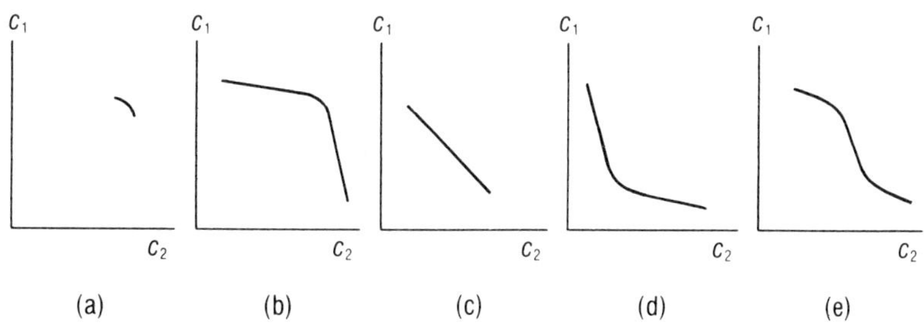

Fig. 10-1. Patterns of Pareto optimal sets for two criteria.

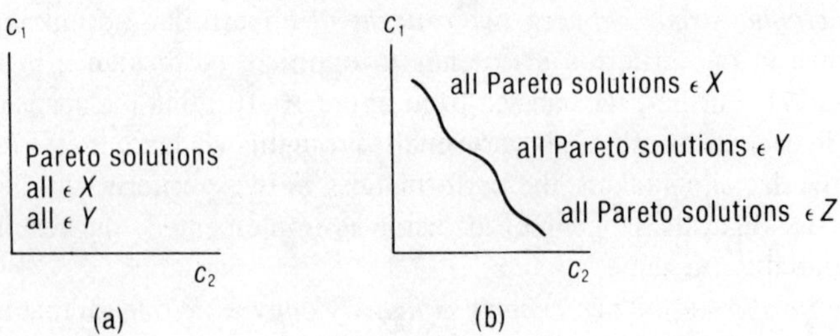

Fig. 10-2. Patterns of solution/performance relationships for two criteria.

variables. The following two characteristics (shown in fig. 10-2) identify the most important patterns:

(a) *Uniform characteristics appear in Pareto solutions.* We sometimes find that all Pareto solutions share some design characteristic and/or that no Pareto solution displays some other design characteristic. We learn that our design choices should, respectively, embrace or avoid such characteristics.

(b) *Patterns of change in characteristics appear in Pareto solutions.* We sometimes find that all solutions with Pareto performances in a particular region of the criteria space share some characteristic that differs from the corresponding characteristic of solutions with Pareto performances in another region of the criteria space. From this, we learn about the relationship between design decisions and desired performances.

EXAMPLE: ESTABLISHING SUITABLE SPANS FOR STRUCTURAL SYSTEMS

Rules of thumb for structural systems are traditionally based on years of experience in the course of which they have demonstrated their reliability and established their limitations. Because of this, they tend to be available for traditional materials only: timber floors, stud walls, and brick walls are well covered; while concrete floors, steel roofs, and precast concrete wall panels are not well covered. It would be useful to develop rules of thumb that apply to today's materials and ensure an acceptable performance in all the necessary functions of the structural element—just as the old "span over two plus one" rule (take the span in feet, divide two, add one, and we have a guide to the joist depth in inches) ensured that a timber floor under construction would be strong enough, would not be subject to excessive deflection, and would be reasonably economical. Here, we shall look for rules of thumb for the design of one-way concrete floor slabs in office buildings. Because such rules must apply to the general case, this exploration seeks to define and analyze field rather than point solutions to design problems.

We consider a live load of 3.5 kN/m^2 (73 lbs/ft^2) and one of the following three possible structural systems: reinforced concrete, steel decking permanent formwork, and prestressed concrete construction. The range of feasible values for the design variables is shown in table 10-1, reflecting current practice in Sydney, Australia. We seek a slab design that, ideally, will combine maximum span with minimum cost and minimum thickness, while satisfying engineering code and deflection constraints. To derive rules of thumb, we consider variable spans and find the Pareto set for three criteria. Deflection is only considered as a code constraint on feasible solutions. Figure 10-3 shows the projection of the Pareto optimal performances onto axes of cost/span, slab thickness/span, and cost/thickness. To clarify the graphs, we have added contours of equal span and contours of equal structural system.

There are roughly 1,500 feasible solutions shown for this problem with the given design variables, but only 35 of these remain after Pareto optimization; all the other feasible solutions are dominated by one or more of these Pareto optimal solutions. In the cost/span diagram (fig. 10-3(a)), we find that the steel decking structural system provides the cheapest solutions for spans of 8, 10, and 12 meters (26, 33, and 39 feet), and that prestressed concrete provides the cheapest solution for spans of 14 and 16 meters (46 and 52 feet). In fact, with the given design parameters the steel decking system proves to be infeasible for spans of 8 meters (26 feet) and greater. The Pareto set solutions offer a considerable range of costs at the shorter spans (with steel decking offering significant savings over the other systems), whereas this range is very small at the longer spans.

In the slab thickness/span graph (fig. 10-3(b)), the prestressed concrete structural system dominates the other systems across the whole range of spans. At the shorter spans, the range of thickness among the Pareto set solutions is small, but at the longer spans (10 and 12 meters (33 and 39 feet)), the range is very large indeed. Moreover, the cost/thickness graph (fig. 10-3(c)) shows that, at spans of 8 meters (26 feet) and greater, a considerable decrease in thickness can be achieved with little increase in cost. At 12 meters (39 feet), for example, the least-cost (reinforced concrete) solution has a thickness of 480 mm (19 inches), while the least-

Table 10-1. Design variables and fixed parameters for a one-way concrete floor slab design problem.

The design options are:

Structural system: reinforced concrete, steel decking, or prestressed concrete
Concrete strength: (a) 20; (b) 25; (c) 30; (d) 35; or (e) 40 MPa (2,900, 3,600, 4,400, 5,000, or 5,800 psi)
Floor thickness: 100–280 mm in 10-mm increments (4–11 inches in approximately $^3/_8$-inch increments)

for all systems, and for reinforced concrete systems:

bar size: 10–18 mm in 2-mm increments ($^3/_8$–$^3/_4$ inch in approximate $^3/_{32}$-inch increments)
steel strength: 275 or 415 MPa (40,000 or 60,000 psi)

for steel decking system:

deck gauge: #20 or #18 (1.3 or 1.4 mm)

for prestressed concrete system:

steel strength: 410 MPa (60,000 psi)

The fixed parameters are:

Concrete cost: (a) 77.0; (b) 79.4; (c) 82.6; (d) 84.5 or (e) 87.7 $/m^3 (2.8, 2.24, 2.34, 2.39 or 2.48 $/ft^3)

for all systems and for reinforced concrete systems:

steel cost: $0.59/kg (for 275-MPa strength) or $0.7/kg (for 415-MPa strength) ($0.27/lb or $0.32/lb for 40,000 or 60,000 psi strength, respectively)
formwork cost: $25/m^2 ($2.32/ft^2)
concrete cover: 20 mm (approximately $^3/_4$ inch)

for steel decking:

steel cost: $0.7/kg ($0.32/lb)
fire protection cost: $10/m^2 ($9.29/ft^2)
propping cost: $4/1 row; $5/2 rows or $6/3 rows
deck cost: $0.8/kg (for #20) or $0.9/kg (for #18) ($0.36/lb or $0.41/lb)

for prestressed concrete:

steel cost $0.7/kg ($0.32/lb)
formwork cost: $25/m^2 ($2.32/ft^2)
tendon cost: $3.1/kg ($1.40/lb)

thickness (prestressed concrete) solution has a thickness of 250 mm (10 inches) at very little increase in cost—a tradeoff well worth accepting. The precise values of the design variables (concrete and steel strengths, reinforcement sizes, and so on) to be chosen within these structural systems can be traced back through the optimization procedure.

Listed below are some examples of rules of thumb that can be derived from these results. Some of these rules are immediately apparent from the Pareto set displayed in figure 10-3, while others have involved tracing the Pareto performances back to the corresponding design decisions, and still others have relied on regression analysis to establish relevant relationship formulas. We should point out that these rules are presented for illustrative purposes only and depend on the particular set of decisions allowed in

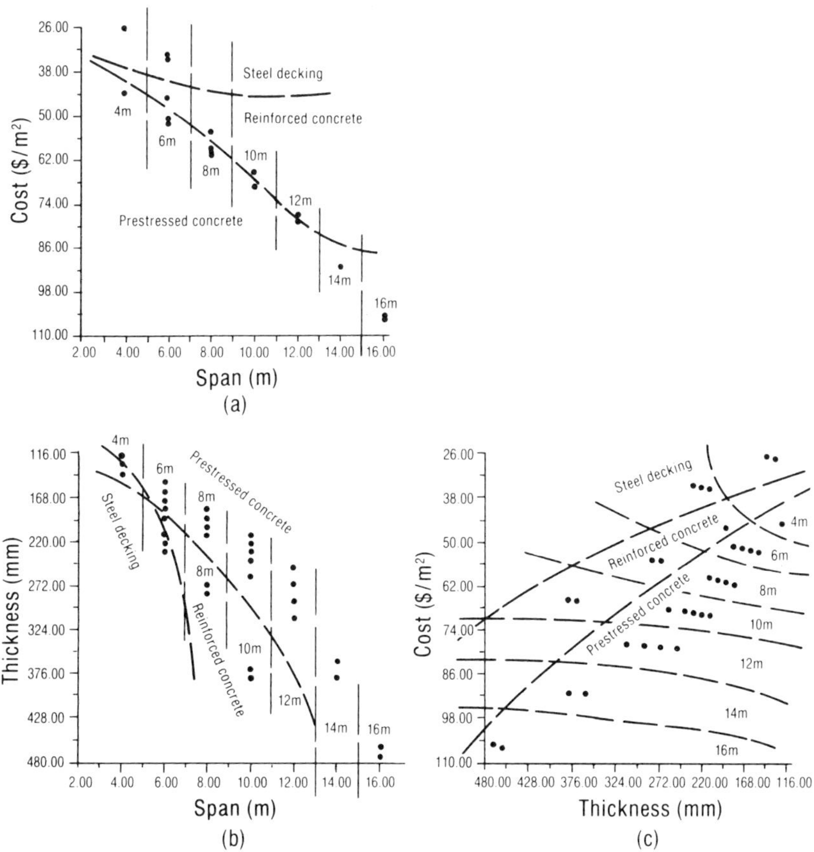

Fig. 10-3. Pareto performances for cost, thickness, and span criteria.

generating the Pareto set. For example, only one layer of reinforcement is allowed in the reinforced concrete slab design, and this seems to affect the feasible Pareto solutions for spans of more than 10 meters (33 feet). We believe, though, that they suffice to demonstrate the kinds of qualitative and quantitative knowledge that can be derived from Pareto optimization in computer-aided design.

RULE 1. *For minimum thickness, one ought to use prestressed concrete.* This is a clear message from figure 10-3(b), where the prestressed concrete system provides the thinnest floor thickness over the whole range of spans. This will hardly be news to an engineer, but it is included here as a demonstration of a kind of rule that may not be obvious in other design situations.

RULE 2. *Thickness = (15 × span) + 60 (thickness in mm; span in meters), for prestressed concrete floors for spans of less than 10 meters (33 feet).* The Pareto set for criteria of minimum thickness and minimum span exhibits a straight line relationship between thickness and span of 4 to 10 meters (fig. 10-3(b)). The rule, of course, assumes that the remaining design decisions are commensurate with a minimum-thickness design.

RULE 3. *Thickness = (31 × span) + 11 (thickness in mm; span in meters), for reinforced concrete floors for spans of less than 10 meters (33 feet).* This also comes from figure 10-3(b). It is interesting to compare this rule with the effective span-to-depth ratio cited in the SAA (Standards Association of Australia) code for reinforced concrete design, which is span/31—since our rule is approximately span/32. A rule derived from Pareto optimization has turned out to be very similar to a rule based on experience. The difference is that the ratio in the SAA code is intended only as a check on deflection, whereas the rule above is intended to provide a rule of thumb on the smallest possible slab thickness that will satisfy the requirements for bending moment, shear, and deflection. As with rule 2, this rule assumes that the remaining design decisions are appropriate.

RULE 4. *Steel decking systems are cheap, but only for spans of up to 6 meters (20 feet).* This is clear from figure 10-3(a).

RULE 5. *One ought to design for minimum thickness when dealing with spans of greater than 8 meters (26 feet).* In figure 10-3(c), we find that for 4- and 6-meter (13- and 20-foot) spans the Pareto subset ranges over a significant portion of the cost axis, but that for spans greater than 8 meters (26 feet) there is so little difference in cost between the minimum thickness and minimum cost solutions that the former is clearly a better choice.

RULE 6. *Cost* $= 25.96 + (1.95 \times span) + (0.19 \times span^2)$ *(span in m; cost in \$), for reinforced concrete design.* This is a bit complex for a rule of thumb, but it is arrived at by fitting a polynomial equation to the Pareto subset for reinforced concrete in figure 10-3(a). The cost is in Australian dollars, and this must, of course, be a rule for particular local conditions. As for the span/thickness relationships, the rule assumes that the remaining design decisions conform to the Pareto set.

RULE 7. *Cost* $= 39.0 + (1.06 \times span) + (0.19 \times span^2)$ *(span in m; cost in \$), for prestressed concrete design.* This is derived by fitting a polynomial equation to the Pareto subset for prestressed concrete in figure 10-3(a).

RULE 8. *Use high-strength concrete in prestressed concrete design.* This rule is derived by tracing back to the design decisions that led to Pareto solutions. Of five possible concrete strengths allowed in the design (20, 25, 30, 35, and 40 MPa (2,900, 3,600, 4,400, 5,000, or 5,800 psi)), 57 percent of the Pareto prestressed concrete solutions (including all the least-thickness solutions—see rule 5) use concrete strengths of 35 or 40 MPa (4,400 or 5,000 psi); while only 5 percent (one solution) use a concrete strength of 20 MPa (2,900 psi). Computer programs have been written specifically for the purpose of inducing such rules from Pareto sets.

KNOWLEDGE FOR EXPERT SYSTEMS

An expert system has been defined as a computer program that embodies sufficient organized knowledge concerning some specific area of human expertise to perform as a skillful and cost-effective consultant. Expert systems can be readily broken into two major components. The first, which is concerned with controlling knowledge, aims to model the domain-independent rational behavior of an expert and is called an *expert system shell*. The second component is the domain-dependent knowledge itself, called a *knowledge base*. While much guidance is available for the construction of an expert system's reasoning and control structure, very little is available to guide the expert system builder in the area of knowledge acquisition. Since expert systems require a knowledge base on which to operate, this knowledge acquisition process is crucial.

Knowledge is generally encoded in expert systems as rules (more formally, via production rules or first-order predicate logic). The derivation of rules of thumb extracts the knowledge contained within the Pareto set from its position within an optimization process and its associated display mechanism. Using knowledge engineering concepts, it is possible to encode these rules separately as knowledge within an expert system for concrete slab design or within a wider knowledge-based computer-aided design system for general building structures. We could encode our rules 1 and 2 in the following terms:

> RULE 1: structure should be prestressed concrete if minimum thickness is critical.
>
> RULE 2: thickness is (15 × span) + 60 if structure is prestressed concrete, and span is less than 10 meters, and design is Pareto optimal.

Knowledge engineering is the art (and science) of designing knowledge-based computer programs. We can use concepts from it to derive our rules of thumb—rules that we have been deriving manually. We could reverse the procedure we have been employing, so that—instead of manually looking for a pattern in the data representing the Pareto optimal set, and then translating it into a rule encoded in an expert system—we could set up a series of prototypical expert system rules that could be treated as hypotheses for rules for thumb. We could then write a program that tested the various hypotheses against the available data and extracted the hypothesis that offered the closest match. Thus, we could directly acquire the knowledge for the expert system.

Rules of thumb represent a short-hand way of encapsulating experience as knowledge. We now have the potential to produce systems that automatically learn certain knowledge. Expert systems and knowledge engineering in structural design, however, represent a new area that has yet to be exploited. Pareto optimization offers a useful approach to the generation of qualitative and quantitative information that can be treated as knowledge by an expert system and can be acquired either manually or automatically by the system.

KNOWLEDGE ENGINEERING IN DESIGN BY OPTIMIZATION

Knowledge engineering, a subfield of artificial intelligence, is concerned with symbolic reasoning and representation of knowledge. The tools and techniques available in this field allow us to move from the traditional method of *algorithmic computing* toward that of *inferential computing*. Such systems are referred to as *knowledge-based systems*. The development of knowledge-based systems has resulted from attempts to emulate the human process of problem solving. The power of knowledge-based systems comes from the way their underlying knowledge is represented and manipulated so that the systems can exhibit "intelligent" behavior. The stored segments of knowledge are known as the *knowledge base*. The mechanism that is used to manipulate the knowledge base is referred to as the *inference engine*. Because a knowledge base is concerned with a specific area of human knowledge, it is always domain-specific—unlike the inference engine, which may be domain-independent and can be used for a wide range of applications.

The aim of any representation scheme is to allow knowledge to be expressed (for subsequent use on a computer system) more explicitly than is possible using conventional programming techniques. Among the many representation schemes that have been suggested are logic-based representations, procedural representations, semantic networks, production systems, and frame systems.

The representation method we have selected falls in the category of *production systems*. Production systems permit the representation of knowledge in a highly uniform and modular way. Knowledge represented in production rules is both accessible and relatively easy to modify. A further advantage of the production system's formalism is the ease with which one can express certain kinds of knowledge. In particular, statements about what to do in predetermined situations are naturally encoded into production rules. Furthermore, it is these kinds of statements that are most frequently used by human experts to explain how they do their work.

Two strategies are employed in problem solving using production systems: forward chaining, and backward chaining. The forward-chaining process starts with a collection of facts and tries all available rules over and over, adding new facts as it goes, until no rule is applicable. In doing backward chaining, a problem solver starts with an unsubstantiated hypothesis and tries to prove it. Their strategy involves finding rules that demonstrate the hypothesis, and then verifying the facts that enable the rule to work.

Knowledge as a Control Mechanism

When a designer begins generating the Pareto optimal set (or an approximation of it), the generation of an individual solution is carried out independently of the control of the process that is used to generate it. The three methods described in chapter 8 simply transform a multicriteria problem into a single-criterion optimization process. This process does not make use of the knowledge of the overall Pareto optimal set in order to perform more efficiently. One possible way to improve the performance of such methods is to provide better controls, based on the available knowledge of the shape of the Pareto optimal set.

In the NISE method, for example, the decision about which segment to use for the generation of the next solution is taken on the basis of an error criterion. Using this strategy, considerable effort may be expended generating closely spaced solutions that do not enhance the overall Pareto set. Four appropriate rules for carrying out this control more usefully, in order to provide an outline of the whole Pareto set, are given below.

If S_iS_{i+1} is the maximum unexplored segment length
and S_iS_{i+1} is greater than the minimum acceptable distance
then generate the next solution between S_i and S_{i+1}

If S_iS_{i+1} is the maximum unexplored segment length
and S_iS_{i+1} is less than the minimum acceptable distance
then terminate the solution generation process

If all segments have been explored
then there is no other solution outside the current boundary

If the same solution optimizes both objectives
then there is no conflict between those criteria

The value of minimum acceptable distance is designated as a percentage of the length of the primary line segment S_1S_2 (fig. 10-4).

The first rule given above is a declarative statement of the procedural control knowledge that will produce a better approximation to the shape of the Pareto set for the same computational load. The second rule is simply the procedural terminating condition. The third rule adds the knowledge that another way to terminate is to exhaust all possible Pareto solutions. The final rule adds domain-specific knowledge related to one of the boundary conditions in multicriteria optimization.

Knowledge to Select Alternate Generation Processes

The NISE method, supplemented with the knowledge stated above, would require fewer solutions to provide the overall outline of the Pareto optimal

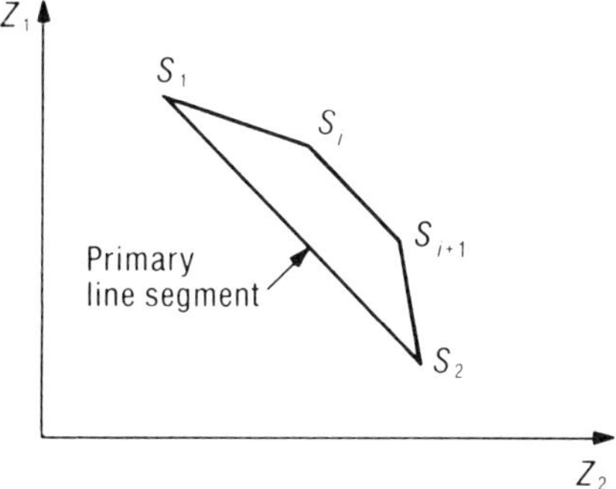

Fig. 10-4. Points S_1 and S_2 represent the optimal solutions of Z_1 and Z_2 individually.

set. But the NISE method is incapable of generating the Pareto optimal solutions in either nonconvex or flat portions of the set. The constraint method, on the other hand, generates convex portions as well as nonconvex portions of the Pareto set and can thus be used to generate solutions in the gaps created in the Pareto set by the NISE method. The knowledge required to perform this task can be encoded by means of the following rule:

If the NISE method has failed to generate solutions between S_i and S_{i+1}
and the length of S_iS_{i+1} is greater than the minimum acceptable distance
then generate solutions between S_i and S_{i+1} using the constraint method

This rule simply encodes the knowledge used to decide when an alternate method of generation can be used.

Knowledge from the Pareto Optimal Set

In design decision making, the shape of the Pareto optimal set provides qualitative knowledge that is of importance to the designer. Such knowledge and the knowledge required to identify the shape of Pareto optimal curves can be encoded as rules, so that the shape information can be inferred automatically. The following rules are useful in this regard:

If the gradients of line segments steadily decrease
and the rate of convexity is high
then the Pareto optimal curve is heavily convex

If the gradients of line segments steadily increase
and the rate of concavity is high
then the Pareto optimal curve is heavily concave

If the shape of the Pareto optimal curve is heavily convex
then less conflict is likely for the Pareto set
and the best compromise solution lies in the northeast corner of the curve

If the shape of the Pareto optimal curve is heavily concave
then there is considerable conflict for the Pareto set
and the compromise solution depends on the designer's preference

Knowledge to Recognize the Optimization Models

Current technology allows us to increase the role of computers in optimization problem solving using knowledge engineering. Nonetheless, we need to be able to identify an optimization model described in algebraic form and to select the appropriate method for solving the problem. Some of the knowledge required for recognition of models and for selection of methods is expressed in the following rules:

If all the variables are of continuous type
and all the constraints are linear
and the objective function is linear
then conclude that the model is linear programming
and execute *LP*-algorithm

If all the variables are of continuous type
and all the constraints are linear
and the objective function is nonlinear and quadratic
then conclude that the model is quadratic programming
and execute *QP*-algorithm

If all the variables are of discrete type
and all the constraints are linear
and the objective function is linear
then conclude that the model is integer linear programming
and execute *IP*-algorithm

If all the variables are of continuous type
and all the constraints are posynomial
and the objective function is posynomial
then conclude that the model is geometric programming
and execute *GP*-algorithm

Clearly, for this knowledge to be computable, it must include inference rules for recognizing variables, the algebraic relationships between variables in the constraints and the objective function, and the type of variables themselves. This recognition of appropriate models is fundamental to design decision problems; the concepts are applicable quite generally.

CONCLUSION

An approach in which optimization is used as a substitute for or supplement to historical case studies can be used to derive rules for design in structural engineering and in other design fields. The formalization of such rules gives them a role as design knowledge that can be applied to comparable design problems—either by human designers or by computer expert systems. It is still necessary, of course, to be able to recognize the comparable problems; a rule derived from the optimization of office floors will not be appropriate for warehouse floors, nor will it be appropriate when the types and strengths of available concrete or reinforcing are different (to quote just the example we have given in this chapter). Nevertheless, if design knowledge can be extracted and become available for use without repeating the often demanding optimization process, both the benefit from and the motivation for using optimization become much greater.

The future of computer-aided architectural design lies, we believe, with design systems that incorporate increasing amounts of design knowledge in themselves instead of relying on the human designer for that knowledge. Some of this knowledge will come from the existing theory and practice of the field; some will be generated for the particular design problem by simulation, optimization, or other techniques; and some will be extracted from simulation and optimization studies and used without reexecuting the model. The search for better design knowledge is one of the greatest motivations for using optimization.

FURTHER READING

The structural system example is drawn from:

Gero, J. S., and Balachandran, M. 1986. Knowledge and design decision processes. In *Applications of Artificial Intelligence to Engineering Problems,* ed. D. Sriram and R. Adey, pp. 343–52. Berlin: Springer-Verlag.

The knowledge as control mechanism, knowledge from the Pareto optimal set, and knowledge to recognize optimization models examples are drawn from:

Radford, A. D.; Hung, P.; and Gero, J. S. 1984. New rules of thumb form computer aided structural design—acquiring knowledge for expert systems. In *CAD 84,* ed. J. Wexler, pp. 558–66. Guildford, England: Butterworths.

Good introductory texts on expert systems include:

Hayes-Roth, F.; Waterman, D.A.; and Lenat, D., eds. 1983. *Building Expert Systems*. Reading, MA.: Addison-Wesley.

Jackson, P. 1986. *Introduction to Expert Systems*. Wokingham, England: Addison-Wesley.

Waterman, D.A. 1986. *A Guide to Expert Systems*. Reading, MA.: Addison-Wesley.

Applications of knowledge engineering in computer-aided design can be found in:

Gero, J.S., ed. 1985. *Knowledge Engineering in Computer-Aided Design*. Amsterdam: North-Holland.

Sriram, D., and Adey, R., eds. 1986. *Applications of Artificial Intelligence in Engineering Problems*. Berlin: Springer-Verlag.

Knowledge engineering and expert systems are only now beginning to find a place in design by optimization. Further material on this confluence can be found in:

Balachandran, M., and Gero, J.S. 1986. Formulating and recognizing engineering optimization problems. In *Proceedings of the 10th Australian Conference on the Mechanics of Structures and Materials,* ed. G. Sved, pp. 223–28. Adelaide: University of Adelaide.

Gero, J.S., and Balachandran, M. 1985. A comparison of procedural and declarative programming languages for the computation of Pareto optimal solutions. *Engineering Optimization* 9(2): 131–42.

Gero, J. S., ed. 1987. Special Issue–Artificial intelligence and engineering optimization. *Engineering Optimization* 12(2):223–26.

Mackenzie, C. A., and Gero, J. S. 1987. Learning design rules from decision and performances. *Artificial Intelligence in Engineering* 2(1):2–10.

Further material on knowledge engineering and expert systems related to computer-aided design can be found in:

Gero, J.S. 1983. Knowledge engineering—future uses of computers in engineering. In *Computers and Engineering*, pp. 159–62. Canberra: Institute of Engineers Australia.

Gero, J.S., and Coyne, R.D. 1986. Developments in expert systems for design synthesis. In *Expert Systems in Civil Engineering*, ed. C. N. Kostem and M. L. Maher, pp. 193–203. New York: American Society of Civil Engineers.

Gero, J. S., ed. 1987. *Expert Systems in Computer-Aided Design*. Amsterdam: North Holland.

Rosenman, M.A., and Gero, J.S. 1985. Design codes as expert systems. *Computer-Aided Design* 17(9): 399–409.

CONCLUDING REMARKS

Design optimization fundamentally involves two issues: how can we do it, and what can we do with the results? To make use of optimization at all, we need to be able to formulate the design problem in a way that is amenable to an optimization technique, and parts 2 and 3 of this book have described some techniques that have proved useful in design. We need more general, more efficient, easier-to-use optimization techniques; research into such things is the province of mathematicians, although designers—in trying to push existing methods into new areas to solve new problems—can make and have made contributions to optimization theory. Faster, more powerful computers have helped extend the applicability of optimization methods, but simply adding computational speed and computer memory will never by itself allow us to explore the enormous number of possible solutions to most design problems.

For designers, the more interesting issue is what to do with the results of optimization, and much of this book has discussed the meaning of such results—how they provide the designer with qualitative and quantitative information, and what supporting information on such factors as sensitivity, stability, and tradeoffs is needed. The thrust of our argument has been that the role of optimization in design is to provide a means for increasing the designer's understanding of the design problem and the nature of good solutions to some of the design objectives.

The notion of there being a single, optimal response to all of the myriad aims and ideals in most design problems is facile. Design requires judgment and tradeoffs, but judgment should be based on the best available information. Optimization can sometimes provide that best information. Much more than in developing mathematical optimization techniques, designers can contribute and have contributed to the creative use of the results of optimization and to the development of better ways of displaying and making available those results.

All of this book has presupposed the use of computers; without them, we would be restricted to very small and less interesting problems. The role of computers is changing from one of machines that do calculations to one of machines that contain and make available knowledge. Optimization, in a sense, is a generator of knowledge: it can be used to discover what are good solutions, what performances those solutions achieve, and how stable and sensitive those solutions are. We have shown in chapter 10 how knowledge can be induced from Pareto sets and represented as rules for a computer expert system.

Optimization is not about mathematics and computer programs, although these are necessary tools. It is about striving for the best, about seeking solutions to human needs, about looking for the elusive ideal answer to our problems. It cannot provide all the answers or replace the design process with a mathematical procedure, but it can provide new levels of understanding. It is up to designers to exploit and extend its power.

INDEX